Living the Quran
with Joy and Purpose

The Modern Muslim World

10

This series will provide a platform for scholarly research on Islamic and Muslim thought, emerging from any geographical area and dated to any period from the 17th century until the present day.

Living the Quran
with Joy and Purpose

Selections on *Tawhid*
from Said Nursi's *Epistles of Light*

Translated, annotated and introduced by

Yamina Bouguenaya

Isra Yazicioglu

GORGIAS
PRESS
2020

Gorgias Press LLC, 954 River Road, Piscataway, NJ, 08854, USA

www.gorgiaspress.com

2020 ܒ,

ܠ
ܩ
܀

ISBN 978-1-4632-4269-5

Library of Congress Cataloging-in-Publication Data

A Cataloging-in-Publication Record is available from the Library of Congress.

Printed in the United States of America

TABLE OF CONTENTS

ACKNOWLEDGMENTS

The editors would like to thank Kelly Tan for her excellent editing and extremely helpful comments. Many thanks to Ailya Vajid for her thoughtful feedback on earlier drafts, to Eric Hoffman for proofing, and all others who read and offered comments on parts of this translation. Many thanks to Ayse Tunc for the cover art.

A sabbatical grant from St. Joseph's University enabled Isra Yazicioglu to make substantial progress on the project. She is also grateful to Dr. Ali Mermer for his kind encouragement.

A NOTE ON ABBREVIATIONS AND DIACRITICS

RNK is the abbreviation for *Risale-i Nur Külliyatı*, a comprehensive compilation of Nursi's books totaling over 2,000 pages (Istanbul: Nesil Yay., 1996) in two volumes. In citing a book by Nursi, we first reference the title of the book in Ottoman Turkish, then note its location in RNK by giving the volume number and then page number.

The majority of the key terms in the *Risale-i Nur*, written in Ottoman Turkish, are loanwords from Arabic and are often derived from Quranic vocabulary. Given that Arabic is more used in Islamic Studies than Ottoman Turkish, when we give transliterations of original terms in brackets, we provide transliterations for Arabic terms. Occasionally we provide both Arabic and Ottoman Turkish renderings, in which case we indicate the latter with 'Tk.' Foreign phrases are italicized, as is the norm. Moreover, in order to attract attention to the Quranic passages in Nursi's work, we italicize quotes from the Quran throughout this book.

PREFACE

Two young fish are swimming in the sea and an older fish passes by them, saying 'the water is nice today, isn't it?' The young fish continue to swim and after a while, one of them asks the other: 'what's water for God's sake?' This famous parable highlights the fact that the most essential things in life often go unrecognized. We would like to use this parable in order to illustrate the core Islamic belief of *tawhid* or the oneness of God, which is so central and yet seldom discussed and examined.[1] What is *tawhid*? Why is it so essential to the teachings of Islam? How does comprehending *tawhid* influence one's perception of reality and consequently, one's behavior and action in the world? In much of the literature on Islam, these questions are often not asked, let alone answered.

In introductory texts on Islam, *tawhid* is merely explained as 'that which is not polytheism.' More advanced scholarly texts focus on the early theological controversies regarding the attributes of God; how divine attributes are related to God's essence. While such abstract discussions may have their significance, they remain peripheral to the Quranic focus on teaching humanity how to witness the stamp of *tawhid* present in all things. Finally, works on Sufism or Islamic spirituality, explain *tawhid* in terms of union with God, through foregoing the ego's claims to self-sufficiency. These texts offer rich resources for the implications of *tawhid* and fortunately

---

[1] The term *tawhid* is derived from Arabic root *w-ḥ-d* and literally means to 'unify.' Since we use this term frequently in this book, we omitted full diacritical rendering, which is '*tawḥīd.*'

have received relatively good attention. Yet, these mystical works may remain elusive for a contemporary audience.

The present book will offer a window into the meaning and practical implications of the central Quranic teachings of *tawhid*. By providing annotated excerpts from a distinguished contemporary Quranic exegete and theologian, Bediuzzaman Said Nursi (d. 1960), this volume will guide the way to a refreshing journey into the intellectual, spiritual and life-transforming implications of *tawhid*.

The book is intended not only for scholars of Islamic theology and the Quran, but also for educated readers interested in understanding belief in God in Islam. In addition, many Muslims are taught from a young age that the oneness of God lies at the heart of Islam and that idolatry is *the* unforgivable sin according to the Quran, but they are provided with little to no discussion as to why that is so. They will hopefully find it illuminating that this book delves into the why and how of *tawhid*.

Furthermore, this book will be enriching to readers interested in understanding the potential of monotheism for humanity at large. Monotheism is a key theme in all of the Abrahamic traditions of Christianity, Islam and Judaism, and resonates with certain interpretations of Hinduism, Chinese religions, and native Indian traditions. When explaining monotheism in the context of Judaism and Christianity, scholars often cite the famous biblical command: 'Thou shall not have any other gods before me, I am a jealous God.' Why is God so jealous? There must be something other than divine caprice going on here, but what could that be? Readers intrigued by such questions will hopefully find insights in this Muslim theologian's deep reflections on *tawhid* as he comments on Quranic passages. Before we summarize some of his key insights, a biographical sketch about Nursi is in order.

Bediuzzaman Said Nursi (1877–1960) was an exceptional Islamic theologian of the twentieth century. His lifetime spanned the final decades of the Ottoman Empire, its collapse and dissolution after the First World War, and the first thirty-seven years of the nascent secularist Turkish Republic, which severely constrained religious freedom, especially until the 1950s. Nursi felt a strong sense of solidarity with the global Muslim community, which faced major intellectual and political challenges, including colonialism, modern criticisms of religious beliefs, and the failure of traditional structures. Living at a time of immense change, Nursi approached the Quran as a dynamic text speaking to the core of the human being and enlightening his world. Similar to profound scholars before him, Nursi read the Quran as utterly relevant to all time periods, including his era of rising religious skepticism.

Referring to an inner transformation he went through around the age of forty-five, Nursi divides his life into two phases, the 'Old Said' and the 'New Said'. In the 'Old Said' period (1890–1922), Nursi was a notable scholar of Quranic interpretation, Islamic theology, and ethics. He also briefly served as an expert scholar at the highest religious institution in the Ottoman Empire at the time, *Daru'l Hikmet-il Islamiye*, which was founded to resolve contemporary intellectual and social issues. Throughout this period, he was also a public intellectual who offered insightful Islamic perspectives for crucial social and political challenges of the time.[2] He proposed educational reforms to the Ottoman Sultans 'Abd al-Hamid (d. 1918) and Mehmet Reshad (d. 1918). His aim was to bring the traditional seminary (*madrasa*) training, Sufism (*taṣawwuf*), and the modern sciences in conversation with each other. He finally secured state funding for his new university project but the First World War erupted and interrupted Nursi's venture. The Russians invaded Nursi's native town and captured him as a war-prisoner. For two years, Nursi lived in Siberia as a prisoner until he managed to escape during the upheavals of the Communist Revolution.

---

[2] For instance, he argued that the era of one caliph acting on behalf of an entire nation was over, and a representative government was needed. Nursi also supported the abolishing of the special status of religious minorities, a change that made all citizens equal before the Ottoman law. Though committed to a religious revival of the caliphate, he distinguished between day-to-day transactions of governance and its religious duties and argued that according to the Sharia, non-Muslim citizens could become governors and have equal say in the parliament as civil servants. Old Said was also enthusiastic about progress in the sciences and what he considered as the end of dogmatism in Europe. For details, see: Isra Yazicioglu, 'Sa'id Nursi,' 110–112.

In 1922, when the Turkish populace was celebrating their victory over European colonial powers, Nursi wrote about a serious danger infiltrating the society; namely positivistic and naturalist ideas and the resulting weakening of belief in *tawhid*. That year also marked Said Nursi's inner transformation from the 'Old Said' to the 'New Said.' With the birth of the 'New Said', his understanding of Islamic revival shifted radically. Nursi now directed his energy on spiritual growth, and the reviving of the hearts and minds with the help of the Quran. He asserted that belief based on imitation (*al-īmān al-taqlidī*, Tk. *taklidi īmān*) cannot survive in this age, and in order to ensure happiness in this world and in the next, belief had to be expounded based on evidence (*al-īmān al-tahqiqi*, Tk. *tahkiki īmān*).

New Said totally abstained from engaging in politics. He was convinced that holding any political agenda while serving the Quran was harmful. While he admitted that political power could be useful for restraining misguided people from corrupting the society, Nursi contended that such people were a minority whereas the majority of people who strayed away from the truth were actually open to it but were unaware of it. The light of the Quran had to be made available to them without any connection to politics, lest they think that the call to the Quran is a means for gaining power. Thus, Nursi abstained from politics.

Persecuted by the secularist state for his efforts on religious revival, New Said lived much of his remaining life in prison and in exile (1925–1956). During this very difficult period, Nursi composed the *Risale-i Nur* (lit. 'Epistles of Light') a six-thousand-page collection seeking to expound the Quran and nurture a life infused with belief and love of God. He also sought to revive *kalām*, Islamic theology, and offer a Quranic theology that is accessible not only to scholars but also to a broader public. Banned by the state, his writings were secretly disseminated and hand-copied by thousands of people, many of whom were also persecuted, imprisoned and even tortured. Despite severe state persecution, the number of Nursi's followers increased over time as his writings were avidly read in different parts of the country. The ban was finally lifted few years before Nursi's death, when Turkey transitioned to a multiparty political system that allowed more civil liberties. Nursi also made it a point to share some of his writings internationally, with Muslims in the Arab world and in Southeast Asia, to encourage deeper engagement with *tawhid*. And, as a gesture of interfaith collaboration ahead of his time, he even sent a selection of his works to the Pope.[3] According to Nursi, despite their disagreements, Muslims and Christians should work together to uphold faith in God in the contemporary age.

Nursi's diagnosis of the weakening of faith is noteworthy, especially when compared with some of his contemporary Muslim revivalists. Unlike many others, he recognized that faith is not inherited and therefore one cannot be a believer simply by being born into a believing family or in a particular geographical location. Nursi seems to suggest that such passive affiliation with faith may have been viable in the pre-modern era, but with the conflicts and challenges this contemporary age faces, such imitative faith will not survive. In this regard, Nursi also perceptively distinguishes between 'not denying God' versus 'believing in God and confirming *tawhid*.' As he writes in one of his letters to his students, 'It is one thing to not deny God; but it is a completely different thing to confirm His existence and unity...'[4] A person may have been born into a faith community and may not be rejecting its beliefs, but that does not mean they are confirming and bearing witness to the truth of such beliefs. [5] Given his awareness of the need to live with conscious and grounded faith,

---

[3] Nursi, *Emirdag Lahikasi-I*, RNK 2: 1834. Unless otherwise noted, our English rendering of the Quranic verses, we made use of Muhammad Asad's *The Message of the Quran*, with occasional modifications based on our reading and other translations such as S. H. Nasr's *Study Quran* and Abdelhaleem's *Quran: A New Translation*.

[4] Nursi, *Emirdag Lahikasi-I*, RNK 2: 1764–1765.

[5] Nursi is not the first theologian in Islamic history to question belief based on mere adherence to traditions. For instance, the medieval Muslim scholar Ghazali (d. 1111) also raised this question. Early in his youth, Ghazali had an existential crisis when he asked questions such as 'Why am I a Muslim? Is it simply because I was born in a particular family?' It is these questions that set Ghazali on the quest for certainty and evaluating the sources of his knowledge. See: See Ghazali's autobiography, as translated by W. Montgomery Watt in Ghazālī, *Faith and Practice of al-Ghazālī*, 21.

Nursi's works are a great choice for the purpose of elucidating this book's theme, namely why does belief in *tawhid* matter?

Nursi's approach to the Quran is also noteworthy. His exploration and explanation of belief in God is guided by the Quran but not in a dogmatic or circular way. That is, he does not simply use the Quran as an authority to be blindly followed. Rather, he takes the Quran for what it claims to be, a guide. He uses the Quran as a map and engages with it to understand its *reasons* for and *implications* of belief in one God. In other words, Nursi aims to show the reader how to appreciate the Quranic reasoning on why and how to believe. Are the signs of God that the Quran talks about really there? How do we perceive and verify them? How does belief in God satisfy my heart and enlighten my life? He follows the Quranic cues in this journey of discovery, without demanding blind faith, without the circular reasoning that 'since the Quran says so, you must accept it.' Such a claim would go against the Quranic view that belief is a choice made after seeing signs, evidences and indications. In other words, Nursi's *Risale-i Nur* makes a noteworthy case for how *tawhid* makes sense intellectually and spiritually, as the selections in this volume will illustrate. His theological discourse also connects to ethical formation of the individual. This book will offer some examples of how he argues that acting with awareness that God is the only sustainer of all that exists is the best and most fulfilling way of being human. Worshipful and ethical living starts with affirming *tawhid*, which in turn leads to fulfilment in this world and the next.

Moreover, the *Risale-i Nur* is refreshing in its relative accessibility. While engaging with profound intellectual and spiritual concerns, overall the *Risale-i Nur* avoids the dryness of many theological and philosophical texts by sharing reflective insights of personal investigatory experiences. In fact, unlike his earlier works written in dense scholarly language, Nursi wrote the *Risale-i Nur* for the common reader. Through the use of metaphors, analogies and helpful explanations, the *Risale-i Nur* makes profound theological and spiritual topics much more readily accessible to the general reader, even though it surely does not make for a casual reading. It is not just the avoidance of technical vocabulary and dense language that makes the *Risale-i Nur* accessible. Rather, Nursi's overall attitude makes his discourse open to a wide audience; especially his insistence on reading the Quran as a living text, speaking to everyone, here-and-now. Moreover, meant for a universal audience, Nursi's text speaks to all humanity and not just those from a Muslim background.

The following chapters will give a taste of how Nursi supports his claim that *tawhid* is a deep human calling. Nursi suggests that faith in one God can nurture rich flourishing of human potentials. In the contemporary era, especially in our Western societies, it has become commonplace to overlook the link between belief and virtue. Many tend to assert that anyone can be a good person independently of his or her beliefs. Such assertion is helpful in the sense that it does not limit moral behavior to cultural or religious labels. Yet, it is also not quite accurate because our worldviews and beliefs *are* relevant to the way we feel and act in the world. Nursi's works highlight the connection between *tawhid* and how it contributes to the betterment of human beings. He argues that belief in one God brings light to a dark world. Without awareness of one God, the world appears to be futile and meaningless and everything seems to be constantly flowing towards death. It is through the perspective of *tawhid* that the purpose and meaning of the world is revealed. The darkness of meaninglessness is replaced with the light of purpose and beauty. Indeed, Nursi asserts that belief in God uncovers the divine art reflecting on the human being, showing that they are an honored guest of the Eternal Sustainer. Moreover, belief in *tawhid* enables human beings to perceive all the glimpses of beauty in the world as indicating transcendent and lasting beauty, and therefore encourages the believers to be conscious mirrors to that Eternal Beauty. Furthermore, Nursi argues that belief in One Source of all power and perfection can release human beings from the debilitating fears and concerns of death and transience, and provide them with the strength to tackle the challenges of life. The excerpts from Nursi translated in this volume will give a peek into such a world where belief, beauty and courage are intimately and organically interconnected.

Having offered a brief overview of the contents of this volume, we shall now note some technical considerations. First, the translation is from Ottoman Turkish, which is the language used in the *Risale-i Nur*. While the study of Nursi's works is still quite limited in English, an English translation of eight volumes of his *Risale-i Nur* is available. The translator, Sukran Vahide, prioritized being faithful to the literal wording of the text, by keeping sentences as close as possible to the original Ottoman Turkish style, in which sentences tend to be rather long. Besides, many key words in the original text, which are of Arabic and Persian origin, do not quite have an exact English term corresponding to them. Vahide's translation encounters this major challenge by occasionally constructing new English terms or by employing unfamiliar expressions, such as 'dominicality' to correspond to *rubūbiyya*, and 'Eternally Besought One' to correspond to *al-ṣamad*. For those interested in the most literal translation and in philological connections, her work will continue to be of help. For those who would like a text easier to follow in English, new English translations of the *Risale-i Nur* are needed. We hope this volume will be one of them.

Accordingly, in our translation, we have tried to make the text as accessible as possible. We often split long sentences in the original into shorter ones. To make the translation more flowing in the English idiom, we also frequently paraphrased a sentence instead of translating it according to its Ottoman Turkish structure. We have also chosen to update some cultural references, like replacing 'dirham' with 'cents.' Furthermore, we edited some of the strong language, such as the occasional reference to the 'absurdness' of *shirk*. Nursi uses such language to highlight logical inconsistency but we have found that such wording is often misunderstood in the English-speaking audience as a personal attack or as ad hominem argument. Perhaps for Western readers, critical analysis of idolatry or unbelief evokes painful memories of inquisition and bigotry in the European medieval and early modern past. Regardless of whether such associations are fair or exaggerated, it is clear that Nursi is simply criticizing the idea, not attacking anyone. Finally, when we rarely skipped a part in the text, we indicated it with '...'.

As noted earlier, the *Risale-i Nur* is an engagement with the Quran. There are explicit references to various Quranic verses throughout. Nursi usually starts the chapters with one or more verses from the Quran. Moreover, the *Risale-i Nur* elaborates on Quranic concepts throughout, such as *tawhid*, surrender, the Beautiful Names of God (*al-asmā al-ḥusna*), gratitude, and signs (*ayāt*). Additionally, the text contains implicit references to various Quranic verses through the use of Quranic phrases or idioms. These references would be obvious to any reader who is familiar with the Quran. We have added notes to the translation where we have indicated such allusions to Quranic idioms and famous passages. Such notes are not meant to be exhaustive of all the Quranic verses indicated or implied in the text. Rather, they are meant to be examples of how Nursi weaves Quranic concepts into how one perceives the world and acts accordingly.

In addition to such annotated translation, we prefaced each translated selection with an explanatory introduction. These brief introductions highlight the key points of the translated sections and also draw attention to the ways in which Nursi's explanations of *tawhid* relate to his Quranic interpretation. In terms of referencing the original text, we have identified the passages with original markers of the text (which is helpful especially when no corresponding Vahide's English translation was referenced) such as '*Words*, Second Word, Third Station, Sixth Point,' so that it will be easier to locate the original texts as published by various publishers. (We hope that such practice of referencing will be adopted in other studies on Nursi's works, so as to make looking up references from the *Risale-i Nur* easier.) Now, before we finally let you journey into these selections, we shall offer a brief overview of Nursi's approach to the Quran.

INTRODUCTION:
NURSI'S QURANIC HERMENEUTICS[1]

> The Quran surpasses all other speech...Indeed, four things en-
> hance the power, beauty and greatness of an utterance: *the
> speaker, audience, purpose and context*. In other words, it is not
> just the context that matters, unlike what the literati suppose.
>
> B. Said Nursi, Mesnevi-i Nuriye

In the above quote, Nursi highlights the importance of the factors
that determine the meaning of an utterance in addition to its content. The very same sentence can have completely different meanings
depending on who is saying it. For instance, if it is my boss who tells
me 'you are fired,' it will have a grave consequence, whereas if it is my
friend, it may just be a tease. Thus, identifying 'who' is speaking in a
text is as crucial as its semantic content, i.e. the words uttered.[2] The

---

[1] An earlier version of this chapter has been published as 'Said Nursi's
Quranic Hermeneutics,' *The Companion to Said Nursi Studies*, 51–66.

[2] Nursi himself gives an example from a Quranic verse. As part of the story
of Noah's ark, the Quran states *And the word was spoken: 'O earth, swallow
up thy waters! And, O sky, cease [thy rain]!' And the waters sank into the
earth, and the will [of God] was done.* (Q. 11:44) According to Nursi, since
the speaker here is God, i.e. the One who has genuine power over the earth
and the heavens, such command to earth and the sky is eloquent. In contrast, if it were a human being who was uttering the same command, it
would not be eloquent; rather, it would convey mere wishful thinking and
delusional talk. The meaning and value of the sentence completely differs

same applies to all the other elements of speech, such as context, audience and purpose; each is essential to interpretation and is as important as what is being said in the speech. Hence, in understanding the content of the Quran, Nursi takes the following four factors into account in interpretation: (1) speaker (*mutakallim*), (2) audience (*mukhātab*), (3) purpose (*maqṣad*), and (4) context (*maqām*).[3] Let us look more closely into each of these factors so as to understand Nursi's approach to the Quran.

Nursi defines the Quran as a universal address from the Creator of the heavens and the earth. To be sure, ordinary human beings and even animals also receive direct inspiration from their Sustainer. Yet, the Quran is the highest form of Divine speech to humanity. In regards to the purpose of the Quran, Nursi identifies the *maqāṣid*, or overall aims, of the Quran. The idea is that a faithful reading of the Quran is only possible by reading its parts in view of these overall purposes. Traditionally, there have been slightly different views of what these main aims of the Quran are. In general, however, it has been agreed upon that the main aim of the Quran is belief in one God, *tawhid*, and the establishment of human life in connection to and in response to God, who is known through his different attributes, such as powerful, compassionate and wise. According to Nursi, the Quran's major purpose is to guide us in answering core human questions about the meaning of existence and to solve the 'riddle' of the universe. More specifically, Nursi suggests that the purpose of the Quran is to establish four major points: (1) *tawhid*, or the oneness of God, (2) prophethood (*al-risālah*), i.e. that God guides human beings through messengers; (3) resurrection (*hashr*) or life after death; and (4) justice (*'adāla*) and worshipful response to one God,

---

depending on who the speaker is. (Nursi refers to speech because the Quran is regarded as Divine speech (*kalām allah*) and it was written down only after being communicated as recitation to the Prophet). Nursi, *Mesnevi-i Nuriye*, RNK 2:1363.

[3] Nursi, *Sözler*, RNK 1:195–96; Nursi, *Mesnevi-i Nuriye*, RNK 2:1363; Nursi, *Words*, 443–44.

(*'ubudiyya*).[4] The first is the key to the rest: only as we grasp the oneness of the source of all the power, beauty, and perfection reflected in the world can we appreciate the other main themes.

According to Nursi, any particular issue mentioned in the Quran is discussed not for its own sake but only as a *means* to convey these major aims and elucidate their implications. Indeed, Nursi notes that the Quran never talks about things for their own sake but rather for the sake of their signification of God's attributes, i.e. things are signs of God signifying/indicating meanings beyond themselves. In other words, the Quranic purpose is never about giving technical information about history, social norms, or nature, or about providing literary entertainment. Rather, whatever the Quran mentions—from a prophetic narrative, to a description of end of times, to a bee making honey, to financial contracts—the aim is to make the Transcendent known to its audience. That is why, the Quran emphasizes that it is not 'poetry' or 'fables of the ancients.'[5]

PUTTING THE QURAN IN ITS COSMIC CONTEXT

Nursi defines the Quran as 'an eternal commentary on the great book of the universe.'[6] This short description is a profound reconceptualization of the Quran for it describes the Quran primarily as an *explanation*, rather than something that is to be explained. The Quran uncovers and reveals the meanings of the universe we exist in.

---

[4] For a helpful survey of *maqāsid* of Quran in classical scholars, as well as Nursi's, see al-Daghamin, 356–58.

[5] Nursi, *Sözler*, RNK 1:161; *Muhakemat*, RNK 2:1986.

[6] In a similar vein, he defines the Quran as 'the pre-eternal translator of the mighty Book of the Universe; the post-eternal interpreter of the various tongues reciting the signs of creation; the commentator of the book of the Worlds of the Seen [Manifest] and the Unseen; the revealer of the treasuries of the Divine Names hidden in the heavens and on the earth; the key to the truths concealed beneath the lines of events; the tongue of the Unseen World in the Manifest World; the treasury of the post-eternal favours of the Most Merciful and of the pre-eternal addresses of the Most Holy, which come from the World of the Unseen beyond the veil of this Manifest World...' Nursi, *Words*, 376–377.

Such definition of the Quran as a commentary on existence is also intriguing because it highlights the indispensability of the Quranic message in understanding reality. Unlike some classical Muslim philosophers, Nursi does not consider even the sharpest human intellect capable of figuring out the meaning of existence simply by observing and examining the universe. Without the cues provided explicitly by the Creator via the Quran (or earlier authentic divine revelations), human being cannot solve the purpose and meaning of the world.[7]

Hence, both the Quran and the cosmos complement each other in making known the Transcendent Being, the Creator. The Quran complements the universe in that only through its guidance one can decipher how the world is pointing to its Maker. And the universe complements the Quran in that it is a witness to the Quranic message. For instance, the Quran discloses Divine power, wisdom and compassion in the world and the world bears witness to them. In fact, Nursi considers the creation and the revelation as two types of speeches of God: the Quran is God's verbal speech sent through the messengers of God (*kalām al-tadwinī*), and the universe is God's speech through creating (*kalām al-takwinī*). The two speeches of God complement each other, just as an artist's speech and act complement each other: 'in order *to describe His act both to the eye and the ear,* the Maker describes His act while performing it. As a true Artist, He unravels His art as He works it. As a true Bestower of bounties, He explains His blessings as He carries out the very act of bestowing.'[8] Reading the Quran without paying attention to the universe would be like listening to an incredible artist describe her artistic activity, without looking at the artistic activity itself.[9]

---

[7] Nursi, *Sözler,* RNK 1:141.

[8] Nursi, *Words,* 444 (italics added).

[9] Nursi, *Words,* 444; *Sözler,* RNK 1:196. See also Mermer and Ameur, 'Beyond the Modern: Sa'id al-Nursi's View of Science,' 126–127. In fact, Nursi suggests that the actions speak even louder than words. The Quranic description of God as merciful refers to God's actions in the world. Similarly, how could one understand the Quranic references to God's wisdom, without observing divine wisdom instantiated in the world? Of course, for

For Nursi, then, the Quran is like a treasure map, disclosing treasures of meaning embedded in—or expressed through—the world around us and within us.[10] References to the 'treasures of *al-asmā al-ḥusna*' embedded in the dynamic flow of the universe is a major theme in the *Risale-i Nur*. Only through the help of the Quran, one can understand that while things come into existence and go and pass away, they express enduring meanings related to the Eternal One. In Nursi's words, 'the activity of [divine] power in the cosmos and the flow of beings is so meaningful in that the All-Wise Maker is making all the beings in the universe speak through such activity... Thus, the dynamism and transience in the universe...is *speech* glorifying God. The constant activity in the universe is a *silent speech*...'[11] Through the guidance of the Quran, one learns to recognize and understand this silent speech of the universe. Otherwise, one experiences life like a deaf person watching a movie; he can perhaps guess a little about what is going on but he cannot truly understand the significance of this flow of existence; he cannot fathom the purpose and meaning of the world around—and within—him. Through the light of the Quran the world starts making sense. The continuous flux of life stops being a source of pain in its apparently endless reenactments of separation and death. Rather, life becomes an enjoyable display of the continuously renewed reflections of the various beautiful qualities of God. Nursi elaborates on how the beautiful qualities of God shine through the contrast of sickness-health, difficulty-ease, need-fulfillment, hunger-sustenance and life-death. Through Quranic enlightenment, the human being starts understanding how the world reveals the beauty of justice, wisdom, healing, generosity and life-giving power of the Eternal Creator. Nursi also intriguingly describes the universe as the macro-Quran (*al-qur'ān al-kabīr*). And, with a subtle allusion to the literal mean-

---

Nursi, in order to 'read' the signs of mercy and wisdom in the universe, one needs to be trained by the Quran in understanding its 'sign language.'

[10] Nursi, *Words*, 376–377.

[11] Nursi, *Mektubat*, '24. Mektub, Ikinci Remiz,' RNK I: 481. (Our translation, italics are added); Nursi, *Letters*, 340.

ing of the term 'Quran', which means 'recitation', he suggests that 'In the great mosque of the universe, the Quran is reciting the universe. Let us listen to it.'[12]

Such appreciation of the Quran's decisive role in deciphering the meaning of existence is a conspicuous trait of Nursi's Quranic interpretation. For instance, in his treatise devoted to interpreting Quranic verses on gratitude, he notes: 'Just as the Wise Quran shows gratitude to be the purpose of creation, similarly this *macro-Quran of the universe, (qur'ān al-kāinat al-kabīr)* demonstrates that gratitude is the most important result of creation.'[13] Similarly, he shares his reflections on the Quranic verse *Behold, then, these signs of God's mercy—how He gives life to the earth after it had been lifeless!* (Q. 30:50) only after making extended retreats by himself in the countryside and meditating on nature. His reflective activity resulted in the *Treatise on Resurrection*, which explains the ways in which the universe bears witness to the truth of life after death in the light of the Quran.[14] Once again, the 'signs' (*ayāt*) of the verbal Quran enlighten the 'signs' (*ayāt*) of the 'macro-Quran' and in turn the signs in the world embody and corroborate the message of the Quran.

---

[12] (Tk. 'Kâinat mescid-i kebirinde Kur'ân kâinatı okuyor, onu dinleyelim.') *Sözler*, '7. Söz', RNK 1:12; Nursi, *Words*, 44. At this point, we may note that Nursi's reference to the universe as the meta-text of the Quran and his focus on the cosmic phenomena as signs of the Beautiful Names of God has precedents in classical scholars such as Abu Talib al-Makkī (d. 998), Abu Hamid Muhammad al-Ghazālī (d. 1111), and Muhyiddin Ibn 'Arabi (d. 1240) as well as Jalal al-din al-Rumī (d.1273). In the classical literature one finds various references to the universe as 'book of creation' (e.g. *kitab al-kawn, kitab al-sun'*, and *kitab al-khalq wa al-tadbīr*.) Ibn 'Arabi, for instance, regarded the Quran as a *kawn masṭūr* or 'logo-cosmos' that manifests the macro-cosmos, which is itself a manifestation of the divine Reality (*al-Haqq*). See: Akkach, *Cosmology and Architecture in Premodern Islam*, 96 and Chittick, *Self-Disclosure of God*, 3–16.

[13] Nursi, *Mektubat*, '28. Mektub, 5. Mesele' [24th Letter, 5th Section, 'Treatise on Gratitude'], RNK 1:520–522.

[14] Nursi, *Sözler*, '10. Soz' [10th Word], RNK 1: 19–43; *Words*, 59–132.

Indeed, a crucial consequence of such recognition of the cosmic context of the Quran is the 'confirmation' of the Quranic message. Nursi suggests that there are two types of Quranic commentaries, one that mainly focuses on explaining the semantics of the Quran, and the other that gives 'evidences' for the 'truths' of the Quran. He considers traditional line-by-line commentary genre to mainly (albeit not exclusively) to fall into the first category. He places the *Risale-i Nur* in the second category in that it focuses on 'demonstrating the truths of the Quran.'[15] The Quranic invitation to reflect and meditate on the world calls its readers not to simply accept but to discover, and eventually witness and confirm, the Quranic truths manifesting in the world. Considering the metaphor noted earlier, the best reading of a treasure map is to utilize it to discover the treasure, and as the treasure is found, the truthfulness of the treasure map is confirmed. Similarly, as we read the Quranic message with an attention to discover and interpret the silent speech of the universe, we will be able to experience the truthfulness of the Quranic message in reality. According to the Quran, the addressees of the Quran will be shown *signs* both in the cosmos, and 'within' themselves, *fi al-āfāqi wa fi anfusihim*, so that its truthfulness will be become evident (Q. 41:53).

Such an approach means that the reader pays attention to how the Quranic message enlightens his world and how it is confirmed by the reality. This approach also brings together the 'outer' and 'inner' worlds. That is, to witness how the Quran unlocks the meaning of the world is to also realize how the Quran is relevant to *me*. Nursi often uses the metaphor of 'telescope' to convey such transformative encounter with the Quran. Many times, in the *Risale-i Nur,* Nursi shares his personal experience in this regard, (examples of which we shall include in the selected texts in this book). In each case, he notes how he felt disappointed, lost or even frustrated at what he perceived to be an ugliness, injustice or tragedy in the world. But then he looks through 'the telescope of Quranic verses' and the true nature of the world is revealed to him and brings him much relief and joy. In these instances, Nursi notes how one not only confirms the truth of the

---

[15] Nursi, *Şualar,* '14. Sua RNK 1:1089; *Rays*, 513.

Quranic perspective but is also relieved by the messages it reveals. In this regard the person also experiences how the Quran is a healing to the hearts, which is another Quranic notion.

In order to further appreciate how Nursi reads the Quran in its cosmic context, let us look at his interpretation of the following Quranic passage and compare it with some of the predominant trends in traditional *tafsir*.[16]

> *Let human being, then, consider* [the sources of] his food: [how it is] that We pour down water, pouring it down abundantly; and then We cleave the earth [with new growth], cleaving it asunder, and thereupon We cause grain to grow out of it, and vines and edible plants, and olive trees and date-palms, and gardens dense with foliage, and fruits and herbage, for you and for your animals to enjoy. (Q. 80:24–32, emphasis added).

In the well-known traditional line-by-line commentaries like Abu Ja'far Muhammad al-Tabari's (d. ca. 923) or Ibn Kathir's, the passage is interpreted by paraphrasing its semantic content. In other words, the text is read simply as a declaration, and the Quranic invitation to actually consider the cosmic phenomena is glossed over. Ibn Kathir (d. 1373) mainly interprets the passage as saying that the believer should be thankful to God for food, while al-Tabari spends the bulk of his exegesis on the etymology of the words. Though the information contained in these interpretations may be accurate, they do not occasion an understanding of the Quran in its cosmic context, i.e. they do not inquire how the verse helps the reader to discover truths or signs of God manifest in the world. In contrast, the classical theologian-exegete Fakhr al-din al-Razi (d. 1209) notes that the above Quranic passage discloses signs in the universe. He suggests that if one were to look at natural phenomena closely, such as the growth of plants, one would discover deep meanings in them, revealing God's

---

[16] Of course, the traditional line-by-line commentaries we shall refer to do not represent the entire vast genre of *tafsir*. Our aim is simply to highlight some of the widely known and popularly read medieval exegetes as a foil to discuss Nursi's hermeneutics.

agency and qualities. Though al-Razi does not explain *how* to proceed in order to discover these meanings, he does go beyond mere semantic analysis and connects the verse to the universe.[17] Nursi takes al-Razi's approach further, explaining more clearly *how* the food and its growth in the world, function as signs revealing the treasures of God's beautiful attributes, *al-asmā al-ḥusna*. Let us look at this approach in more detail.

Nursi first highlights the last part of the Quranic passage: 'for you and for your animals to enjoy.' He suggests that by highlighting the 'purposeful sequence' in the growth of vegetation, the Quranic passage teaches how to perceive the 'hidden' agency of God implied in natural processes. The Quran invites its audience to pay attention to the beneficial results of these natural processes as they indicate purpose and care. And since the natural causes involved in this process of growth of grains and fruits lack the capacity to consciously plan out things or have mercy, it is understood that these purposeful events reveal the agency of a wise and merciful One. In Nursi's words:

> [The Quran] is in effect saying: 'Rain comes from the sky in order to produce food for you and your animals. Since water does not possess the ability to have mercy for you and your animals and thus produce food accordingly, it means that *the rain does not come [on its own], it is sent.* And the earth cleaves up and yields forth food for you. But lacking feelings and intelligence, it is far beyond the ability of the earth to think of your sustenance and feel compassion for you, so it does not produce the food on its own...'[18]

Thus, the Quran explains how this natural process is a sign. Or to use Nursi's metaphor, the Quran enables its audience to hear the 'silent speech' of phenomena praising God by indicating his beauti-

---

[17] We accessed Tabari's, Ibn Kathir's and Razi's commentaries on this passage through the comprehensive scholarly *tafsir* database maintained by Jordanian Ministry of Religious Affairs at <www.altafsir.org>.
[18] Nursi, *Words*, 435 (modified translation and italics added). For original text, see: *Sözler*, '25. Söz, 7. Sırr-ı Belağat,' RNK 1:192.

ful attributes. The flourishing of fruits and grains are means through which mercy, generosity, and wisdom of the Unseen Creator is manifested.

In light of this Quranic passage as well as others that speak explicitly about cosmic phenomena, Nursi suggests that one of the main aims of the Quranic discourse is to rectify our superficial understanding of the world. More specifically, Nursi perceptively suggests, like his predecessors such as Jalal al-din al-Rumi (d. 1273), that correcting our misunderstanding of natural causality is a main purpose of the Quran since it is directly connected to the reality of tawhid. The Quran teaches the reader to notice the surprising 'gap' between what we habitually call the cause and its effect. Many tend to think that natural causes are responsible for cosmic phenomena, while in reality they are simply 'apparent' causes, being themselves created and employed by the Causer of causes, the Creator. The Quran discloses that between a seeming cause and what seems to be its effect there exists a transcendental gap. Indeed, these seeming causes lack qualities such as wisdom, knowledge, power, mercy and so on, that are required to create and sustain the results attributed to them. Hence, contrary to our conventional assumption, unconscious, unknowing clouds cannot create rain, lifeless rain cannot sustain life, parents are not the creators of their children, and so on. Nursi offers a metaphor that illustrates our superficial perception of causal processes: it may at first seem that mountains are joined to the sky at the horizon. But when one pays closer attention and gets closer, he sees that there is a huge distance between the mountains and the sky, and it is within this vast distance that 'the stars rise.' So too, says Nursi, 'the distance between [seeming] causes and effects is such that it may be seen *only with the light of the Quran* through the telescope of belief.' And 'it is within this long distance between seeming cause and its effect that the Divine Names (*al-asmā al-ḥusna*, lit. 'Most Beautiful Names,' or 'attributes of perfection') each rise like stars.[19] The place of their rising (*maṭla'*) is this distance.'[20] In Nursi's

---

[19] As Muhammad Asad in his Quranic commentary on verse 7:180 notes, '*al-asmā al-ḥusna* (lit., 'the most perfect [or 'most goodly'] names'), which

hermeneutics, therefore, both the cosmic *ayāt* and the Quranic *ayāt* are places where flashes of the Most Beautiful Names 'rise up' and emerge.[21]

In the above passage, the Quran calls the audience to look at the growth of grains, fruits and other vegetation, and thereby teaches how 'numerous Divine Names... like All-Compassionate, Provider, Bestower, and All-Generous' are disclosed through those cosmic phenomena.[22] Nursi's interpretation of this passage shows how the Quranic message deciphers and reveals the meanings of the creational signs (*ayāt*). It also exemplifies how a believer can experience and witness the unfolding of the meaning of the Quranic message in the world and thereby confirm its truth.

Another striking example of Nursi's reading of the Quran in its cosmic context is his interpretation of the Quranic phrase *bismillah* or 'In the name of God,' which is the first selection in this volume. *Bismillah* is not simply an invocation that a believer is called to utter. Rather, it is a key expression that the entire universe expresses. In other words, cosmic phenomena unfold in God's name, *bismillah*, disclosing the hidden divine agency through which everything happens.

Nursi's awareness of the cosmic context of the Quran is relevant not only for the passages explicitly mentioning cosmic phenomena, which make up a large part of the Quran, but also for the passages that are often thought to be unrelated to the interpretation of the universe. For instance, the verse stating *There shall be no coercion*

---

occurs in the Quran four times—i.e., (in 7:180 as well as in 17:110, 20:8 and 59:24) it is to be borne in mind that the term *ism* [singular of *asmā*] is, primarily, a word applied to denote the substance or the intrinsic attributes of an object under consideration, while the term *al-ḥusna* is the plural form of *al-aḥsan* ('that which is best' or 'most goodly'). Thus, the combination *al-asmā' al-ḥusna* may be appropriately rendered as 'the attributes of perfection'—a term reserved in the Quran for God alone.' (Asad, *The Message of the Quran*, 231).

[20] *Words*, 435 (modified translation, with italics added).

[21] Ibid., and see also *Sözler*, '25. Söz, 7. Sırr-ı Belagat,' RNK 1:192.

[22] *Words*, 436.

in matters of faith (2:256) would mean not only that one should not force faith upon others, but that the reality is such that faith and coercion 'cannot *ontologically* co-exist...because faith is a free choice and a state of being willingly open to the divine speech; it is a state of grateful surrendering to the grace of God. The use of force would negate all these qualities and the result would not be faith but hypocrisy.'[23] In a similar fashion, Nursi interprets the Quranic descriptions of *shirk* or attributing partners with God as 'an awesome injustice' as reflecting a cosmic reality. As will be made clear in the selections in this volume, Nursi explains how *shirk* disconnects the universe from the Eternal One, and thus constitutes an extremely unfair insult against all beings by reducing them to random things.[24] Similarly, the Quranic statement that belief marks the distinction between the highest and lowest form of human existence (Q. 95:4–6) can be confirmed by looking at the universe, and how belief makes a difference in the actual unfolding of human nature and in fulfilling his full potential.[25]

Nursi's approach of reading the Quran in its cosmic context is also reflected in his approach to the Quranic stories of the prophets. He reads these prophetic stories as communicating universal principles, helping human beings to discern the signs of God in the world, in nature and life events. For instance, Nursi interprets Adam being taught 'all the names' (Q. 2:31) as representing key truths about the purpose of human beings and their unique mission and potential as humans. The story teaches us that all humanity is gifted with the potential of discovering the purpose of the world around them and consequently to know their Creator with all His Most Beautiful Names.[26] Hence the story of Adam in the Quran provides cues to understanding how we can fulfill our human potential; as a result,

---

[23] Mermer, 'Islam: A Dissenting Prophetic Voice,' 83.

[24] Nursi, *The Rays*, 19–20.

[25] Nursi, *Words*, 319–327. Similarly, Nursi interprets the verse about not bragging (Q. 3:188) in light of reflection on nature, and the verse about hearts being only satisfied with remembrance of God (Q. 13:28) in cosmic context. See, respectively: *Words*, 139–140 and *Words*, 692.

[26] Nursi, *Words*, 253–254.

we can confirm the Quranic message by reading the story in relation to our own reality. In this volume, we offer excerpts from his interpretation of Jonah's story in the Quran.

Such an approach to the prophet stories also explicitly takes into consideration the author, audience and purpose of the Quran in appreciating its content. These stories are not being told for the sake of narrating a historical account; the Wise Creator speaking in the Quran would not simply give information that would have no implication for human beings here-and-now. If the divine voice in the Quran is referring to an interaction between Adam and the angels, it is for the purpose of edifying the audience. When the Quran narrates that angels prostrated before Adam and Satan refused to do so, (Q. 2:34), it is teaching us the Adamic human potential of going beyond the angels through human capacity of knowing "countless disciplines and branches of knowledge" and thereby the Creator with all His beautiful names. Moreover, it indicates that "most of the physical beings in the universe and their representatives and appointed beings are subjugated to human being, and that human being's senses are predisposed and amenable to benefiting from all of them." While there lurks a serious enemy in the path of man's progress represented by "evil matter and its representatives that corrupt human nature and drive him down wrong paths."[27] Similarly, the miracle stories teach us that the order in nature is not necessary in itself. Rather, the One who is behind the impressive order in nature is not bound by the regularities of his creation. He maintains order in the world for our benefit, 'He has the power of *Be and it is.*' (Q. 16: 40)[28] Whether it is the Dhulqarnayn's story, the golden calf incident, Mary's virgin birth, Abraham's search for God, or Job's prayer in affliction, for

---

[27] Nursi, *Words,* 254.

[28] According to Nursi, it is God's freewill that makes human freewill possible. If the seeming causes were actually effective in determining events, then because they cannot customize situations according to human choices, it would make human will impossible. See: Nursi, 'Treatise on Destiny, 26th Word, Second Topic, Sixth [Point].' For a brief discussion of Nursi's view of God's will and human freedom and unique connection to God's mercy, see Yazicioglu, *Understanding Quranic Miracle Stories,* 153–154.

Nursi every Quranic story is told with the aim of revealing a truth that enlightens the reader's way of being in the world and hence connects him to his Sustainer (*rabb*).[29]

When he defines the Quran as a truthful commentary on the universe, Nursi is clearly aware that there are other interpretations of reality. For instance, there is the non-theistic interpretations of reality, such as naturalism. There are also various 'imbalanced' spiritual approaches. Nursi compares their understanding of the cosmos with the Quranic perspective. First, he contrasts 'philosophy' with 'Quranic wisdom.' He uses the term 'philosophy' not to denote philosophy in general, but a particular form of philosophy that reject or ignore Divine guidance as it is revealed in the Quran (or in earlier divine revelations), which we will render as 'godless philosophy,' for lack of a better term. He outlines a number of key problems with such approaches to the universe. First, unlike the Quranic approach, such godless philosophy completely misses the truth about the universe. For it refuses to recognize that the world points beyond itself, to its Creator. Nursi offers a helpful metaphor to contrast the Quranic worldview with godless philosophy. The latter looks at the world like a clueless chemist looks at a calligraphy written in a language that is foreign to him. The chemist may give a superb analysis of the quality of the ink and paper, but he fails to understand the meaning communicated through the calligraphy. In fact, he not only cannot read the text, but also does not know that the calligraphy before him *is* actually a piece of writing that signifies meaning. Similarly, godless philosophy fails to note that the world is a dynamic book, filled with indications or signs pointing to the Transcendent.[30] Moreover, such an approach places the ego at the center of everything and considers that everyone's mission is to promote their ego. It fails to realize the fact that the ego is 'indicative,' i.e. it reveals and

---

[29] See: *The Flashes*, 17–20; 147–150; *Words*, 254. For an engagement with Nursi's approach to Prophet Job in the Quran, see Bouguenaya, 'Scriptural Approach to the Problem of Evil' and Yazicioglu and Mermer, 'Affliction, Patience and Prayer: Reading Job (p) in the Quran.'

[30] Nursi, *Words*, 143–145.

reflects the beautiful qualities of the One Who sustains it in life.[31] Furthermore, Nursi contrasts the social implications of godless philosophy with that of Quranic wisdom. While the former sees power as the arbiter of truth and at the driving force for social dynamics, Quranic wisdom places truth in place of power: truth has power, that is, 'right is might, rather than might is right.'[32]

Being aware of the failure of human attempts to understand reality without guidance from the Quran, Nursi recognizes the need for Quranic wisdom regardless of scientific and technological discoveries. To use the previous metaphor, even the most skillful chemist needs instruction in realizing that the ink on the paper which he regards as mere shapes is actually a piece of paper with meaning. Similarly, even as science improves, we remain in need of the Quran which reveals the *meaning* of existence, a point we shall return to later in this chapter.[33]

Another interesting contrast between Quranic wisdom and 'godless philosophy' that Nursi offers is related to the way each of them interprets regularities in the world. 'Godless philosophy,' (which again in Nursi's works is *not* a label for a school of philosophy but more an attitude that even an illiterate person can display), fails to perceive how the regular occurrences in the world are significant. Instead, it regards the regularities in nature as 'normal,' and finds 'freaks' and exceptions to the norm interesting and worthy of attention.[34] Conversely, the Quran invites us to appreciate that regularities are actually extraordinary signs, pointing to a wonderful maker

---

[31] Ibid. 144. While the Quranic view reveals that our life, for instance, is not truly ours but a gift of the Bestower of life, given to us, to reveal His beauty and then taken away according to divine will. For a detailed discussion of such contrast between Quranic wisdom and 'godless philosophy' see Nursi, *Flashes*, 159–166.

[32] Nursi, *Words*, 146.

[33] For a discussion of how Nursi sees the relation between the Quran and modern science, see Yazicioglu, 'Perhaps their Harmony is not that Simple,' 339–355.

[34] Nursi, *Words*, 150.

behind the scenes.[35] For Nursi, one of the main aims of the Quran is to cut through the veil of familiarity (*ulfa*).

As the Quran rejects the denial of the signs of God, it also dissociates itself from a sentimentalist subjective approach to the universe. Let us consider how Nursi understands the Quranic verses that dissociate the Quran from being poetry, such as *And We have not imparted him [the Prophet] poetry, nor would it [poetry] have suited this [message]* (Q. 36:69; see also 37:37; 69:41; 52:30). By rejecting its identification as poetry, the Quran dissociates itself from being a depiction of reality based on unguided subjective feelings. In other words, the Quran's elucidation of beings and events as signs of God is about seeing things as they are, which is not to be confused with arbitrary 'poetic' responses to the world.[36]

Nursi also distinguishes Quranic wisdom from spiritual approaches that he describes as 'imbalanced.' He argues that coming from the comprehensive perspective of the Creator, the Quran offers the keys to the truths of existence, unlike various spiritual explorers whose limited visions lead them to focus on one aspect of the reality at the expense of others. Hence, the Quranic perspective balances the manifestations of Divine majesty and beauty, as well as Divine immanence and transcendence manifest in the universe. The Quran reveals the truths of the Most Beautiful Names of God manifesting in the universe in a *balanced* way, within a comprehensive vision.[37]

We should also note that Nursi's emphasis on the cosmic context of the Quran makes it more accessible to a non-specialized audience. Any general reader who is willing can learn to read the 'signs' of God in the cosmos in light of the Quranic guidance. In contrast, by privileging semantics over semiotics, traditional exegesis frequently favors the linguistic expert over the general reader. To be sure, himself being an expert in Arabic and Quranic eloquence (*balāgha*),

---

[35] Similarly, the famous Muslim sage, Jalal al-din al-Rumi (1207–1273) regards that the main message of the Quran and of all the prophets is to deconstruct seeming causality and thereby to reveal *tawhid*. (See, for instance, *Mathnawi*, Book 3, 2525)

[36] Nursi, *Sözler*, '13. Söz' [13th Word], RNK 1:53, *Words*, 151.

[37] Nursi, *Words*, 453–457.

Nursi appreciated and made use of the benefits of such an expertise.[38] Nevertheless, by focusing on the semiotic reading of the
Quran and using the semantics as a tool in its service, Nursi's approach enables the general readers to access the Quranic meanings,
despite their lack of expertise in Arabic linguistics.

Another frequent motif in traditional exegetical literature is the
genre of *asbāb al-nuzūl* or occasions of revelation. Given that he is
attentive to universal lessons communicated through specific stories,
it is not surprising that Nursi de-emphasizes this genre. The literature of occasions of revelation are often unreliable in terms of their
historical authenticity, and also their use often narrows down the
Quranic guidance to a particular historical circumstance and detracts
the reader from its cosmic context and personal implications. An
interesting example is Nursi's reading of the Quranic verse *God has
purchased the lives and possessions of the believers in return for Paradise* (Q. 9:111). *Asbāb al-nuzūl* literature places the verse in the context of the oath of Aqaba in late Meccan Period. This oath was taken
by a small group of men and women from Medina, who accepted
Prophet Muhammad's message and invited him to migrate to Medina to escape religious persecution. They promised both to worship
only One God and to defend the Prophet from physical attacks as
they would defend their own selves and families. While he was certainly aware of such reports, Nursi does not mention them in his
interpretation of this verse. Rather, he places the verse in its 'cosmic
context,' as pointing to a universal bargain available to everyone. The
transaction referred in the verse is the transaction that is extended to
every human being. Things in the universe are in a constant flux,
continuously arriving and departing, coming into existence and then
vanishing. And human being wonders: is there a way to salvage anything from this unceasing flow towards death? Is it possible to find a
way to stability and eternity in the midst of all this transience? The
verse offers a solution: sell yourself and your possessions to God in
return for eternal paradise. The trade is *not* about giving up one's self

---

[38] Nursi's fine command on Arabic *balāgha* is manifested in his *Ishārat al-
i'jāz*.

or possessions per se, but rather it is about transforming their use by shifting from using them in the name of ego to using them in the name of God. Nursi explains that the selling of one's self to God in return for Paradise means using one's body and faculties, such as reasoning, heart, and senses, in God's name, *bismillah*. Nursi also explains that such a 'transaction' perfectly matches the reality and can be confirmed in light of the signs in universe. For instance, when one does not sell one's intellect to God, it means that he uses his reasoning in a way that overlooks or rejects the indications or signs of God in the universe. In this context, the intellect only serves to recognize the darkness of a transient world. It becomes like a tool of torture, as it recognizes the sorrows of the past and uncertainties of the future, and perceives the wretchedness and finitude of the transient world around him. When one refuses to sell the intellect to God, then, one finds himself in a world disconnected from the beautiful divine names, and thus cut off from eternity and enduring meaning.[39] This is the pain contained in not selling the intellect back to its maker. In contrast, Nursi explains that the Quran invitation to sell the intellect to God refers to using the intellect to uncover the indications to Divine beauty and majesty reflected in the world and thereby connecting with the Eternal One. Such a transaction yields relief and happiness in this world as well as the world to come. Hence, Nursi reads the verse as enabling human beings to interact meaningfully with the world and transcend transience here and now.[40]

---

[39] Nursi says: 'The intelligence is, for example, like a tool. If you do not sell it to God Almighty, but rather employ it for the sake of the soul, it will become an ill-omened, noxious and debilitating tool that; it will descend to the rank of an inauspicious and destructive tool. It is for this reason that a sinful man will frequently resort to drunkenness or frivolous pleasure in order to escape the vexations and injuries of his intelligence. But if you sell your intelligence to its True Owner and employ it on His behalf, then the intelligence will become like the key to a talisman, unlocking the infinite treasures of Compassion and the vaults of wisdom that creation contains.' *Words*, 39.

[40] Such connection to a universal bargain has also precedents in the tradition in that in the *tafsir* literature one encounters the saying attributed to

In sum, while Nursi is aware that the Quran has been revealed over a period exceeding two decades under a variety of different circumstances, he does not use its initial historical context in a way that overshadow the overall purposes of the Quran and its cosmic context. Indeed, for Nursi it is a remarkable feature of the Quran that it is an overall unified text with relevance for all types of readers across the ages, despite being revealed over a period of two decades under many different circumstances of revelation.[41]

Interestingly, Nursi notes that the Quran frequently talks about seemingly petty things, even though it claims to be from God and full of wisdom. For instance, various stories about ancient people are narrated in the Quran: why would a sacred text care to narrate such an event of the past? As noted earlier, for Nursi, the answer is that the purpose of these stories transcends mere particular events. Rather each of these stories is the 'tip' of an iceberg of meaning, they represent a universal reality manifest in the cosmos. For Nursi, since the Quran speaks to all classes, and all ages, and the majority of people are common people, these stories are narrated so as to convey 'universal lessons' in a form accessible to all. Thus, for instance, Mo-

---

Imam Jafar al-Sadiq or Hasan al-Basri that this transaction includes every believer in the world. Similarly, Fakhr al-din al-Razi also suggests that the *jihad* reference in the following part of the verse includes forms of striving in God's path that are other than defense in the battlefield. Nursi's exegesis takes such references further and explains *how* the bargain can indeed be universally applicable to all audience of the Quran.

[41] *Sözler,* '25. Söz, 2. Sule, 1. Nur,' RNK 1:187. Here, Nursi refers to classical scholars such as al-Zamakhshari (d.1143), Sakkaki (d.1229), and Abd al-Qahir al-Jurjani (d. 1078) as having demonstrated the connections across the verses and the overall coherence of the Quran. He adds that while the various circumstances of revelation do not disturb the internal unity and harmony of the Quran, they have some effect on the flow of the text. Their effect is enriching like the 'bumps and excrescences appear on a tree, not to spoil the harmony of the tree, but to produce fruit which will be the means for the tree reaching its adorned perfection and beauty.' In other words, 'these factors stick out their knobbly heads in order to express meanings which will enhance the Quran's fluent [order]'. (*Words,* 426–427).

ses' insistence that his people sacrifice a cow in response to the divine command is a crucial lesson about confronting idolatry. Nursi uses information about the historical context as a means to uncover the Quranic message. He notes that the Children of Israel had spent a long time in Egypt, where cows had become an object of veneration because of their indispensability for agriculture and therefore for survival. The Children of Israel must have internalized the tendency to misperceive this animal not just a *means* but a *source* of their survival. The story of their struggling to sacrifice a cow is thus a story about a people confronting their idol in tangible terms and refusing to renounce it.[42] Through this story, the Quran conveys a valuable lesson in *tawhid* that can be applied to our own moments of idolizing a created thing. The Quran is cautioning us against turning a blessing of God into an idol worthy of adoration in itself and against depriving ourselves of the eternal source of that blessing.[43]

Nursi also de-emphasizes the *israiliyyat* or the haggadic stories borrowed mainly from Jewish and Christian oral sources used in some traditional commentaries to 'fill in' the assumed 'missing' details in Quranic stories. As is well known, aversion from *israiliyyāt* is a common tendency in contemporary Muslim approaches to the Quran. The 'lack of detail' in the Quranic narratives in comparison with the biblical and haggadic stories is increasingly recognized in a positive light. For instance, the Quran does not hold Eve as responsible for Adam's eating of the forbidden fruit. Unlike some medieval interpreters who were eager to 'augment' the Quranic story with extra-Quranic stories about how Eve is to be blamed, contemporary Muslims are increasingly recognizing that the absence of such a remark in the Quran is meaningful in itself.[44] In a way similar to these

---

[42] *Words*, 254–255.

[43] Similarly, for Nursi, miracle stories in the Quran also convey crucial principles of interrupting our familiarity (*ulfa*) with the cosmos that leads to a superficial attitude. For a detailed analysis of Nursi's interpretation of Quranic miracle stories, see Yazicioglu, *Understanding the Qur'anic Miracle Stories in the Modern Age*, (University Park, Penn.: Penn State University Press, 2013), 123–163.

[44] See Ingrid Mattson, *The Story of the Qur'an*, 192–194.

contemporary trends, Nursi regards silence of the Quran in narrative details as meaningful in itself and worthy of note. He criticizes the use of extra-Quranic stories when it overlooks Quran's cosmic context and purpose of connecting human beings to their Creator. Such uncritical use of *israiliyyāt*, even when found in classical *tafsir*, is not a genuine *exegesis* of the Quranic meanings but a distortion.[45]

At this point, we may also note that Nursi affirms the classical Islamic understanding that the Quran, being a discourse from the Eternal, contains endless meanings that are accessible to various audiences all at once, and across the ages till the end of time. In the next and final section of this chapter, let us take a closer look at how the Quran speaks to a contemporary audience from Nursi's perspective.

READING THE QURAN IN THE CONTEMPORARY AGE

As time grows older, the Quran grows younger.

B. Said Nursi, *Mektubat*

For Nursi, the Quran speaks to all periods of history and to all classes of people. Since it is coming from the Eternal One, unlike other texts, it does not become outdated or 'old' as time progresses. Rather, the Quran is an unending, inexhaustible treasury of guidance, whose treasures are revealed even more as time goes on. Indeed, each age has a special share from the word of God, in addition to the universal message of the Quran of making God known with His Most Beautiful Names that is pertinent across all ages.[46]

A fascinating aspect of the modern age is the advance in the exploration of the universe. Nursi notes how scientific disciplines have undergone exponential growth, giving rise to the creation of disciplines within disciplines in order to study natural phenomena. If there had been no order or consistency in the world, it would not be possible to study phenomena and consequently sciences could not progress. Therefore, according to Nursi, these developments in the study of nature relate anew to a crucial aspect of the Quranic dis-

---

[45] Nursi, *Muhakemat*, RNK 2:1985–1988.
[46] Nursi, *Letters*, 456.

course: its constant reference to the universe as *ayāt* or 'signs.'[47] When interpreted in light of the Quran, various scientific discipline can be utilized to confirm and elucidate the Quranic interpretation of the cosmos as pointing to the wisdom and other Most Beautiful Names (*al-asmā al-ḥusna*) of God. Interestingly, referring to the verse *We have adorned the lowest heaven with lamps and made them [missiles] for stoning devils...* (Q. 67:5), Nursi suggests that when interpreted in the light of the Quranic teachings on *ayāt*, each scientific discipline can enlighten different aspects of the order in the universe, each becoming like a star (*al-najm al-thāqib*), piercing through the darkness of disbelief, defeating doubts about God cast by the devils.[48]

Nursi of course was not naïve; he was aware that modern scientific discourse often brought with it a particular philosophical baggage, that of materialism and atheism. It is a popular notion that the scientific description of reality undoes the need for belief in God. For instance, it is suggested that rain was associated with God in the past because people did not know enough about the formation of rain. It is surmised that since today we have a scientific description of the water cycle, we do not need to believe in or rely on God anymore. Nursi challenges such understanding; it is a misunderstanding of reality and that is why we need the Quranic guidance in understanding the universe. Nursi suggests that the *fact* that we can describe, for instance, the water cycle in the world and predict rain does not mean that we therefore do not depend on the source of power and mercy that sustains the water cycle. Modern science seems to provide a description and reliable weather forecast, but it does not eliminate the crucial *interpretive* question: Can the formation of rain, which is clearly a purposeful, useful and life-yielding process, be attributed to purposeless, blind, and lifeless natural causes, such as heat, water particles, clouds, coldness, and gravity? Or, do these natural causes together with the effects associated with them point to a merciful and wise Life-Giver who employs them purposefully and creates life out

---

[47] Nursi, *Muhakemat*, RNK 2:1986.
[48] Nursi, *Iṣarat al-iʿjāz*, RNK 2:1216.

of them? It is only when one hastily skips over this important questioning and critical analysis that s/he can disregard the need for belief in God. Nursi deconstructs such misunderstanding. He also shows that when properly contextualized, information about the world can be used to appreciate the Quranic message better. When science brings in more data about the orderliness and purposefulness of the world, we should ask more intently: what does this regular and beneficial process 'say' to us?[49]

Living at a time of great social and political upheavals, Nursi also saw the Quran as relevant in contemporary socio-political contexts.[50] In interpreting various Quranic commandments, Nursi notes a crucial principle: in the Quran, the divine author speaks not with a limited human vision but with a comprehensive view on human life and cosmic realities. Moreover, Nursi notes that the Quranic injunctions address not only ideal but also non-ideal conditions, like in the case of polygamy and divorce. He also notes that the Quran sometimes offers general principles (*'āmm*) that need to be interpreted when applied to a particular situation (*takhṣīṣ*), like in the case of relations with 'people of the book.'[51] Although he occasionally offers insightful interpretations of implications for the sacred law or *sharia* in the Quran, Nursi's works are not focused on Islamic Law in interpreting the Quran, unlike the predominant trends in the current Islamic discourse. Instead, Nursi focuses on the commonly underappreciated cosmic and existential context of the Quran.

His treatise on *ijtihad* or legal interpretation, was interestingly written as an interpretation of the Quranic verse *if they referred it to the Messenger and those in authority among them, those seeking its meaning would have found it out from them* (Q. 4:83).[52] Here, Nursi stresses the importance of a holistic approach to *sharia* that is based

---

[49] For a detailed analysis of Nursi's interpretation of natural phenomena, see Yazicioglu, *Understanding Quranic Miracle Stories*, 135–147.

[50] For a brief discussion of Nursi on contemporary politics, see Yazicioglu, 'Sa'id Nursi,' 110–112.

[51] See: Nursi, *Münazarat*, RNK 2:1944, 1955.

[52] English translation is from Abdel Haleem's *Qur'an: A New Translation*, 58.

on the Quranic spirit instead of a piece-meal approach motivated by trumping lasting spiritual priorities with a misunderstanding of what is perceived as the 'needs of the times.'[53]

As a contemporary interpreter of the Quran, Nursi also engaged with some of the contemporary criticisms of the Quran. One criticism was about repetitiveness; it was claimed that the Quran repeats itself over and over again. Nursi responds by highlighting not only the basis of the Quranic content but also the basis of the interaction between the Quran and the reader's life. He suggests that the Quran is 'nourishment' for the human heart and the mind, and like 'light and water' for the human spirit. Repetition is boring and problematic only when it does not meet a need. In contrast, if the need keeps renewing, repeating the meeting of that need becomes pleasurable. For instance, we eat every day and breathe every moment. Nobody finds breathing every moment or eating when they are hungry boring. Similarly, the Quranic statements enlighten and nourish the spirit and the heart and that nourishment is needed on a regular basis. The Quran is nurturing for a reader who is aware of his spiritual needs.[54]

Another criticism directed at the Quran was its supposed lack of organization. As is well known, the Quran does not follow linear organization: it does not follow a timeline or a narrative plot nor is it organized in the order it was received by Prophet Muhammad. According to Nursi, the wisdom behind such lack of a rigid order is that it frees each verse to interconnect with many other verses at once. In his profound book on Quranic hermeneutics, *Muhakamat* (Ar. *Muḥākamāt*), composed in Arabic and translated by his brother Abdulmejid Nursi into Ottoman Turkish, Nursi offers the metaphor of concentric figures in a painting where 'one and the same dot becomes the eye of a character, the silhouette of another's face, the mouth of another and the nasal opening of yet another figure... Similarly, there are such intersecting relations across the words of the Di-

---

[53] Nursi, *Sözler*, RNK I: 212–216; *Words*, 495–502.
[54] Nursi, *Words*, 251, 767.

vine speech.' [55] In a similar vein, Nursi gives the metaphor of stars in the sky so as to describe the relationship between Quranic verses. When one looks at the sky at night, it seems at first that the stars are scattered randomly without any organization. Whereas, they are of course organized, otherwise there would be havoc in space. Yet, they are organized in a way that does not marginalize any particular star. For, if there is no definite center, there is no periphery; one could take any star as the center and see the other stars from its angle. Similarly, the verses of the Quran are like stars, and each can become a center for the rest. The loose organization of the verses constitutes the Quran's intra-textual richness, strength and flexibility. [56]

Nursi's response to contemporary criticisms of the Quranic style is quite original. Viewed in the background of some of the recent trends in Quranic Studies, we may better appreciate his approach. Recently, several scholars noted the need to question our expectations of a linear organization from the Quran. A typical linear text inevitably limits the interrelationship across its parts, by requiring a beginning, climax, end and particular flow of its chapters. In contrast, as Michael Sells highlights, the Quran (lit. 'recitation') is a primarily oral text, which allows for dynamic relationship across its passages. [57]

---

[55] Nursi, *Muhakemat*, RNK 2:2017.

[56] Nurs, *Words*, 151.

[57] See: Michael Sells, *Approaching the Qur'an* and Daniel Madigan, *The Qur'an's Self-Image: Writing and Authority in Islam's Scripture*. Similarly, William Graham and others have analyzed the dynamic aspect of the *kitāb* or book in the Quran, suggesting that the Quranic discourse flows like a dynamic conversation that any reader could enter at any point, without feeling left out for not having heard or read the 'beginning' of the message. In this connection, we may also note that Nursi's understanding that the major themes of the Quran, which are repeated in various forms, are contained in all parts of the Quran. In other words, like a hologram, the major themes of the Quran are found everywhere in the text, in every *sura*, every *aya* and sometimes in a single word even. Nursi suggests that there is a profound wisdom and compassion in this style: since not everyone can read entire the Quran at short intervals, each chapter, including the short ones,

In sum, Nursi approaches the Quran with an emphasis on taking into consideration its author, audience, purpose, and its cosmic context. The Quran is like a treasure map for existence filled with treasures of meaning pointing to the majesty and beauty of the Transcendent. Indeed, the Quran is a dynamic 'recitation' or commentary on the cosmic show unfolding each moment. Nursi's striking attitude to the Quran reflects a deep grasp of the Quran's main themes and its overall purpose and it enables the audience to relate to the Quran here-and-now. With such an understanding, Nursi interprets various Quranic passages, whether they are referring to nature, prophetic stories, or commands, in a way that allows the reader to both relate to and confirm the text. Building on some of the most insightful approaches within the classical Islamic tradition and displaying profound awareness of the challenges and opportunities of a contemporary world, Nursi is a crucial Quranic interpreter worth studying further. The selections in this book will offer a glimpse of the way in which the primary Quranic theme, oneness of God, is enlightening, relevant and fruitful for the contemporary reader.

---

are packed with the essential nutrients that represent the gist of the entire Quran, so to speak, and thereby fulfill a recurring human need for meaning and for connecting to the Creator. (Nursi, *Words*, 250).

SELECTIONS FROM EPISTLES OF LIGHT
(RISALE-I NUR)

I

BISMILLAH: IN THE NAME OF GOD

This epistle explains a key Quranic phrase, *bismillah,* by elucidating its reality in the universe. Using wonderfully simple language and short parables, this treatise explains how all things in nature constantly declare *bismillah.* They say *bismillah* not necessarily verbally, but with their 'tongue of disposition' (*lisān al-ḥāl*), i.e. through their way of being and functioning.

In order to show how this is the case, Nursi first highlights that clearly beings accomplish tasks beyond their capacity. When we recognize this state of affair, it becomes easy to conclude that they are accomplishing such results through a greater power. Nursi provides a parable to communicate this crucial reasoning and make it accessible to his audience. If we see that a person is able to make a whole town obey him, we can deduce that he is not acting in his own name as a mere citizen, in which case no one would take him seriously and submit to his orders. Obviously, he must be acting in the name of an authority that holds power over the citizens, such as the government. Similarly, we repeatedly observe beings accomplishing results well beyond their abilities. This indicates that they must be acting *in the name of* an All-Powerful One, and not on their own initiative, in their own name. Thus, with a careful reflection on natural events, we can recognize the agency of an Unseen Powerful One who enables a tiny seed to flourish into a huge tree, a tree to bear abundant fruit, animals to produce nourishing milk, and so on.[1] To add to Nursi's examples, we can think of a spider spinning an intricate web or muscle tissue in our vocal cords producing sophisticated and precise sounds. In each case, beings are accomplishing tasks far beyond their capacities. That means they are acting through an all-encompassing power, i.e. in the name of God, *bismillah*.

After having explained how natural causes act in God's name, Nursi then makes a connection to the miracle passages in the Quran. Miracles are often considered to be exceptional moments where things or people act in ways beyond their power, such as the references in the Quran to an infant speaking (a miracle of Jesus), a staff becoming a snake (a miracle of Moses), a virgin conceiving (a miracle of Mary), fire not burning (a miracle of Abraham), and so on. Nursi reads these extraordinary events mentioned in the Quran as inviting us to pay attention to ordinary miracles all around us. For instance, in the Quran, upon God's command Moses strikes with his staff at a time of need and, miraculously water gushes forth from the rock for his people to drink. (*And We said, 'O Moses, strike the rock with your staff'—whereupon twelve springs gushed forth from it...* Q. 2:60) Nursi sees this verse as a commentary on the natural world. He notes that this miracle story is actually played out in everyday life. For instance, when a delicate root pierces through the soil to reach to a water resource, it is a re-enactment of Moses' miracle of splitting the rock with his staff and bringing forth water. Just as the performance of Moses's staff was wondrous, in the sense that it exceeded the capacity of an ordinary staff, the delicate rootlets of a plant piercing through hard soil is amazing. For such a feat exceeds the capacity of the seeming natural causes associated with it.[2] By using Quranic mir-

---

[1] Both the logic of Nursi's argument here and most of his examples from nature are borrowed from the Quran. (See: Q. 2:22, 6:95, 6:141, 7:57, 14:32, 16:66, etc.)

[2] The word for 'miracle' in the original Turkish text is '*mucize*' from the Arabic '*mu'jiza.*' The latter is derived from the root '*a-j-z*, which indicated inability or powerlessness. Nursi uses this term in the sense that all causes are unable ('*ajiz*) to produce their effects. In this sense, all created beings

acle stories as a revelatory insight into the natural world, Nursi notes how events in the world can take place only 'in God's name,' i.e. through Divine power and will. This is an example of how through Quranic guidance, one discovers the speech of the universe, how all things declare *bismillah*.

It is worth noting that in this treatise, as elsewhere in other parts of the *Risale-i Nur*, the so-called 'ordinary' events are amazing not because the natural causes associated with them have not yet been discovered. Rather, it is because such 'seeming causes' (*al-asbāb al-ẓāhiriyya*) do not have the capacity to produce what is happening. The causes can only 'work' if they are empowered by 'Causer of all causes' (*musabbib al asbāb* or *musabbib al-haqiqi*). In the case of rootlets piercing through hard soil, for instance, we may discover that these delicate leaves release a secretion or enzyme with which the soil is pierced. Yet, our discovery of this liquid does not at all decrease our awe; on the contrary it increases the evidence that the whole process occurs *bismillah*. For, the production and secretion of such a liquid in a plant's roots are acts of comprehensive wisdom and knowledge. And the liquid's seeming ability to penetrate the hard soil is an act of power. All these qualities of wisdom, knowledge and power far exceed the capacity of the fragile, ignorant, blind and powerless roots. The frail and unconscious rootlets from which the liquid comes forth cannot be responsible for producing such enzymes and piercing through the hard soil. Therefore, the rootlets, together with their enzymes, must be acting in God's name. In other words, they are declaring *bismillah*. Thus, even after we acquire detailed knowledge of how the delicate roots produce enzymes and pierce through hard soil, the event remains just as amazing, if not more so. All these are signs to comprehensive wisdom, knowledge and power, and therefore indicate an all-wise, all-knowing and all-powerful being.

After taking the reader through the dynamic 'pages' of nature under the guidance of the Quran and showing how the universe acts

---

and events are *mujiza*, in the sense that they are inimitable and they put causes to impotence (*i'jaz*).

in God's name, the treatise then turns to human choices. This is an example of how Nursi reads the oneness of God as relevant to the reader's life here-and-now. If the entire universe *is* functioning through the Sustainer's power, in His name, if this *is* the reality of existence, then human beings are no exception. The only difference is that human beings have the capacity to consciously acknowledge this truth or to reject it. Nursi argues that recognizing the true power behind all, the giver of blessings is the most reasonable, honest, truthful, and meaningful choice for human beings. Thus, the treatise ends with encouraging the reader to choose to consciously act in God's name; and to affirm that the power, wisdom, compassion, beauty, that is reflected in their actions point to the Source of all power and beauty, i.e. to God. Hence, human beings are to gratefully accept the blessings granted to them as signs to the One & True Bestower of all Blessings. This is what it means to live in God's name, *bismillah*. To utter *bismillah* at the beginning of all actions as it is the custom among Muslims is simply a reminder of this profound cosmic reality of *tawhid*.

***

ON BISMILLAH[3]

In the Name of God, the Merciful, the Compassionate.
And from Him we seek help.
All praise be to God, Sustainer of all the worlds.
Peace and blessings be upon our master Muhammad
and upon his family and his companions.

Bismillah, 'In the Name of God,' is the start of all goodness. Let us also start with it. Know, Oh my ego (*nafs*)![4] This blessed phrase is

---

[3] This is the title we gave to Nursi's 'First Word,' in *Sözler* [*Words*], RNK 1:3–4.

[4] 'Nefis' in Ottoman original is from *nafs* in Arabic, which has various meanings and uses. Sometimes it simply denotes self, soul or person. Other times, it is used to indicate a part in human being that is stubborn, shortsighted and resistant to faith. In the above context, it seems to refer to the

not only a mark of Islam, but it is also ingrained in the creation as all beings constantly recite it through 'the tongue of their disposition' (*lisān al-ḥāl*). If you want to understand how *bismillah* holds an awesome and unending strength and how it is a vast and endless treasure, listen to the following parable:

Once upon a time, two men went on a journey through the deserts of Arabia. In order to travel safely and survive in the harsh desert, one had to take the name of a tribal chief in the area in order to enter under his protection. For surely, a traveler on his own would perish in the face of the difficulties in meeting his needs compounded with the innumerable challenges of journeying through the desert. One of the two men was humble, the other arrogant. The humble man took the name of a tribal chief, while the arrogant man did not. The first one traveled safely wherever he went. If he encountered bandits, he would say: 'I am traveling in the name of tribal leader so-and-so,' and they would leave him alone. If he came across a tent, he would again mention the tribal chief's name and he would be hosted generously in the tribal chief's honor. In contrast, the arrogant man had a horrible time throughout his journey. He was constantly trembling in fear and begging from others. He was both humiliated and ridiculed.

Now, my arrogant soul (*nafs*), you are that traveler. And this world is the desert in the story. Your weakness ('*ajz*) and poverty (*faqr*) are boundless. Your enemies and needs are endless. So, take the name of the Pre-Eternal Ruler and Post-Eternal Sustainer of this desert and be saved from begging before the whole universe and trembling before all kinds of events.

Indeed, this phrase, *bismillah* is such a blessed treasury: it connects your infinite vulnerability, weakness ('*ajz*) and poverty (*faqr*) to the source of infinite power and mercy. It makes your weakness

---

latter category, i.e. the egoistic soul, hence our rendering as 'ego' so as to highlight its negative connotation. The Quran distinguishes between the evil-commanding soul (*al-nafs al-ammāra*), the blaming soul (*al-nafs al-lawwāma*), and the soul that is at peace (*al-nafs al-muṭma'inna*). See Q. 11:53, 75:2, 89:27.

and poverty an excellent intercessor in the Court of the All-Powerful, Compassionate One (*al-qadīr al-rahīm*). Indeed, the person who acts *bismillah*, in the name of God, is like a government official who acts in the name of the government. Unlike an individual with no authority who is acting in his own name, such a person fears nobody. He performs every matter and withstands all challenges in the name of the law and the government.

In the beginning we said that *all beings* recite 'in the Name of God' (*bismillah*) through their 'tongue of disposition,' (*lisān al-ḥāl*). How is that?

Consider the following. Say, you saw that a person walked into a town and made all its inhabitants move to another location and start working on a project. Given that this one person is able to accomplish such results beyond his personal power, you would be certain that he had not acted in his own name. Rather, you would know that he was an official, acting in the name of the government and relying on its power.

In a similar way, all things act in the name of Almighty God because, for instance, tiny things like seeds and grains accomplish things beyond their power: they grow into huge trees, raising loads like mountains on their tiny shoulders. Clearly, in accomplishing such wondrous tasks all these trees proclaim, *in the Name of God*, and fill their hands from the treasury of Divine mercy, and offer them to us. Similarly, all gardens say: *in the Name of God*, and become huge cooking pots from the kitchens of Divine power in which numerous varieties of foods are prepared. All blessed animals like cows, camels, sheep, and goats, say: *in the Name of God*, and become like fountains pouring milk from the abundance of mercy, and offering it to us as a most delicate and pure nourishment in the name of the Provider (*al-razzāq*).

The roots and rootlets of plants, trees, and grasses soft as silk, say: *in the Name of God*, and pierce and pass through hard rock and earth. When they mention the name of God, the name of the Most Merciful, everything becomes subjected to them. Indeed, roots spread through hard rock and earth and yield 'fruits' [such as potatoes, carrots, and other root vegetables] as easily as branches spread through air and produce fruits. What is more, the delicate green leaves retain their moisture for months in the face of extreme heat thereby challenging and silencing Naturalists who explain events by referring them to nature itself. It is as though they are saying: 'Even heat and hardness, in which you trust so much, are under a divine command. Indeed, like the Staff of Moses (peace be upon him), each of those silken rootlets conform to the command of, *And We said, O Moses, strike the rock with your staff,* (Quran, 2:60) and split the rock. And the delicate leaves fine as thin paper recite the verse, *O fire be coolness and peace* (Quran, 21:69) against the heat of the sun, each like the body of Abraham (peace be upon him).'

Now, since all things say: *in the Name of God,* and bear God's gifts and blessings in God's name, and offer them to us, we too should declare: *in the Name of God.* We should give in the name of God and take in the name of God. And we should not take from heedless people who neglect to give in God's name.

Question: We make payments to people for things, even though people are only the conveyor of God's blessings. What should we 'pay' to God, Who is the true owner of the gifts?

The Answer: The price that the True Bestower of blessings wants in return for those valuable gifts and goods can be offered in three ways: one is through *remembrance (dhikr),* another through *gratitude (shukr),* and the other through *reflection (tafakkur).* Saying 'In the Name of God' *(bismillah)* at the start of enjoying the blessings is *remembrance,* and, 'All praise be to God' *(alhamdulillah)* at the end is *gratitude.* And, *reflection* consists of contemplating His blessings and recognizing that they are priceless wonders of art, miracles of power of the Eternally Self-Sufficient on Whom everything depends *(al-samad)* and gifts of His mercy. Would it not be foolish to adore a postman for delivering a wonderful gift to you while remaining unaware of the sender of the gift?[5] It is a thousand times more foolish to praise and love the apparent source of gifts while

---

[5] The literal expression used in the text is, 'Would it not be foolish to kiss the feet of a poor man who brings to you a precious gift from a King, while forgetting the real sender of the gift?'

forgetting the True Originator and Bestower of Gifts. O my soul! If you do not wish to be foolish, give in God's name, take in God's name, begin in God's name, and act in God's name. And be in peace!

2

NATURE:
WINDOW ONTO THE CAUSER OF ALL
CAUSES

One of the last chapters of Nursi's crucial work, *the Words*, '33rd Word,' was written during a Ramadan as a response to a question about the Quranic verse: *We shall show them Our signs (ayāt) upon the horizons [of the universe] (afāq) and within themselves (anfus) till it becomes clear to them that it is the truth. Does it not suffice that your Sustainer is Witness over all things?* (Q. 41:53) The questioner requests a brief explanation of this verse, showing how these two major *signs*, namely the 'macrocosm' (that is, the universe), and 'microcosm,' (that is, the human being), reveal 'the necessary existence and oneness of God (*waḥdāniyya*) and his attributes and 'essential qualities' (*shu'unāt.*)' The unnamed questioner also provides the reason for such request: 'For the unbelievers have gone too far,' as they are now questioning the need for praying to God.[1]

Nursi responds by noting that all the chapters of *Words* can be read as an exegesis of the quoted verse, as a 'drop' from the verse's 'ocean.' Before he sets out to offer 'thirty-three windows' that show existence and oneness of God, he offers a parable. Think of a wondrous person who builds a vast magnificent palace. He first sets forth its foundations with a wise and purposeful plan. Then he details the

---

[1] Nursi, *Words*, 683.

parts of the palace, constructs its various rooms and subsections. Then he decorates the palace exquisitely, installs various technology in it, and constantly changes and renews the palace so as to display amazing skills and generosity. This amazing maker also opens up a window from each room showing his abode and places a 'phone line' in each room. Nursi then unpacks how this is a parable for this world and its Peerless Glorious Wise Maker. Among the important points[2] he makes pertains to the 'windows': 'From each 'room,' level, universe, species and individual, [God] has opened up windows onto Himself, showing His existence and unity. He has placed a phone line in each heart. Now, it would of course be beyond our capacity to talk about all these innumerable windows. Referring them to the all comprehensive Divine knowledge, we shall just offer thirty-three windows as lights from the *ayat* of the Quran....' In keeping with the 'blessed number' thirty-three associated with daily prayer invocations, Nursi then offers thirty-three 'windows,' six of which are selected below. The Quranic passages in the beginning of each 'window' is from the original text. We added a short introductory note to each selected window within square brackets.

***

10TH WINDOW

[This 'window' talks about the interconnectedness of the universe as a sign to the Sustainer's existence and unity. The fact that unconscious and ignorant things are acting in cooperation for beneficial results shows that they are all being employed by the Maker of all.]

And [God is the one who] sends down water from the sky, and thereby brings forth [all manner] of fruits for your sustenance;

---

[2] Another important point he mentions is that the Creator sustains the universe according to universal laws but He also grants exceptions for individuals 'crying out at the constraints of those laws.' Indeed, 'within those universal and general principles He has special favours, special succour, special manifestations, so that everything may seek help from Him and look to Him at all times for every need.' Nursi, *Words*, 684 (modified translation)

and He has made ships subservient for you, so that they may sail through the sea at His behest; and has made the rivers subservient for you; and has made the sun and the moon, both of them constant upon their courses, subservient for you; and He has made the night and the day subservient for you. And He gives you from all what you ask of Him. And if you would count God's blessings, you could never compute them.[3]

(Quran, 14:32–34)

All beings in this universe help each other, respond to each other and support each other thus showing that they are under the care of one single caretaker (*murabbi*), directed by one single planner and director (*mudabbir*), managed by one single governor (*mutaṣarrif*)[4] and demonstrating that they are the servants of one single Sustainer.

Look at the principle of cooperation at work in the universe: With command of the Sustainer, the sun 'cooks' the necessities required for the life for living beings. Similarly, the moon serves as a calendar for computing the passing of time, and light, air, water and nutrition hasten to the aid of living beings. Moreover, plants hasten to the aid of animals, and animals hasten to the aid of human beings. Likewise, organs in a body support each other and nutritive particles hasten to the aid of the cells in the body.

In other words, *unconscious* and *lifeless* beings help and support each other with wisdom and generosity and they heed each other's needs, thereby manifesting a principle of generosity, compassion and mercy. This reality clearly shows that they are the servants, employees, and creations of the One and Unique (*al-wāḥid al-aḥad*) Necessarily Existent Self-Sufficient One on whom everything depends (*al-fard al-ṣamad*), the All-Powerful, All-Knowing, All-Merciful, and All-Generous.

---

[3] The earlier part of the Quranic passage starts with 'God is the one who...' This is another example of how the Quran describes who God is through what we observe in the universe.

[4] In Arabic, *mutaṣarrif* is the active participle of the verb *taṣarrafa*, which means to act without restriction and have the right of disposal over something.

O bankrupt philosopher—what would you say to this 'window'? Can you explain away any of these facts with blind coincidence?

11TH WINDOW

[This 'window' is on how the human heart shows the One and Only Creator. It builds on the interconnectedness of the universe explained in the previous window. Given the interconnectedness of all things, logically it is extremely difficult to explain even one being without *tawhid*. However, what is at stake here is not just finding logical consistency. Rather, the peace of the heart is implicated. *Shirk* is problematic not only for logical thinking but also, and perhaps especially so, for the heart. Thus, connecting the heart and the mind, this window shows that the 'remembrance of God,' *dhikr*, which is mentioned in the Quranic verse cited below, involves both the heart and the mind.]

> *Truly, in the remembrance* (dhikr) *of God hearts do find their rest.* (Quran, 13:28)

All the souls and hearts pained and tormented by the suffering and confusion that misguidance engenders can only be relieved by knowing the One and Only Creator. They are saved by attributing all beings to only one Maker. They find peace with the mention of only One God.

Indeed, if all beings are not attributed to one single being, then every single thing would have to be ascribed to innumerable causes, as it is clearly shown in the 22nd Word.[5] In that case, the existence of one single thing would be as difficult as the existence of all beings. In contrast, if we attribute all things and beings to God, it means that we are attributing them all to one single being.

---

[5] Keeping in mind that the above selection is from 33rd Word, reference to '22nd Word,' is a reference to an earlier chapter in *Words*. Due to its length, we placed our translation of 22nd Word at the end of this volume (chapters 12 and 13).

If we do not attribute them to God, then it implies that we are attributing the existence of every single thing to innumerable causes. In that case, the creation of a single fruit would become as complicated as the creation of the entire universe, and may be even more difficult than that. Indeed, if we give the command of one soldier to a hundred officers, hundreds of difficulties would ensue. Whereas if a hundred soldiers were to be commanded by one officer, their management would become as easy as commanding one single soldier. Similarly, it is extremely difficult and complicated for numerous diverse causes to converge in order to produce a single thing while the creation of many things by one single being is very easy.

Therefore, it is crucial to confirm the oneness of the Creator and to know God as the sole Maker of everything. Indeed, it is only through knowing God as the sole Creator that human beings can be saved from the endless torments that arise from the curiosity and desire for truth inherent in their nature. Clearly the path of denial (*kufr*) and associating partners with God (*shirk*) is precluded and baseless since it involves manifold difficulties and pains. Whereas there is limitless ease in confirming Divine oneness; an ease that corresponds to the ease, abundance and excellent artistry observable in the creation of beings. Without doubt, the path of Divine oneness is necessary and it is the truth.

You see how dark and painful the path of misguidance (*dalalah*) is. Why do you insist on following it? Look, how easy and joyful the path of belief and *tawhid* is. Enter that path and be saved.

19TH WINDOW

[This 'window' offers a reflection on a key point in the Quran: that everything in the heavens and the earth glorifies God. Nursi reflects on this Quranic notion by using the examples of a flower and a tree. In order to 'hear' their glorification, Nursi pays close attention to the order and balance in them. Moreover, he highlights the embellishment and beauty in them. The adornment of things indicates that their Maker is a 'Beautiful Generous One' who is 'making himself known and loved.' Just like the flower and the tree, all living beings and rest of the creation are constantly speaking of their Maker and revealing His beautiful qualities. The universe is like a huge symphony of praise and this window offers a lively 'trailer' from the speaking universe. To choose to remain deaf to this symphony and to pretend that the creation is mute is a huge loss. In fact, as Nursi explains elsewhere, (such as in Chapter 9 of this book), it is an insult and injustice to the creation.]

> *The seven heavens extol His limitless glory, and the earth, and all that they contain; and there is not a single thing but extols His limitless glory and praise: but you [O human beings] fail to grasp the manner of their glorifying Him! Verily, He is forbearing, much-forgiving!* (Quran, 17:44)

As this verse indicates, the Glorious Maker has placed so much wisdom and meaning in the celestial bodies that it is as if in order to show His majesty and beauty, He has embellished the skies with the 'words' of the suns, moons, and stars. He has also placed such wisdom, meaning and purpose to the beings in the air that it is as if He has made the sky speak through the 'words' of the thunder, lightning, and raindrops to show His perfect wisdom and beautiful compassion. Furthermore, He has made the face of the earth like a head with many tongues speaking, with meaningful words such as animals and plants, thereby displaying the perfectness of His art...He also makes the plants and trees speak with the 'words' of leaves, flowers, and fruits, thereby declaring His perfect art and beautiful compassion. As to these flowers and fruits, He also makes them speak through the 'words' of their seeds, thus revealing His subtle art and perfect sustainership (*rubūbiyya*) to conscious beings.

Now from among these endless 'words' of glorification (*kalimāt tasbiḥiya*), let us listen to the speech of just one shoot and one flower, to see how they bear witness to their Maker. Indeed, each plant and each tree reveal its Maker in so many ways, speak in so many 'tongues,' that they amaze the mindful people and make them exclaim 'Glory be to God (*subhanallah*), how beautifully they are bearing witness to their Maker.'

Yes, the glorification of each plant as it flowers and sprouts, and its smiling 'speech' is as beautiful and as clear as the plant itself. For we see *wisdom* within the *order* uttered by the beautiful 'mouth' of each flower and by the 'tongue' of each orderly shoot, and by the 'words' of each well-arranged seed. And this order is within a *balance*, which demonstrates that all of this is done with *knowledge*.

Likewise, this balance is within an *artistic tapestry* which demonstrates the skillfulness of this art. And that artistic tapestry is within *embellishments* which *demonstrate munificence (lutf)* and *generosity (karam)*. And those embellishments are wrapped in lovely *smells*, which demonstrate *compassion (raḥma)* and *beneficence (iḥsan)*.

All these meaningful features one within the other constitute such a 'tongue' of witnessing that speaks of the Beautiful Maker [al-ṣāniʿ] with His names. This 'tongue' of witnessing also describes Him with His attributes, and expounds the manifestation of His names. And, it expresses His making Himself loved and known.

Now, if you can hear such a testimony from one single flower, can you imagine how strong would be the testimony of all the flowers in all the gardens on the face of the earth declaring the necessary existence and oneness (waḥda) of the Glorious Maker. Can any conscious human being resist this powerful testimony? What doubts and what heedlessness (ghafla) can remain?

Now come let's look at a tree carefully. Can you see it's lovely 'mouth' testifying to its Maker through the orderly coming out of its leaves in spring, the balanced opening up of its flowers, and the growing of its fruits with wisdom and mercy, and their dancing at the blowing of the breeze like innocent children in the embrace of the branches? Observe how

- the 'tongue' of the leaves turning green at a hand of generosity,

- the 'voice' of the flowers smiling with the joy of received kindness,

- and the 'words' of the fruits laughing by on account of a manifestation of mercy

all declare a wise order. And within that wise order, we can see a just balance. And within this balance that reflects justice, there are refined arts and embroideries. Within the skillful art and embellishments, there are various delicious tastes and pleasant scents that indicate compassion (raḥma) and beneficence (iḥsan).

And within these delicious tastes and pleasant scents, we can see seeds and kernels that are truly miracles of divine power (muʿjizāt al-qudra). All these show very clearly the necessary existence, unity, beautiful compassion and perfect sustainership (rubūbiyya) of a

Wise, Generous, Compassionate, Beneficient, Bestower, Beautifier and Exalter Maker and Artist. (*sāni', ḥakīm, karīm, raḥīm, muḥsin, mun'im, mujammil, mufaḍḍil*)

Thus, if you can listen to the speech of all the trees on the earth as they speak through their way of being and tongue of disposition, you will see and understand what beautiful jewels there are in the treasury of *all that is in the heavens and the earth glorifies God.* (Q. 59:24)

O heedless soul plunged into ingratitude! Do you think you have been left idle in this world? The Beautiful Generous One is making himself known and loved through all these innumerable 'tongues,' expressions, and glorifications. Simply by ignoring those discourses, you cannot silence them. So, come to your senses and heed them. For the universe does not fall silent just because you close your ears. And beings do not stop speaking; they continue to testify to unity of the Maker (*waḥdāniyya*). They shall of course convict you.

23RD WINDOW

[This 'window' addresses how life reveals attributes and qualities of the One Creator. Life is like a focal point on which lights of various beautiful names of God converge and shine clearly. Here, Nursi also refers to the attributes and essential qualities of God revealed through life by using a new term: *shu'unāt*. This term comes from *'shu'n'* in Arabic, which is the plural of *'sha'n'* meaning 'task.' It is used once in the Quran: *everyday He is upon a task.* (Q. 55:29) It is a rare term in Islamic theology as well. The famous Islamic scholar and mystic Imam al-Rabbani Ahmad al-Sirhindi (d. 1034 AH/1624 CE) 'uses it to refer to one of the stations that is closest to God's essence (*dhat*) in the Sufi practice of 'the journey to God.'"[6] As Mustafa Tuna notes, Nursi refers to *shu'un*, 'often doubly pluralizing it as 'ṣuūnāt'—as a stage of contemplation in which one can come closest to God's essence, which itself remains beyond human comprehension according to a Prophetic tradition that defines the limits of con-

---

[6]Tuna, 'At the Vanguard of Contemporary Muslim Thought,' 331.

templating God in the Sunni Islamic tradition.' Since 'the specific connotations that the term *shu'unāt* acquires in Nursi's usage ...defy a comprehensive translation and go far beyond referencing a station in the journey to God that is experienced yet not describable,' it is difficult to give an adequate translation.[7] Therefore, we kept the Arabic original in brackets whenever we offered an approximate rendering of the term.]

He who has created death as well as life (Q. 67:2).

Life is the brightest and loveliest miracle of divine power. It is the strongest evidence for the oneness of God (*waḥdāniyya*) as well as the most comprehensive and luminous mirror to the manifestations of the Self-Sufficient One on whom everything depends.

Indeed, life shows the Ever Living and Self-Subsistent Source of All Being (*al-Hayy al-Qayyum*) with all His names and 'essential qualities' (*shuu'nat*). For life is like sunlight which is comprised of seven colors or like a healing concoction of various ingredients mixed together. Accordingly, life is a truth made of many attributes. Some of these attributes expand through the senses that are differentiated as they grow like [like hearing or seeing]. While most of the attributes associated with life reveal themselves through the emotions that are disclosed by bubbling up out of life.

Moreover, life includes the sustenance, compassion, support and wisdom that are manifest throughout the governance and management of the universe. It is as if life pulls them along wherever it goes. For instance, when life enters a body, it makes its home and orders it with wisdom thus manifesting the name All-Wise. Similarly, life manifests the name Generous (*al-karīm*) by organizing and arranging the body according to its needs. Likewise, the name Compassionate (*al-rahīm*) manifests through granting all kinds of blessings for the continuation and perfection of life. Moreover, the manifestation of the name of Provider (*al-razzāq*) emerges through the

---

[7] Tuna, 'At the Vanguard of Contemporary Muslim Thought,' 330 (also see 331–336).

production and storage of both physical and spiritual nourishments for the maintenance and unfolding of life within the body.

Thus, life is like a point of convergence in which various attributes intermingle. to the point of becoming one and the same. It is as if life in its entirety is knowledge, and at the same time it is power, while it is simultaneously wisdom and compassion, and so on. Its comprehensive quintessence makes life a mirror to the Eternally Self-Sufficient One on whom everything depends *(mir'at ṣamadiyya)*, reflecting the qualities of the Sustainer's Essence *(shu'ūn al-dhāt al-rabbānī)*.

It is because of this mystery that the Necessary Existent Being, who is the Ever Living and Self-Subsistent Source of All Being *(al-ḥayy al-qayyūm)*, creates life abundantly and profusely, and He spreads and disperses it widely. He puts everything at the service of life. For life's task is great. Indeed, it is neither an easy nor a trivial duty to be a mirror to the Eternally Self-Sufficient One on whom everything depends.

In sum, we see before our eyes at all times countless new lives as well as souls that are the origins and essences of these lives being sent into existence expeditiously out of nowhere. These show the necessary existence of the Ever Living and Self-Subsistent Source of All Being and His sacred attributes and Most Beautiful Names, just as sunrays show the sun. If someone were to reject the sun, then he would have to deny the sunlight that permeates the day. Similarly, if a person does not recognize the Sun of Divine oneness that is the Ever Living and Self-Subsistent Source of All Being and the Giver of Life and Death, then he would have to deny the existence of living beings that fill up the face of the earth from the past to the future. Such denial would mean utter ignorance and foolishness.

24ᵀᴴ WINDOW

[This 'window' explains how like life, death is a sign pointing to the Wise Creator. Nursi is making use of the Quranic approach which brings to attention growth and decay as signs of God. If things did not wither away or die, we would mistake them as sources of the qualities that they display, such as life and power.[8] Their death and decay is therefore a declaration that the source of life—and power, beauty, wisdom and so on—lies elsewhere. Hence, death is as bright a window as life, revealing *tawhid*.]

> *There is no deity except Him. Everything is bound to perish, except His [eternal] countenance* (wajh). *With Him rests all judgment; and unto Him shall you all be brought back.* (Q. 28:88)

As the Quranic verse *[the One] who has created death as well as life* (Q. 67:2) indicates, death is *not* non-existence, execution, vanishing, or extinction. Death is *not* a deterioration without an agent or maker. Rather, death is a release from duty, a transfer from one place to another, a change of body; it is retirement from the duty of this world and the prison of this body. Thus, death is an orderly and wise act carried out by a Wise Maker (as explained in more detail in the 'First Letter').

Indeed, the 'artworks' and living beings on the sentient face of this earth show the necessary existence and oneness of a Wise Maker. Similarly, through their death, these living beings are bearing witness to the eternity and oneness of the Eternally Living One. In the 'Twenty Second Word,'[9] we have already explained and demonstrated how death is a very strong evidence of oneness and eternity, so here we will explain only one important point.

Through their existence, living beings indicate the existence of a Necessary Existent One. Similarly, through their death those living beings also bear witness to the eternity and oneness of an Eternally Living One. For instance, the face of the earth, which constitutes a single living being, indicates the Maker through its organization and various situations and states. When it dies—when the winter covers the face of the earth with a white shroud—it attracts the attention of human beings away from itself. Seeing the passing 'funeral' of the

---

[8] This point is explained in the river metaphor that Nursi uses in other places, see for instance: *Rays*, 'Second Ray, First Station, Third Fruit,' translated in Chapter 11.

[9] See Chapter 12 and 13 for its translation.

spring, human beings turn their gaze to the past and notice a wider perspective. That is, human beings are reminded of all the past spring seasons, each of which filled up the face of the earth with life. Human beings also foresee the coming of future spring seasons, each of which is a wonder of divine power bringing forth abundant life on the face of the earth. The death of the earth in winter, therefore, brings to mind a vast and bright vision of the past and future. All together this succession of seasons strongly bear witness to the necessary existence, oneness and eternity of a Glorious Maker, a Powerful One Possessor of Perfection, an Enduring and Eternal One, an Eternal Sun. They reflect such brilliant proofs that they clearly show the truth of *I believe in the Single and Unique God.*

In sum, as indicated by the Quranic verse *[God is the one who] gives life to the earth after it had been lifeless* (Q. 30:19), this living earth points to the Maker in the spring. Likewise, the 'death' of spring turns our attention to all the spring seasons, which are wonderful miracles of Divine power, lined up in the past and in the future. Instead of one spring, it reveals many springs. In place of one short-lived and transitory miracle, thousands of miracles of divine power are brought to mind.

Moreover, each of the past springs is a clearer witness [to God] than a present spring occurring right now. As a matter of fact, past springs have disappeared *along with their seeming causes (al-asbāb al-ẓahiriyya).* The fact that new springs came after the ones that vanished shows that seeming causes are naught, they have no effect.[10] The death of living beings along with their seeming causes shows that they can only be created by a Powerful Glorious One who, with His wisdom connects life with seeming causes.

---

[10] For if the seeming causes were real causes of existence, they themselves could not have lost existence. To give an example, we may be tempted to think that parents give life to their offspring. But when a parent dies, it becomes clear that she was not the sources of life for her children. After their death, we see more clearly that parents are only *seeming* causes. In reality, both parents and their offspring are given life by the Giver of Life. (Translators' note).

Similarly, future springs testify more brightly to the Everlasting and Living One than a current spring. For the future springs will also emerge after the death of the face of the earth and life will appear again from out of nowhere, and new living beings will be sent to duty on earth and then they too will perish and pass away...

Oh, the one who has been stuck in idolizing nature and who is about to suffocate from that confusion. Think carefully. How can anyone other than the One whose wisdom and power encompasses the past and future have a part in creating life on earth? How can blind chance and nature be responsible in any way? If you want to be delivered from this confusion, and approach the truth, say: 'Nature is at best a record of Divine power. As for chance, it is a veil of our ignorance concealing a hidden Divine wisdom.'

27ᵀᴴ WINDOW

[This window offers an insightful reflection on the Quranic verse that describes God as the creator and 'wakīl over all things.' As Muhammad Asad explains, 'The term wakīl denotes 'one who is entrusted with the management of (another person's) affairs,' or 'is responsible for (another person's) conduct.'' When used 'in combination with the phrase 'alā kulli shay'in (as, e.g., in Q. 6:102 or Q. 11:12)' it is used in the sense of 'the One who has everything in His care.''[11] Nursi uses the verse as a guide to understanding the causal order in the world. At a superficial glance, it seems like natural elements are making things happen: giving life, designing, providing sustenance, creating beauty, and so on. In reality, one Creator—who is frequently described here as the 'All-Wise Artist-Maker'—is creating everything. This window offers three major ways in which this reality can be witnessed in the world (which are summarized in its final paragraph). The window offers another example of Nursi's exe-

---

[11] Asad, *The Message of the Quran*, 418, fn.4. Asad also notes 'the term *wakil* is sometimes used in the sense of 'guardian' (e.g., in Q. 3:173), or 'defender' (e.g., in Q. 4:109). In the present instance [Q. 17:2] (as well as in 39:62) the term evidently alludes to God's exclusive power to determine the fate of any created being or thing.' (Ibid.)

gesis of the Quranic verses in a way that connects the 'signs' in revelation with 'signs' in nature, thereby leading to confirmation of the 'Quranic truths.'[12]]

> God is the Creator of all things, and He is Guardian over all things [wakil]. (Q. 39:62)

When we look at the things in the universe that appear to be causes (asbāb) and effects (musabbabat), we see that the most sophisticated cause is unable to create the simplest effect. Therefore, we can conclude that these causes are like a veil and that the real maker of the effects is someone else.

For instance, let us take a small example from amongst countless creations: the faculty of memory placed in a tiny space in human brain. We see that it is like a comprehensive library in which one's entire life is preserved with incredible precision. What cause can possibly be responsible for such a miracle of power? The brain folds? Simple and unconscious particles in the brain cells? Winds of chance?

Such incredible artistry can only be the art of a wise maker who creates it as a small sample of the major record of human deeds in order to be an evidence for the Day of Judgement, when human beings will be held accountable for each of their deeds. We may consider all eggs, kernels and seeds as comparable to the human faculty of memory. Likewise, other effects may be compared to these tiny yet comprehensive miracles. Indeed, whatever effect and artful creation we look at, we perceive such an amazing art that far exceeds the capacity of its simple seeming cause. What is more, the artistry in these effects transcends the capacity of all causes combined together. For instance, let us consider the sun, which looks like a major cause. Can it create a fly? If the sun possessed consciousness, it would state its incapacity as follows, 'Thanks to my Creator's gifts, I have plenty of light, color, and heat in me. However, things that constitute a fly,

---

[12] In Nursi's words, *Risale-i Nur* is a type of exegesis that 'demonstrates the Quranic truths.' Nursi, *Şualar*, '14. Sua,' RNK 1:1089; *Rays*, 513. See the Introduction of this volume.

like eyes, ears, and life, I do not have and they are beyond my capacity.'

Moreover, the wonderful art and embellishment in effects dismiss seeming causes. Instead, they indicate the Necessarily Existent One, the Causer of all causes (*al-musabbib al-asbāb*) to whom all affairs go back, as it is expressed in the verse *to Him return all affairs* (Q. 11:123)

Similarly, the purposes, results, and benefits associated with the effects clearly show that these effects are the works of a Generous Sustainer and a Compassionate Wise One. For, unconscious causes cannot in any way think purposefully and act accordingly. Yet, we see that each created being comes into existence in accordance with not only one purpose, but many purposes and wisdoms. Therefore, a Wise and Generous Sustainer must be creating them and making such benefits their purposes of existence.

Consider the rain for example. The seeming causes of the rain clearly do not have the capacity to think of the needs of living beings and have compassion on them. Therefore, rain is clearly sent to the assistance of living beings through the wisdom of a Compassionate Creator, who has created living beings and has guaranteed their sustenance. That is why rain is often called 'mercy' (*raḥma*).[13] For, many compassionate benefits are included within the rain—it is as if compassion has become embodied in the form of rain, and is coming down in drops.

Likewise, the ornaments in plants and the embellishments and impressive skills in animals clearly demonstrate the necessary existence and unity of a Glorious One, who wants to manifest and endear Himself behind the veil of the unseen. This means that the beautiful aspects of beings and their embellishments clearly indicate the *attributes* (*ṣifāt*) of revealing and endearing oneself. And, these attributes

---

[13] In the Quran (as in Q. 42:48) as well as in the *hadith* rain is described as being sent from God's mercy. This may be a reason why in many traditional Muslim cultures, rainy weather is often considered as good weather rather than 'bad weather.'

clearly show the necessary existence and unity of a Powerful Maker (*ṣāniʿ qadīr*) who is known (*maʿrūf*) and loving (*wadūd*).

In sum, seeming causes point to the Creator in three ways. First, causes are simple and weak in comparison to the effects ascribed to them which are very precious and display incredible artistry. Second, the purposes and benefits of an effect shows that its ignorant and unconscious causes cannot be its creator, rather only a Wise Artist-Maker (*ṣāniʿ ḥakīm*) can be the creator. Third, the embellishments and skills in the effects point to a Wise Artist-Maker who wants to show his power to conscious beings and make Himself loved.

O poor worshipper of seeming causes (Tk. *asbabperest*)! How can you explain away these three important truths? How can you delude yourself? Use your reason, rend apart the veil of seeming causes, give up *shirk,* and say *He is the only One, He has no partner* (*waḥdahu lā sharīka lahu*). And, be saved from endless delusions.

3
ONLY ONE GOD:
GOOD NEWS AND HEALING

O humankind! There has now come unto you an exhortation from your Sustainer, and a healing for what is in the hearts, and guidance and mercy unto the believers.

—Quran, 10:57

He who ascribes partners to God [shirk] is like someone who is hurtling down from the skies—whereupon the birds snatch him up, or the wind blows him away to a distant place.

—Quran, 22:31

And yet, they worship, instead of God, things that can neither benefit them nor harm them...

—Quran, 25:55

The selection below illustrates how the Quranic emphasis on *tawhid* (the oneness of God) is deeply relevant for human life. By explaining the joyful consequences of *tawhid*, the text clarifies the meaning of the Quranic verses that reveal *shirk* as futile and painful and *tawhid* as a source of relief and blessings, as mentioned above.

More specifically, the selection provides an exegesis of the well-known invocation of *tawhid* by Prophet Muhammad: *There is no deity except God. He is one; He has no partner. To Him belongs everything. To Him all praise is due. He gives life. He deals death. He is ever-living, and dies not. All good is in His hand. He has power over everything. And with Him is all journeys' end.* Every phrase of this

53

prophetic invocation also occurs frequently in the Quran, and in the excerpt below, Nursi focuses on the 'good news' and 'healing' each one provides. He explains how *tawhid* illuminated by these phrases relieves human beings of their burdens and heals their existential wounds opened up by transience and vulnerability. By making human beings honored guests of the Eternal One, *tawhid* discloses the profound meaning of life and the resulting immense delight of the heart and spirit.[1]

***

GOOD NEWS AND HEALING IN *TAWHID*[2]

In His name, Glory be unto Him.[3]
There is nothing that does not glorify Him with praise.
In the Name of God, the Merciful, the Compassionate.
There is no deity except God. He is one; He has no partner. To Him belongs everything [mulk]. To Him all praise is due. He gives life, He deals death. He is Ever-living, and dies not. All good is in His hand. He has power over everything. And with Him is all journeys' end.

It is very beneficial to recite this invocation after the morning and evening prayers. According to a reliable narration from the Prophet

---

[1] In this selection, Nursi focuses inward: explaining how *tawhid* makes perfect sense for the human heart and soul. In the original text, there is second part that follows the part excerpted here, which revisits the same phrases in the Prophet's invocation by reflecting on nature, showing how each phrase not only offers great news for human life but also contains evidences for *tawhid* from the universe. Taken together, the two sections nicely mirror the Quranic notion of the signs [*ayat*] of the One God in the inner self and in the outer world: *We shall show them Our signs in the <u>horizons</u> [of the universe] and <u>within</u> themselves, until it becomes clear to them that it is indeed the truth.* (Quran, 41:53, emphasis added)

[2] *Mektubat*, '20. Mektup Birinci Makam' (*Letters*, '20th Letter, First Station'), RNK 1: 449–451. Title is added.

[3] Italicized part is in Arabic in the original.

(peace and blessings be upon him) this expression of *tawhid* reaches the level of the Highest Divine Name (*al-ism al-a'ẓam*). The invocation contains twelve phrases. Each phrase brings in good news as well as unfolds a new horizon onto the unity of sustainership (*tawḥid al-rubūbiyya*) and each phrase contains a sign to the majesty and perfection of the One. Leaving the details to the rest of the *Risale-i Nur*, in the following two sections, we shall offer a brief summary of the meanings of *tawḥid* contained in this invocation. But let us start with an introduction.

INTRODUCTION

The highest purpose of existence and achievement of human nature (*fiṭra*) is found in belief in God (*īmān billāh*). The greatest level of humanity and its greatest progress lies in knowledge of God (*ma'rifatullah*), which flourishes from belief in God. And, the most exciting happiness and loveliest pleasure for humanity lie in the love of God (*muḥabbatullah*), which springs from knowledge of God. Finally, the highest joy for the human spirit (*rūḥ*) and human heart is the spiritual pleasure that ensues from loving God.

Indeed, all genuine happiness, true joy, and pure pleasure emanate from knowing God and loving Him. The former cannot be without the latter. If you know and love God, then you receive—or acquire the potential to receive—endless happiness, blessings, light, and mysteries. If you do not truly know and love God, then you are afflicted with endless hardship, pain and worries, emotionally, spiritually and physically.

After all, even if you were the ruler of the entire world, what value would it have without belief in God? Even as a ruler of the world, you would still be a vulnerable, needy human being, tossed around in a miserable and messy world, without any protector or any enduring outcome for your life. Any fair and honest person will acknowledge that if we do not know our Sustainer, our existence in this passing, finite, and broken world amongst the lonely human race is simply tragic. In contrast, when we find our Sustainer and know our Owner, then we can seek refuge in His infinite compassion and rely on His endless power. Then our tragic world will transform into a pleasing abode and profitable marketplace.

FIRST STATION: GOOD NEWS IN *TA WHID*

Let us see how in each of its eleven phrases, this invocation of *tawhid* provides good news, healing and spiritual pleasure.

First phrase: *La ilaha illallah* (There is no god except God.)

This phrase bears the following good news. Our spirit faces many needs and is helpless in front of so many adversities. In realizing that there is no deity except God, our spirit finds an incredible recourse, a source of help (Tk. *nokta-i istimdad*), which fulfills all of its needs by opening to it a treasure of infinite mercy.[4] It also finds a source of support (Tk. *nokta-i istinad*) against all its enemies and challenges in the absolute power of its owner and creator; its sole object of worship, as this phrase indicates and reveals. Thereby, our hearts are saved from incredible horror and our spirits are spared painful sadness. Appreciating *there is no deity except God* and confirming its truth brings about eternal relief and lasting joy.

Second Phrase: *wahdahu* (He is the only one)

This phrase contains healing, joyful good news.

Our hearts and spirits are involved with so many things. We feel connected with countless people and beings, and we care deeply about the world around us. With such intense involvement, our hearts and spirits are overwhelmed with the mess and confusion of the world. It is then that 'He is the only one' ('*wahdahu*') comes to the rescue and becomes a refuge and a protector against all the confusion and misery. The phrase *wahdahu* announces to us:

'God is one. Do not tire yourself begging from others. Do not debase yourself before anything or feel indebted to them. Do not tremble before them, or debase yourself by trying to please them.

---

[4] By using the term 'treasure' (like 'infinite treasure' or 'treasures of mercy') Nursi is making use of a Quranic concept as in '*and there is not a thing but its (sources and inexhaustible) treasures are with Us*'(Q. 15: 21). See also Q. 17:100; 52:37; and 63:7.) The specific term 'treasures of mercy' (*khazain rahma*) is also mentioned in Q. 38:9: *the treasures of your Sustainer's mercy, the Almighty, the All Giving.*

There is only one sovereign of the universe. The keys to all things are with the One. He has control over everything. Everything is resolved through His command. If you find Him, you will find all your wishes, and you will be saved from endless indebtedness and fears.'

Third Phrase: *La sharīka lahu* (He has no partner)

This phrase means that just as God does not have any partner in His divinity (*uluhiyya*) and sovereignty, He also has no partner in His sustaining, governance and creating. To appreciate this reality, contrast Divine sovereignty with the so-called human sovereignty. A human ruler may have no partner with him on the throne; he may be the one and only sovereign of a country. Still, to carry out his ruling, he will surely have officials such as governors, ministers, advisers that help him and thus act as his partners.

These partners will not allow ordinary citizens to enter into the sovereign's presence and interact with him directly. They will say: 'you need to request from us.' However, God Almighty the Pre-Eternal and Post-Eternal Sovereign, has no partner neither in His sovereignty nor in His governance and sustaining of creation. He is not in need of any helper whatsoever, and nothing can happen or influence anything else without His direct command and power. Therefore, anything and anyone can directly turn to Him at any time. Since God has no partner or helper, no one can stop anyone from having direct recourse to God; anyone can enter His presence at any time.

Thus, this phrase *He has no partner*, conveys the following good news to the human spirit:

The believing human spirit can enter the presence of the pre-eternal and post-eternal Sovereign in any state, at any time and any place, for any wish without facing any obstacle, hindrance or intrusion. The believing human spirit can turn directly to the Beautiful Glorious One (*al-jamīl dhu'l-jalāl*) and the Powerful, Perfect One (*al-qadīr dhu'l-kamāl*), who owns all the treasures of mercy and happiness. Finding His mercy and relying on His power, the believer will find incredible relief, ease and happiness.

Fourth Phrase: *lahu al-mulk* (everything belongs to Him alone)

This phrase means that everything is completely His. As far as you are concerned, it means that you belong to Him, and you are His property and you work within His property. This phrase proclaims the following healing and joyful news:

'O human being! Do not think that you own yourself. For, you cannot take care of yourself. That is a heavy burden that you cannot carry. You cannot protect yourself or avoid disasters or take care of all your endless needs by yourself. Therefore, do not suffer and cause yourself pain in vain. The property belongs to someone else: to an owner who is both powerful and merciful. Rely then on His power and do not decry His mercy. Give up sorrow and enjoy. Throw away hardship and embrace happiness!'

This phrase also announces a relief regarding your worries about the world. It says: This world that you love, and care and worry about belongs to a Merciful and Powerful One. Surrender the property to its owner. Let Him take care of the world, and you enjoy life, instead of undertaking its burdens that you cannot carry. The Owner is both Wise and Merciful and manages everything as He wishes. Whenever you are overwhelmed, say like Ibrahim Hakkı *'Let us see what the Owner does/ Whatever He does is beautiful.'*[5]

Fifth Phrase: *lahu al-hamd* (to Him belongs all praise)

That is, all praise, acclaim, tribute and gratitude are due to Him. He deserves all thanks and adoration. For, all blessings and gifts (*ni'am*) are His; they all proceed from His eternal treasures of mercy. The good news in this phrase is that His treasures are endless, infinite. This phrase announces:

O human being! Do not be saddened by the passing of blessings. The source of these gifts and blessings is the unending treasure of divine mercy. Do not be devastated by anticipating the end of

---

[5] Ismail Hakkı Erzurumî (d. 1780) was a Muslim scholar and poet from Eastern Anatolia who wrote on Islamic spirituality and ethics in Ottoman Turkish (and partly in Arabic and Persian). The lines quoted are from his famous poem 'Tefvizname.'

what you enjoy. A passing pleasure is just one 'fruit' of an eternal 'tree' of mercy. Since the tree is enduring, there will always be more fruits coming. Do not worry!

Moreover, reflect with gratitude on the incredible honor and privilege that comes with these gifts: the honor and privilege of receiving from the All-Merciful One. Such awareness will increase your enjoyment of the gifts manifold. As you know, if you receive a gift from an eminent person, the compliment received through that gift is much more enjoyable than the gift itself.

For instance, if a great ruler gave you an apple, you would be delighted by the compliment conveyed through that apple thousands of times more than by the apple itself. Similarly, with the phrase *lahu al-hamd* ('*to Him belongs all praise*'), that is, with gratitude and praise, you are able to recognize the bestowal (*in'am*) within the gift (*ni'ma*). As you recognize the bestowal, you will recognize the Bestower of the gift (*al-Mun'im*). Thereby, you will feel His merciful and compassionate compliment and attention to you contained within the gift. You also will remember the endurance of His kindness and generosity. This way, the door to an incredible spiritual pleasure much more delightful than the gift itself opens up to you through this phrase *to Him belongs all praise*.

Sixth Phrase: *yuhyī* (He grants life)

That is, He is the one who gives life, and He is the one who maintains life by providing nourishment, and He is also the one who provides the necessities of life. Moreover, the lofty purposes of life belong to Him and the important results of life pertain to Him; most of the outcomes of life belong to Him.[6] Thus, by announcing Him as the giver of life, this phrase gives great news to the mortal and powerless human being:

O human being! Do not be burdened by the heavy loads of life. Do not grieve at the passing of life! And, do not see only the worldly

---

[6] Literally, 'ninety-nine percent of life's results belongs to Him.' In other words, what we tend to consider as our personal achievements or aims in life is only a fraction of the actual meaning and purpose of our existence.

and insignificant aspects of life and regret coming to this world! Instead, know that your life belongs to the Ever Living and Self-Subsistent Source of All Being (al-Ḥayy al-Qayyūm). He takes care of the expenses and necessities of your life. Know also that your life has many purposes and results that belong to Him. You are a captain in the ship of your being; do your part nicely, receive your payment, and enjoy the ride. Remember that this ship of life is very valuable—it yields so many beautiful results—and that the Owner of this ship is very Generous and Merciful. So, be happy and grateful and know that when you perform your part righteously, all the outcome of that ship will in one respect be credited to your account of deeds (for the hereafter) and it will yield an eternal life.

Seventh Phrase: *yumīt* [He gives death]

He is the one who gives death. That is, He releases you from the duty of life, transferring you out of this impermanent world and emancipating you from the responsibility of service. That is, he takes you from this transient life to an eternal life. Thus, this phrase calls out the following message to mortal human beings and jinn:[7]

Listen to this good news! Death is not execution; it is not obliteration; it is not nothingness. Death is neither eternal separation, nor, a random catastrophe without a maker. Rather, it is an intentional act of release and a change of place brought by a Merciful Wise Doer (fāʾil ḥakīm raḥīm). You are being sent to the realm of eternal happiness, back to your original homeland. Death is the gate to the intermediate realm (barzākh) where you will meet with most of your loved ones.

---

[7] It is interesting that Nursi includes jinn here. The Quran refers to the jinn as invisible beings who have similar challenges and opportunities as human beings. They have choice on how to respond to God by using their freewill and other faculties. Chapter 72 of the Quran contains the longest passage on the jinn (verses 1–15), referring to a group of jinn who listened to the Prophet recite the Quran and confirmed it by repenting from *shirk*. They also note: *among us are such as have surrendered themselves to God—just as there are among us such as have abandoned themselves to wrongdoing...* (v. 14)

Eighth Phrase: *wa huwa hayyun la yamut* ('and He is living and dies not')

You love things in the world because of the beauty, perfection and munificence you see in them. Know that there is One whose beauty, perfection and favor infinitely surpasses them all and whose single manifestation of beauty surpasses the beauty of all beloveds. Such an Eternal Object of Worship, such an Undying Beloved, has an eternal and enduring life free from transience and from any shortcomings or imperfection. Thus, this phrase *and He is living and dies not* addresses jinn and human beings, all conscious beings and all people of love:

Good news to you all! You have an Eternal Beloved who heals your wounds inflicted by the endless separations from your passing beloveds. Since He exists and He is eternal, there is no need to worry regardless of what happens to them. The beauty, munificence, kindness and perfection that you adore in your beloveds are but faint shadows of the manifestation of the eternal beauty of the Eternal Beloved. So, do not be hurt by their passing. For, they are like mirrors to the One. The changing of mirrors only refreshes and enhances the radiance of the manifestation of His beauty. And, since He exists, everything exists. (That is, separation is only temporary and reunion is the ultimate end).

Ninth Phrase: *biyadihi al-khayr* (all good is in His hands)

That is, all good is in His hands. All the good you do is preserved in His records. All your righteous deeds are recorded with Him. Thus, this phrase calls out the following good news to jinn and humans, saying:

O helpless ones! When you enter the grave, do not say: 'Our wealth has vanished, and our efforts are wasted. We have exited this wide and beautiful world and entered the narrow grave!' Do not cry out in disappointment. For, all your possessions are preserved. All your actions have been written down. All your service has been recorded. The One who shall reward your service, who owns all goodness and has power to do all good, will keep you in the grave for a while and then bring you into His presence. Happiness awaits you. Your service and hardships have ended; you are heading toward ease and mercy. It is now time to receive your reward.

Indeed, the Powerful One of Glory (*al-qadīr dhul-jalāl*) who preserves the legacy of last spring in the form of seeds and makes those preserved seeds flourish abundantly the following spring is the same One who will preserve the fruits of your life and will give abundant yield to your service.

Tenth Phrase: *wa huwa ʿala kulli shayin qadīr* (and He is powerful over all things)

That is, He is one (*wāḥid*). He is unique (*aḥad*). He is powerful over all things. Nothing is difficult for Him. For Him, creating the spring is as easy as creating a single flower; creating Paradise is as easy as creating the spring. The countless beings that are created anew every day, every year, and every century testify in limitless ways to His limitless power. This phrase gives the following good news:

O human being! Your service and your worship will not be wasted. An abode of reward and happiness has been prepared for you. In place of this passing world, an eternal Paradise awaits you. Believe and trust in the promise of the Glorious Creator that you know and worship. It is impossible that He would break His promise. He has no reason whatsoever to turn back on His promise. There is no shortcoming in His power whatsoever. Just as He created your small backyard, He can create—and has created—Paradise for you. He promised Paradise to you, and of course He shall take you in.

Look: we see before our very eyes how each spring millions of species are resurrected with utter order and balance, so easily and so quickly. Surely, the Powerful Glorious One who accomplishes this can keep His promise.

Indeed, *given that* such an Absolutely Powerful One:

- creates thousands of examples of Resurrection and Paradise each year,

- announces and promises eternal happiness in all His revelations,

- always acts with truth and integrity,

- whose endless perfection is indicated by all the perfections in the creation,

- has no flaws or deficiency whatsoever,

and, *given that* breaking promises, lying, and deceiving are ugly qualities and are shortcomings...

Surely and certainly such a Powerful and Glorious One, such a Wise and Perfect One, such a Merciful and Beautiful One, will keep His promise. He will open up the door of eternal happiness to you, o believer, and will take you into Paradise, the original home of your ancestor Adam.

Eleventh Phrase: *wa ilayhi al maṣīr* (Unto Him is the journeys' end)

That is, once human beings fulfill the important purposes of their lives, they will return back to their Glorious Creator and Generous Sustainer who has sent them here. We as human beings have been sent to this world in order to perform a precious service and achieve a profitable 'trade.'[8] Once our service and trade are completed, we shall leave this passing world and we shall be honored with the magnificent presence of the Creator in the eternal realm. In other words, we will be saved from the hassle of seeming causes and the dark veils of intermediaries and multiplicity. We will meet our Merciful Sus-

---

[8] There are references here to Quranic verses such as *I have not created the invisible beings and human beings to any end other than that they may [know and] worship Me.* (Q. 51:56) as well as verses in which metaphors of 'trade' and 'profit' are used, such as *O You who have attained to faith! Shall I point out to you a bargain (or trade) that will save you from grievous suffering [in this world and in the life to come]? You are to believe in God and His Messenger, and to strive hard in God's cause with your possessions and your lives: this is for your own good - if you but knew it! [If you do so,] He will forgive you your sins, and [in the life to come] will admit you into gardens through which running waters flow, and into goodly mansions in [those] gardens of perpetual bliss: that [will be] the triumph supreme!* (Q. 61:10–12) The bargain or trade here ultimately refers to the conscious surrendering to the True Owner of everything in return for eternal happiness. For more in depth analysis of the meaning of such 'trade', see Nursi's commentary on the Quranic text *God has purchased the persons and possessions of the believers in return for the Garden* (Q. 9:111, Abdel Haleem tr.), in *Words*, 'Sixth Word.'

tainer and the abode of His eternal kingdom directly without any veils.

Thus, this phrase gives the highest, best good news:

O human being! Do you know where you are going? Are you aware of where you are being taken? You are headed to Paradise, whose one-hour stay is much more pleasurable than a thousand years of happy life on this earth. And you are going to the mercy and presence of such a Beautiful Perfect One that the vision (*ru'ya*) of His beauty (*jamāl*) for an hour is much more beautiful than a thousand years of Paradise. The beauty in the creatures that you love and are attached to is but a pale shadow of His beauty and a weak reflection of His most beautiful names (*al-asmā al-ḥusna*). The entire Paradise with all its splendor is just one manifestation of His mercy, and all forms of longing, love, and attraction are just a spark from His love. You are going to such an Undying Adored One and such an Eternal Beloved! You are invited to His eternal feast, to Paradise. Thus, you should enter through the gate of death with a smile, not with tears!

This phrase, *Unto Him is the journeys' end*, also gives the following good news:

O human being! Do not think that you are going toward extinction, darkness, and nothingness. Do not think that you will just be decomposed and forgotten, and be drowned in 'multiplicity' (*kathra*, Tk. *kesret*).[9] Rather, instead of going into extinction, you

---

[9] 'Finding unity within multiplicity' is a common shorthand in classical texts of Islamic spirituality for seeing the truth of the world in light of *tawhid*. 'Multiplicity' refers to the multiplicity of the creatures—things, events, causes, situations, etc.—in the universe that may become a distraction from their single source, if not perceived for what they are, as signs (*ayāt*) indicating and glorifying the One. They thus seem tantalizing but unsatisfying: perfect and beautiful in some ways, but utterly imperfect and disappointing in other ways. And, most importantly, their glimpses of perfection and beauty are passing and temporary. Such multiplicity is confusing, exhausting, and unsatisfying, when it is not understood that all this is coming from one source and point to the Creator—hence the author's reference to 'being drown in multiplicity.' That is, for the unmindful or heedless (*al-ghāfil*), multiplicity can become a veil to the reality of *tawhid*.

are moving toward eternity. Rather than nothingness, you are being taken to enduring existence. Instead of darkness, you are going to the world of light. You are going back to your real owner. You are returning to the capital of the Eternal King. You will not drown in 'multiplicity'; rather you will breathe in the realm of unity. You are not heading toward separation but toward reunion!

4

IT IS NEVER TOO LATE TO THROW OFF THE YOKE OF *SHIRK*: THE LIGHT OF *TAWHID* IN OLD AGE

When [Zachariah] called out to his Sustainer in the secrecy of his heart, he prayed: 'O my Sustainer! My bones have become weak, and my head glistens with grey hair. But never yet, O my Sustainer, has my prayer unto Thee remained unanswered.'

—Quran, 19:3–4

Behold, those beings whom you invoke instead of God cannot create [as much as] a fly, even were they to join all their forces to that end!

—Quran, 22:73

The selection below is excerpted from a longer treatise called *Treatise for the Elderly*, which beautifully explains *tawhid* and its existential implications for human life, especially the old age. Relevant for both the old and the young, the treatise shows how belief in one God can release human beings from the burdens they bear through making them aware of their connection to the Eternal Merciful One. Nursi prefaces the *Treatise* with the prayer of Prophet Zachariah (Zakariyya) in the Quran, quoted above.

The selection we have excerpted here starts on a personal note, which is a style Nursi frequently utilizes to illustrate the healing power of *tawhid*. Recognizing his own shortcomings, he first depicts his miserable state of living in the illusion and darkness of heedlessness (*ghafla*). Then he illustrates how the light of the Quran enlightened and relieved his pain. Such existential confession serves as encouragement for the journey to find peace and joy through first rejecting *shirk*.

The personal note is about a moment of existential crisis: upon noticing his grey hair in the mirror and feeling betrayed by a good friend, Nursi deeply experiences the painful transience of the world. Furthermore, he realizes how 'seeming causes' cannot satisfy his need for constancy and permanence. Fame, a good profession, close friends—none seemed to cure or compensate for his utter vulnerability, neediness, and transience. Couldn't he turn to the One who can grant him all his needs? He wanted to but there was a block. He was unable to see the light of *tawhid* due to a worldview tainted with *shirk*. The attitude of *shirk* assumes that seeming causes are in charge and imagines God's role in the universe to be minimal. Nursi has to first debunk this myth of *shirk* which is frequently smuggled in under the guise of science, rationality, and scholarship. He needs to purge from his soul all remnants of this dark worldview and invites the reader to do the same.

This process of cleansing from *shirk* is performed in light of reflecting on nature. Using Quranic guidance in observing the evidences of *tawhid* in the world, Nursi fully engages with and debunks the claims of *shirk* and heedlessness (*ghafla*). More specifically, using Quranic passages that teach how even the smallest creations are related to and indicate the Creator's immense power and knowledge, Nursi shows that it is impossible to attribute even 'small' and 'particular' things to seeming causes.

It is noteworthy that this text presents the process of reasoning about nature and discovering the signs of God in the outer world (*al-afāq*) as leading to peace in the inner world (*al-anfus*). In this sense, it is a nice exposition of the Quranic passage that refers to signs of God in the outer and inner world (Q. 41:53). The selection is also an illustration of the Quranic ideal of *hearts wherewith they reason* (*qulūbun ya'qilūna bihā*) (Q. 22:46).[1] In other words, the witnessing and thinking process that the Quran teaches the reader is not a mere intellectual exercise divorced from feelings and existential needs. Rather, reasoning in light of the Quranic guidance is meant to provide healing as well as nourishment to the human heart and spirit.

As noted earlier, Nursi's *Treatise for the Elderly* starts with the Quranic reference to Prophet Zachariah's prayer in old age. The selection translated here connects his prayer with the Quranic emphasis on *tawhid*, recognizing that every single thing is under God's control only. It shows how once we discover the One who creates and sustains the universe with incredible power, wisdom, and knowledge, we can be assured that our profound existential needs for meaning, happiness, permanence and eternity are being met. In this treatise, Nursi insightfully connects the Quranic guidance on the universe with human nature (*fiṭrah*) saying 'one who cannot create a fly cannot hear my deepest wishes and know my spiritual longings. One who cannot create the heavens cannot provide me with eternal happiness. Thus, my Sustainer is the One who can heal my heart, who can send rain through the clouds, and who will transform this world into the next one and open the doors of Paradise to me.'[2] With such understanding—after the explanation of how a perspective of nature that is based on *shirk* is groundless and false—Nursi ends with celebrating the light of *tawhid* that enlightens old age.[3]

---

[1] The Quranic passage suggests that a sound *heart* is one that *reasons* well and is receptive to divine guidance. The earlier part of the verse encourages traveling on the earth and observing, which is an invitation to witness in the world, the signs indicating the Most Beautiful Names of God. Then, the verse highlights the ideal of 'reasoning hearts' and 'hearing ears': *Have they, then, never journeyed about the earth, whereupon they would have hearts wherewith they might understand, or ears whereby they might hear? Yet, verily, it is not the eyes that have become blind—but blind have become the hearts that are in their breasts!* (Q. 22:46).

[2] This quote is from the selection below.

[3] Interestingly, in the treatise, Nursi does not directly mention Prophet Zachariah's prayer for a successor mentioned in the following verses. *'Now, behold, I am afraid of [what] my kinsfolk [will do] after I am gone, for my*

***

THE LIGHT OF *TA WHID* IN OLD AGE[4]

After I returned from captivity during World War I, I lived in a house on Çamlıca hill in Istanbul with my late nephew Abdurrahman. Life was joyful for someone like me. I was free after a long captivity and I had now a prestigious position at a scholarly institution, and I was able to disseminate knowledge. I was residing in one of the most scenic locations in Istanbul. My dear nephew—a great student, assistant, scribe and spiritual son—was with me. I felt like the happiest person on earth. Everything was perfect. But, then, I noticed my grey hair in the mirror.

This prompted a spiritual awakening similar to what I had experienced in the mosque in Kostroma, when I was captive in Russia.[5] I started to question what gave me happiness in life. Each and every one of the reasons turned out to be flimsy and deceptive. Around the same time, someone whom I had regarded as a very close friend betrayed me in a completely unexpected way. This further alienated me from the life of this world. I said in my heart: 'Did I get everything wrong? Have I been totally deceived? The things I relied on for hap-

---

wife has always been barren. Bestow, then, upon me, out of Thy grace, the gift of a successor who will be my heir as well as an heir [to the dignity] of the House of Jacob; and make him, O my Sustainer, well-pleasing to Thee! (19:4–19:6). By starting his treatise only with the first three verses of Chapter 19 (Sura Maryam), Nursi is placing the emphasis on the prophet's attitude in his prayer rather than on his particular wish. What is crucial here for Nursi is that Prophet Zachariah is sharing his deep longing in old age with trust and hope in the One. His prayer is important because it reflects a profound awareness of *tawhid*. Since Prophet Zachariah is aware that his Sustainer is the One who holds power over everything and cares about even secret wishes, he is not overwhelmed with his needs or his weakness in old age.

[4] Nursi, *Lemalar*, '26. Lema, 11. Rica' [*Flashes*, 26th Flash, 11th Hope], RNK 1:710–713.

[5] Having captured by Russians during the invasion of Bitlis, an Eastern Ottoman province, Nursi spent two years in captivity in Russia, 1916–1918.

piness are all unreliable and passing. While I am pitiful, people admire my situation and look up to me. Are all these people insane? Or am I the one who has gone mad for seeing these people who are enamored of this worldly life as insane?'

Anyway...During that intense spiritual awakening catalyzed by my old age I saw the transience of all the passing things to which I was attached. I also looked at my own self and saw my utter vulnerability and powerlessness. At that point, my spirit which longed for eternity and was attached to passing things with the illusion that they were eternal, cried out: 'Since my physical self is mortal, what good can I expect from fleeting, mortal things? Since I am weak, what can I expect from these powerless things? I need an Eternal, Enduring One and an Everlasting, Powerful One who can solve my problem.' I started to look for a solution.

First, I hopefully turned to the knowledge I had gained throughout my scholarly training. Unfortunately, I had mixed up Islamic disciplines with philosophical sciences[6] until then, thinking that they were a means to progress and illumination. In reality, they had sullied my spirit and had blocked my spiritual development. Suddenly, with God's mercy and munificence, the sacred wisdom of the All-Wise Quran came to my assistance. It cleansed the dirt of those philosophical discourses. Let me briefly summarize my situation before and after that cleansing.

The spiritual darkness arising from the naturalist and godless philosophy was choking my spirit by plunging it into a dark universe. No matter where I looked, I could not find any light, only suffocation. The layers of darkness were dispersed by the light of the Quranic lesson of *tawhid, la ilaha illallahu* 'there is no god except God.' I was finally able to breathe. But then my ego (*nafs*) and Satan resisted, attacking my heart with arguments from naturalist godless

---

[6] The term used here is *'ulum al-falsafa*, literally 'philosophical disciplines.' As noted in the Introduction, Nursi's reference to 'philosophy' indicates a particular form of thinking that disregards (either implicitly or explicitly) Divine guidance, and interprets the world without awareness of God. For a scholarly analysis of Nursi's use of the term 'philosophy' see: Mermer and Ameur, 'Beyond the Modern: Sa'id al-Nursi's View of Science,' 124–126.

philosophy. There ensued a struggle within me, which ended with my heart's victory, thanks to God. I have talked about the discussions between my heart and my ego during this process in many other treatises. Here I shall just note one example of the victory of my heart and offer one strong evidence out of many so that it can be of use to some elderly readers like me, whose spirit has been tainted, whose heart has fallen sick, and whose ego has become spoiled in their youth due to the misguidance as well as the distraction coming from godless philosophy and the so-called 'modern sciences.' Their spirits will be freed from the ego's and Satan's attacks on recognizing the oneness of God, *tawhid*. It is as follows:

As the representative of godless philosophy, my ego said to my heart: 'We live in a universe where natural causes effect things by their very nature. Everything is connected to a particular material cause. Therefore, for instance, you should expect the fruits from tree, and the harvest from the land. So, what is the point of praying to God for things, especially small things?'

At that point, the secret of recognizing the oneness of God was disclosed to me with the light of the Quran. My heart replied to my ego:

The smallest thing, like the biggest thing, comes directly from the power of the Creator of the whole universe. There is no other way possible. And the particular natural causes you note are all just a veil, behind which the Creator is acting. For, the smallest things that seem to be the least significant sometimes are 'bigger' in terms of their artistry and creation. For instance, a small fly is no less than a chicken in terms of artistry in its creation. Therefore, it is inaccurate that 'big things' are in need of God whereas 'small things' are not, as though they were not dependent on God creating them and sustaining them into existence. The reality is that there are only two options before us: everything is either a product of material and natural causes, or created and sustained by One God only. The former option is illogical and impossible [since causes themselves are in need of being sustained], and the latter makes absolute sense and is logically necessary. How so? Let us explain.

When you attribute all things to one being, the Eternally Powerful (*al-qadir al-azali*), the existence of every single thing is explained very easily. After all, such a one clearly has all-encompassing knowledge, as demonstrated by the order and wisdom displayed throughout the universe. With this all-encompassing knowledge, the quantity and quality of everything is easily determined. Besides, He is clearly infinitely powerful, as demonstrated by the utter ease with which extremely sophisticated and artistic things and beings come into existence. It is clear from the way things, beings, and events occur—as we explained in great detail in other treatises—that the maker of these things has infinite power. Clearly such an all-powerful and all-knowing one can create with the ease and speed of commanding 'Be' and it is!' (*kun fayakūn*) (Q. 36:82).[7] The extraordinary ease we observe in the world is clearly the evidence to one source of comprehensive knowledge and incredible power...[8] [In other words, the in-

---

[7] The phrase *kun fayakūn* is mentioned in a number of Quranic verses, e.g. 'when We will anything to be, We but say unto it, *'Be'—and it is.*' 16:40 (see also Q. 2:117, 2:163, Q. 36:82, 40:68, etc.). Nursi interprets this Quranic description as emphasizing God's infinite power and knowledge. Regarding this passage, the eleventh century Muslim scholar al-Ghazali said 'The outward meaning of this verse is not possible because if the saying of God 'Be' was addressed to the thing before that thing came into existence, then it would simply be an impossibility since the non-existent does not understand address and, therefore, cannot obey. And if it was addressed to the thing after the thing has come into existence, then it would be superfluous, since the thing is already in existence and does not need to be brought into being.' Thus, the verse must be interpreted as a metaphor for 'conveying the idea of greatest power.' (Ghazali, *Foundations of the Articles of Faith*, 44–45.) In other words, the imagery of things coming into being as an instant response to God's command is an effective way of articulating God's immense power, before which there is no resistance from anything. The verse thus expresses that the willed thing is brought into existence by the Creator with utter ease, without any difficulty or delay.

[8] There is a paragraph here that offers a metaphor, which we skipped for the sake of keeping the text easier to follow. The metaphor refers to a book written in invisible ink. When the appropriate chemical is spread on the book, the entire book suddenly becomes visible. In the metaphor, the invisible ink represents the comprehensive divine knowledge that determines the specific states and forms of created beings. The book's content becoming

credible ease with which the world runs makes perfect sense only if we refer to the comprehensive knowledge and amazing power of the One.]

In contrast, if we do not attribute the existence of all the things to one who is Eternally Powerful and who knows everything, then it would be impossible to explain the existence of even a smallest being like a fly. The fly would have to be constituted by the cooperation of the various elements and species of the earth according to a measure that they agreed upon. Moreover, we would have to say that the particles working in that small fly know in detail the purpose of the fly's creation and its delicate organization. In other words, when we reject the Eternally Powerful and Knowing One, we have to make unreasonable assumptions because natural factors and material causes obviously can neither create from nothing, nor can they give life. Hence, if they are presumed to be the creators, they must be able to create by bringing together various things from all over the world in such a manner as to produce a fly.

For instance, a living being contains many elements that are found throughout the world. Indeed, a living being is like a summary of the entire universe and the production of one seed requires power over the entire tree. Making a living being requires gathering various things from all over the universe according to a delicate plan and considerable knowledge. Can natural causes accomplish this? Not ever, because they are inanimate and lifeless, and they have no knowledge or power. They do not possess knowledge so as to draw out a plan and set out a scheme to distill life from the entire universe and to arrange the particles into a particular pattern...

Yet, we observe right before our eyes incredible planning and precision: beings take a particular form out of innumerable possibilities, particles come together and constitute a specific shape in a very orderly manner, without any physical mold shaping them. Particles unite and collate on top of each other forming orderly living beings.

---

immediately visible represents things coming into being with extreme ease through God's absolute power and will.

How could material and inanimate natural causes be responsible for such wondrous events? It is impossible. It is too far-fetched for material and natural causes to be the real creators or producers of things. Clearly, they are acting at the command of a Creator with infinite, encompassing knowledge and power. Anyone who uses his reason with an open heart will recognize this reality.

That is why the great Quranic verse says, *Behold, those beings whom you invoke instead of God cannot create [as much as] a fly, even if they were to join all their forces to that end!* (Q. 22:73). In other words, even if all the material causes were to be gathered together and even if they had will and choice, they would not be able to create one single fly or any of its organs. Even if they were to combine various elements into a fly, they would not be able to keep it in its particular balance. And even if they were to achieve that, they would not be able to constantly renew the constituents of the fly's body such as cells, atoms and particles and continuously maintain them in a harmonious and orderly fashion; let alone give life to the fly and sustain it. In sum, it is clear that material and natural causes cannot create. Someone else is the real and sole creator and maker, the true owner (*al-ṣāḥib al-ḥaqīqī*).

Indeed, their real maker must be the one who creates all living beings on earth with the same ease as giving life to a single fly—as pointed out in the verse, *the creation of you all and the resurrection of you all is but like [the creation and resurrection of] a single soul* (Q. 31:28). This Maker can bring the entire spring season with the same ease as creating a single flower. For, He is not in need of creating through gathering things one by one, He only says *'Be!' and it is.* (*kun fayakūn*) (Q. 2:117, 36:82, etc.). Every spring, we see how He creates not only innumerable beings with their material constituents, but also their countless forms, qualities and functions. He has the plan and model for everything in His knowledge. All the particles and atoms are under His immediate command; they act with His knowledge and power. Thus, He creates everything very swiftly and effortlessly. Not a single thing swerves from His plan even a tiny bit.

Both the planets and atoms are part of His organized employees. All are part of His forces.[9]

In other words, things rely on pre-eternal power (*al-qudra al-azaliyya*) and work under the principles of pre-eternal knowledge (*al-ʿilm al-azali*). That is why such incredible feats happen. That is why small things are actually big as they yield marvelous results. Look, for instance, how a tiny pine seed becomes a huge pine tree... Through their direct connection to pre-eternal power, things can display incredible artistry that is well beyond the seeming power of the seeming causes associated with them.

In sum, the fact that things come into existence with such incredible artistry and such ease shows that they are created by an Eternally Powerful One. Otherwise, it would be impossible for these things to come into existence...

Through this powerful, profound and clear proof, my ego fell silent. It gave up being Satan's temporary disciple, and a representative of misguidance and materialist philosophy. My ego believed in God. And said:

'Yes, I need such a Creator and Sustainer who will know my smallest wishes and most secret longings, who can take care of the most hidden needs of my soul, and who can transform this huge world into the next world in order to grant me eternal happiness. My Creator and Sustainer can only be the One who can create the heavens as easily as He creates a tiny fly, and can place the sun in its orbit as easily as He places a particle in my eye. Otherwise, someone who cannot create a fly cannot hear my deepest wishes and know the deepest longings of my soul. Someone who cannot create the heavens cannot provide me with eternal happiness. Thus, my Sustainer is the only One who can heal my heart, send rain through the clouds, and will transform this world into the next one and open the doors of Paradise to me.'

---

[9] Nursi's reference to planets and atoms as being part of God's employees or forces may be an exegesis of the Quranic reference to God's *junūd* (lit. 'army' or 'forces') *forces of the heavens and the earth belong to God*. (Q. 48:4; see also 48:7 and 74:31).

Thus, my dear elderly friends, who similarly may have spent part of their lives in the darkness of godless philosophy! See how the repeated declaration of the Quran, *la ilaha illa hu* ('there is no god except the One God'), offers such a strong, unassailable and enduring truth! The Quran gifts to you such a sacred pillar of faith that enlightens all darkness and heals all spiritual wounds! ...

Dear elderly brothers and sisters! Since you have belief (*īmān*) and you have prayers and supplications that enlighten and nourish belief, your old age is like eternal youth. For, you can gain eternal youth through it. The cold, burdensome, ugly, dark and painful old age is not yours, but that of the people of misguidance. They can regret and cry, not you. Dear respected believing elderly, be joyful and grateful, and say *all praise be to God for all situations....*

5
SURRENDERING TO THE ONE:
THE EXAMPLE OF PROPHET JONAH

The prayer of Prophet Jonah quoted in the Quran is well known among many Muslims, who invoke it in time of distress. According to a narration from Prophet Muhammad, whoever prays with this supplication in time of difficulty definitely receives God's help. In the excerpt below, Nursi focuses on the mystery of this prayer, explaining how it is a transformative declaration of *tawhid* in a crisis situation. Prophet Jonah's case sets an example for realizing the truth of *tawhid* at a deeper existential level especially in difficult circumstances or situations that we perceive as unfair. According to Nursi, such deeper revelation of *tawhid* again comes with seeing the 'seeming causes' as merely means to the displaying of Divine power and recognizing that there is no power or help except through the One. As alluded to briefly in the Quran and also as mentioned in this selection, Prophet Jonah was overwhelmed with his prophetic mission to a people who were very resistant to his teachings. And he ran away. As he was escaping, Jonah found himself in a situation where he tangibly experienced that *none* of the seeming causes has any power. Having boarded on a ship to escape, he ended up being thrown into the sea and stuck in the belly of a whale. Nothing and no one seemed to be able to help him out in that impasse. Only then he recognized with 'deepest certainty' (*haqq al-yaqīn*), that every single thing and every event is created purposely and it is under the direct control of the Merciful Creator of All Things.

With honesty and courage, Prophet Jonah admits that he had misinterpreted his situation earlier and turns to the One God in surrender and repentance. Nursi suggests that it is through this deeper realization of *tawhid* and complete surrender to the One that his crisis was transformed into a breakthrough and wonderful salvation. Enemies transformed into friends. At first it had seemed like all were united against Jonah: the people, the night, the whale, and the stormy sea. But then, when he realized that there is no deliverer except the One, Jonah could see their friendly faces that point to their Creator. Indeed, the purpose of 'seeming causes' is to reveal that they are under the direct power of the One who has complete power over everything, and thereby to proclaim *His* power, wisdom, and mercy. Their powerlessness acts like a mirror to divine power. It is then that we can recognize that what seemed as meaningless and hostile are in fact purposefully revealing their Merciful, Wise and Powerful Creator and making Him known to us. Jonah's awareness of *tawhid* meant that he realized that nothing could harm or benefit him without the permission of the One. Indeed, the very whale that seemed to threaten his life was turned into a vehicle that carried him, by the will of God, to the shore of salvation.

Applying Jonah's case to our lives, Nursi explains that when we forget that beings and causes are all interrelated and that they are all acting under the command of the One who has control over all things, then we inevitably fall into despair and darkness. For Nursi, Jonah's stormy sea, the dark night and the whale represent our lives, our future and our desires when we live in forgetfulness of *tawhid*. He explains how Jonah's prayer undoes the illusion of forgetfulness through a threefold affirmation. The first part of the prayer is the declaration of tawhid: *there is no god except You* (*la ilāha illa anta*). It is a recognition of the fact that seeming causes have no power to determine our lives and future. The second part of the prayer declares *Glory be unto You* (*subḥānaka*), which affirms that the Creator is free from injustice and imperfection. With this invocation, we give up our misperception of this life as unfair and transience as the ultimate reality. Surely, the One who made human beings and gave them their needs and their yearning for justice, is free from injustice and imperfection. The final phrase of the prayer declares, *verily I have been among the wrongdoers* (*inni kuntu minazzālimīn*). That is, in the first two phrases the awakened person gives up blaming the world, destiny, and God, and now, he takes responsibility for his

misunderstandings. He realizes that it is his previous distorted perception and choices that made things seem hopeless and ugly. Jonah's
prayer is an invitation to surrender to the Merciful Creator of All
Things and thereby asking for forgiveness, giving up victim mentali-
ty and taking responsibility for one's choices.

This text on Jonah serves as a good example of a well-grounded
Quranic hermeneutics, according to which the stories and parables in
the Quran are not simply told for the sake of storytelling or communicating a historical event. Rather these stories convey profound
'universal principles.' As Nursi puts it elsewhere, particular events
narrated in the Quran are 'tips' of universal truths: 'there are in the
All-Wise Quran numerous minor events behind which are concealed
universal principles, and which are shown as the tips of general
laws.'[1] In the case of this story, the minor event of Prophet Jonah's
salvation points to a universal truth, namely that a needy human
being can only be delivered from the threatening vicissitudes of life
through acknowledging their connection with their Omnipotent
and Merciful Maker. When in a state of heedlessness, human beings
forget that everything is under the control of their Creator, and they
tend to imagine that events befalling them are unrelated and meaningless. Thus, they fall into despair and find it hard to bear the challenges they encounter in life. It is only when they re-affirm Divine
Unity that they can seek refuge in God, take responsibility for their
misperception and responses to events, realize the meanings of those
events, and attain peace in this world and the next.

Finally, it is worth noting that after exegeting Jonah's prayer
('The First Flash') Nursi turns to reflect on the prayer of Prophet Job
(*Ayyūb*) in the Quran ('The Second Flash'). The prayer of Prophet
Jonah in the Quran may be interpreted as a remedy to the 'problem
of evil' in relation to human choices—Jonah was frustrated at his
people's stubborn rejection. While the case of Prophet Job in the
Quran may be interpreted as a solution to what is termed as 'problem of natural evil'—sickness and calamity befell Prophet Job. In his
discussion of Job's prayer in the 'Second Flash,' Nursi suggests that

---

[1] Nursi, *Words*, 253.

difficulties and sickness are a foil for the manifestation of beauty (the Most Beautiful Names of God).[2]

***

PROPHET JONAH'S PRAYER[3]

In the name of God, the Merciful the Compassionate

Then he [Jonah] cried out in the deep darkness: 'There is no god except You! Glory be to You! Indeed, I have been among the wrongdoers.' And so, We answered him and saved him from distress: for thus do We save the believers.

—Quran, 21: 87–88

The prayer of Prophet Jonah (*Yūnus*)—peace be upon Prophet Muhammad and upon him—is a very powerful and effective means for obtaining an answer to prayer. The gist of the celebrated story of Jonah, peace be upon him, is as follows:

He was thrown into the sea and was swallowed by a big fish. He found himself in the belly of the fish, in the midst of a stormy sea, in the deep darkness of the night. He realized that no cause could deliver him, and he cried out, *'There is no god except You! You are limitless in Your glory! Indeed, I have been among the wrongdoers.'* This prayer led to his immediate deliverance.

What was about this prayer that was so transformative? His prayer contains the realization that all the 'seeming causes' are completely powerless. Since the night, the sea, the fish and the weather seemed to be all united against him, he needed someone who has power over all of these seeming causes. In other words, only the one who has power over all these elements could save Jonah, upon him be peace. Even if all people were his helpers and servants, they could

---

[2] Nursi, *Flashes*, 'Second Flash,' 21–28. Also see Mermer, 'Nursi's Scriptural Approach to the Problem of Evil' and Yazicioglu, 'Affliction, Patience and Prayer: Reading Job (p) in the Quran.'

[3] Nursi, *Lem'alar*, 'Birinci Lem'a' [*Flashes*, First Flash], RNK 1:579. The title was added.

not have helped him out of that impasse. Thus, it became clear that seeming causes have no power whatsoever.

When Jonah, peace be upon him, realized with the certainty of seeing ('*ayn al-yaqīn*) that there is no recourse other than the Causer of All Causes (*musabbib al-asbāb*), then the oneness of God became manifest to him.[4] As this prayer highlighted the powerlessness of all the seeming causes, it also immediately subjugated the night, the sea and the fish. Through the power of *tawhid*, his prayer instantly transformed

- the belly of the fish into a submarine;

- the stormy sea into a peaceful and safe place,

- the dark cloudy sky into a clear sky with a shining moon.

The created beings that had been pressing and threatening him from all sides now showed him a friendly face from every direction. Thus, Jonah, peace be upon him, reached the shore of salvation, where, he enjoyed the favor of his Sustainer, beneath a gourd tree. (Q. 37: 146).[5]

Now, we are in a situation exceedingly more awful than that in which Jonah, peace be upon him, first found himself:

- Our night is our future. When we think about the future with forgetfulness of our Sustainer (*ghafla*), our future appears to be much bleaker and more terrifying than Jonah's dark night.

- Our sea is the constantly changing world in which we live. This world is full of death and separation. Indeed, each 'wave' of our sea bears thousands of corpses. Hence, our sea is a thousand times more frightening than Jonah's sea.

---

[4] Literally, 'the light of *tawhid*, recognizing oneness of God, revealed the truth of unicity (*ahadiyya*) to him.' For a discussion of the distinction between *ahadiyya* and *wahidiyya*, see explanation in introduction to Chapter 10.

[5] *And We caused a creeping plant to grow over him [out of the barren soil].* (Quran, 37:146)

- Our whale is the caprice of our ego, which tries to engulf and destroy our eternal life. This fish is a thousand
  times more threatening than Prophet Jonah's. While his
  fish threatened to destroy his limited earthly life, our
  fish seeks to destroy our eternal, everlasting life.

If this is our real situation, then let us take the example of Jonah (p).
Let us turn away from all of seeming causes and take direct refuge
with the Causer of Causes, our Sustainer. Let us say, *There is no god
but You. Glory be unto You! Indeed, I have been among the wrongdoers.*

Let us affirm clearly with the certainty of seeing it (*'ayn al-
yaqīn*): Our future, the world and the desires of our ego all seem to
be united against us because of our forgetfulness of God (*ghafla*) and
misguidance. Only the One who has power over the future, the
world and our ego can protect us against their harm.[6] Indeed,

- Who else other than the Creator of the Heavens and the
  Earth would know the secrets of our hearts and our most
  hidden wishes?

- Who else other than Him can enlighten our future through
  creating life after death?

- Who else other than Him can save us from the pressures of
  the overwhelming vicissitudes of the sea of life?

None other than the Necessarily Existent One can be of help to us.
Nothing whatsoever can help and save us except with His permission
and will.

---

[6] Ultimately, their true lasting harm comes from our misinterpretation of
them. (In the Quranic view, even when someone transgresses against others,
he cannot harm them in the true lasting sense; in the end, the unjust truly
only harms himself.) Human beings perceive the world as united against
them when they forget that it is sustained by One who is Merciful and of
Infinite Wisdom. Similarly, the ego becomes harmful when we do not use
its desires as a means to accessing the signs of God. For a detailed analysis of
the function of the ego see Nursi, *Words*, '30th Word.'

Now, this is the reality of our situation. Given that through Jonah's prayer, the fish became like a submarine for him, the sea became a beautiful smooth abode, and the dark night transformed into a peaceful moonlit night, then in recognition of the truth and power of this prayer, we should also affirm:

There is no god but You. Glory be unto You! Indeed, I have been among the wrongdoers.

- Let us attract Divine mercy into our future by saying *there is no god but You* (*la ilaha illa anta*).

- Let us attract Divine mercy into our world by declaring *glory be unto You* (*subḥānaka*).

- Let us attract God's mercy to our ego; and concede that *Indeed I have been the wrongdoers* (*innī kuntu minaẓẓālimīn*).

This way, through the light of faith (*nūr al-imān*) and the radiance of the Quran, our future will be enlightened. The terror and horror of our world will be transformed into fellowship, familiarity and joy. And in this world of ours, where through death and change, innumerable corpses constantly keep surfacing over the waves of years and centuries, we can take refuge in the 'ship' of *surrender* (*islām*) built in the 'workbench' of the all-Wise Quran (*al-qur'ān al-ḥakīm*). In that spiritual ship, we shall sail in peace through the sea of life and reach the shore of safety and fulfill our life's duty. Instead of terrifying us, the hurricanes and earthquakes of the sea of life will thrill us, like the change of scenes in an exciting movie relating a pleasurable story. That is, these fluctuations in the sea of life will open up enjoyable and soothing horizons for our deliberation and contemplation. Moreover, through the Quranic teachings that enable discernment (*al-tarbiya al-furqāniyya*),[7] our ego will not engulf us [through short

---

[7] Literally 'the edification/education of *furqān*.' *Furqān*, used as adjective here, literally means 'discerning,' and is also used as a description of the Quran in the Quran (for instance, Q. 2:185, Q. 25:1), to revelation given to Prophet Moses (Q. 2:53) and discernment bestowed on believers who have consciousness of God (Q. 8:29).

sighted insistence and obsessions that threaten our eternal future.] Rather, it will be a reliable mount, which we will ride towards eternal life.

In sum, since human beings have a comprehensive nature— through which they connect to so many things—they are also utterly fragile and vulnerable. They can suffer from a fatal disease, be terrified by an earthquake, and fret about the end of the world approaching. Just as human beings are wary of a tiny virus, they are also worried about a potential global catastrophe. Just as they love their home, they also care about the vast world around them. Just as they love their backyards, they also deeply long for the eternal gardens of Paradise. Therefore, the protector, the lord, the sustainer and refuge of such interconnected and vulnerable beings can only be the One in whose hand is the entire universe. Only the One who has command over all things—from tiny particles to planets—can be our refuge. Therefore, human beings are in constant need of seeking His help and invoking Jonah's prayer:

> *There is no god but You. Glory be unto You! Indeed, I have been among the wrongdoers.*

6

YOU ARE THE ARTWORK OF THE ONE GOD AND YOUR SOUL LONGS FOR THE ONE

Thee alone do we worship;
and unto Thee alone do we turn for aid.

—Quran, 1:5

The following selection, which consists of four brief notes or 'indica-tions' (*rumūz*), further clarifies the implications of *tawhid* for human life. Human beings find their true object of adoration through rec-ognizing the oneness of God. *Tawhid* enables human beings to ap-preciate things as ephemeral mirrors reflecting the Eternal One. Through *tawhid*, human beings can orient themselves truthfully in the world. Through *tawhid*, they can set right their priorities in life to nurture and fulfill their potentials so as to yield eternal happiness.

'First Indication' reflects upon the fact that human beings are interconnected with the rest of the world—physically, emotionally, and spiritually. Our body is literally made up of the elements of the earth; we are nourished from air, plants and animals, light, and so on. These facts are signs and indications that we are the handiwork of an amazing Creator who holds the entire universe in His control. Therefore, we should worship the One alone and seek help from Him only. Nursi argues that the only alternative to worshipping one Creator only is to worship a multitude of seeming causes, or nature itself under a variety of appellations. Such worship of created beings does not necessarily take the form of traditional paganism, such as bowing to physical idols. Rather, human beings often tacitly worship 'seeming causes' by assuming that created beings are the source of life and well-being. We implicitly place our hope in them for survival, healing, power and self-worth. Nursi argues that such worship of created beings does not make sense and is also deeply unsatisfying. For, these seeming causes in which we place our hope are utterly weak and they are themselves being constantly made, just like us. The sun, the moon, soil, rain, air, vegetation, etc.—they do not even know us, so how could they be our creators or contribute to our creation? Thus, the 'First Indication' can be read as an exegesis of Quranic verses such as, *To Him [alone] is all invocation of truth. Those whom they invoke instead of Him cannot respond to them any more than someone who stretches out his open hands towards water, [hoping] that it may reach his mouth, though it never reaches him: the invocation of the disbelievers is all in vain.* (Q. 13:14, emphasis added)

'Second Indication' highlights another important point, which is the fact that the world is both beautiful and passing. This short piece connects with early Meccan chapters of the Quran that repeatedly and eloquently remind of the transience of this world.[1] And, again, human beings have two choices in responding to this fact: we either love the world itself or its Eternal Creator and Sustainer. From a Quranic perspective, this world—including our own souls—are signs to the Eternal Artist. That is why they all reflect glimpses of beauty while being fraught with transience and shortcomings. Nursi suggests that worshipping the world and our own souls instead of their Maker is foolish. Using a mirror metaphor, which is a common one in Islamic spirituality, he explains that neither the world nor our own soul is worthy of being idolized or worshipped. Rather, they are signs, inviting human beings to the One to whom all adoration and worship is due.

In 'Third Indication,' Nursi further encourages the reader to 'wake up' to reality and set priorities in life accordingly. We are to invest into the aspect of life that yields eternity, living with awareness

---

[1] See Quran, Chapters 82–89. These early Meccan suras refer to both beauty of the world and its decay and transience. For an eloquent translation, see Sells, *The Early Revelations*.

of what is real, and not allow our precious faculties to be wasted on an illusion of permanence of this impermanent world. *Shirk* is suffocating for the human heart, spirit, and other precious subtle faculties because it betrays our longing for meaning and permanence by drowning us in disappointing illusions. In Quranic vocabulary, which is again the source of Nursi's reflections, we are to seek what we are created for: *So, set thy face steadfastly towards the [one ever-true] faith, turning away from all that is false, <u>in accordance with the natural disposition which God has instilled into human being</u>* (Q. 30:30, emphasis added). That is, we should not waste our lives running after an illusion, a 'mirage.' (Q. 24:39)[2]

Finally, 'Fourth Indication' calls upon the reader to take stock of their perception of life. Human beings are deeply attached to life, and yet life is merely a fleeting moment at the level of corporeality. What is the way out of this dilemma? It is to live at a higher level, at the level of the heart and the soul/spirit. The pleasures of life are meaningful and fulfilling *only when* they are anchored in *tawhid*. Then, they are enjoyed at the level of the heart and soul, with gratitude and in awareness of the indications to the Eternal One.

In sum, all of these four 'indications' offer tips from a Quranic perspective on life. Nursi attempts to show how the Quran reveals the truth of existence with balance: noting both its beauty and transience. The world is not disparaged for being transient, nor is the human being regarded faulty for being limited. Rather in their transience and limitedness, they are like mirrors reflecting glimpses of the beauty and power of the One; they are signs (*ayāt*) to the Eternal Creator. Human beings need to make conscious choices to discern this reality and accordingly direct their love and praises to the one true source.

---

[2] '*But as for those who disbelieve, their deeds are <u>like a mirage</u> in the desert, which the thirsty supposes to be water—until, when he approaches it, he finds that it was nothing: instead, he finds [that] God [has always been present] with him, and [that] He will pay him his account in full—for God is swift in reckoning!* (Quran, 24:39, emphasis added).

***

FOUR BRIEF INDICATIONS ON *TAWHID*[3]

First Indication: You are a Small Universe Bearing Amazing Divine Art

What is amiss with you that you cannot look forward to God's majesty—seeing that He has created (every one of) you in successive stages? Do you not see how God has created seven heavens in full harmony with one another, and made the moon as a light therein and made the sun as a radiant lamp? And God made you grow out of the earth like a plant; and thereafter He will return you to it (in death) and then He will bring you forth (from it) in resurrection. (Q. 71:13–17)

O human being who worships and adores the seeming causes! Let's say you saw a wonderful palace being constructed out of precious rare stones. Some of these stones are only found in China, some only in Spain or Arabia, and others are unique to Far East Asia. If you saw all these special stones brought together with utter ease from various corners of the earth within the same day and used to build a wonderful palace, would you have any doubt that the maker of such a palace is an incredible ruler who has control over the entire globe?

In the same way, every living being is like a divine palace (*qasr ilāhī*), and human beings are the most beautiful and wondrous of those palaces. Some of the precious stones of this 'human palace' come from the world of spirits, some from 'the world of similitude' (*'ālam al-mithāl*), some from the Preserved Tablet (*lawḥ al-maḥfūẓ*),[4] and others from the realms of air, light, and minerals.

---

[3] Nursi, *Lem'alar*, '17. Lema, 14. Nota' [*Flashes*, '17th Flash, 14th Note'], RNK I: 654–655. The subtitles and the Quranic passages in the beginning of each 'indication' have been added by the translators.

[4] The 'preserved tablet' is mentioned in Quran 85:22. In contemporary terms, we might perhaps translate the 'preserved tablet' as a 'secure database' in which everything is recorded. Nursi refers to the 'preserved tablet' in a number of different passages, often referring to the indications to it in

Moreover, the needs of human beings stretch to eternity, their wishes spread to the furthest corners of the universe, and their concerns pertain to this world and the next.

This is your nature, oh human being. Accordingly, your maker can only be the one who manages and governs the earth and the heavens as easily as turning the pages of a book.[5] He can only be the one for whom this world and the next are readily present, and for whom pre-eternity and post-eternity are like yesterday and tomorrow. Only such a being who has control over the earth and the heavens and rules this life and the next can be your true object of worship, your refuge, and your savior.

Second Indication: Do Not Confuse the Mirror with the Sun

Now among His signs are the night and the day, as well as the sun and the moon. Do not prostrate to the sun or the moon, but prostrate to God, who has created them if is He Whom you worship. (Q. 41:37)

Imagine foolish people who are not aware of the sun. When they see the sun reflected in a mirror, they fall in love with the mirror. They eagerly protect the mirror for fear of losing the sun that they see in it. However, once they realize that the sun is actually out there, and that it does not vanish when the mirror breaks, their love will be redirected towards the sun itself. Then, they understand that the sun reflected in the mirror is not bound to the mirror nor does its existence depend on it. Rather, it is the sun in the sky that makes the mir-

---

the world, such as human memory or seeds, which is worth analyzing in a separate project. In this context, he seems to suggest that the coming into existence of a human being clearly shows the existence of a comprehensive prior plan, a divine plan stored in a 'preserved tablet.' See, Yazicioglu, 'A Graceful Reconciliation,' 134 and also Nursi's 'Treatise on Destiny,' in *Words*, '26th Word,' tr. by Vahide, 477–494.

[5] Nursi's use of the metaphor of 'turning pages' to describe the ease with which the Creator manages and sustains the natural world is an indirect reference to the Quranic verse which refers to God *roll[ing] up the skies as written scrolls are rolled up.* (Q. 21:104)

ror shine. The mirror is illuminated because of the sun, not vice versa.

O human being! Your heart and nature are like a mirror. The intense and innate love for eternity contained in your heart is not for the mirror but for the reflection of the Eternal and Majestic One which shines upon the mirror of your heart in proportion to its capacity. Due to your unmindful confusion, however, you misappropriated the love due to the Eternal One for yourself. Now is the time to set the matter right. Turn to Him and proclaim, *O Eternal One, You are the Eternal (Ya Baqī anta al-Baqī)*! That is, since You exist and You are eternal, we do not worry about separation and nonexistence![6]

Third Indication: Exercise Caution—You Have Precious Faculties

...for the earth, despite all its vastness, became [too] narrow for you...(Q. 9:25)

...he holds out promises to them, and fills them with vain desires: yet Satan's promises are nothing but delusion. (Q. 4:120)

O human being! Your Wise Originator (*al-Fāṭir al-Hakīm*) has endowed you with a very strange feature. Sometimes, you feel so suffocated: the earth feels too small for you as though it were a prison, and you long for a vaster place. Yet, at other times, you settle into a tiny space: you get lost in a memory, in a moment, or in a task. Your heart and mind, which cannot fit inside the vast earth, can become stuck

---

[6] In other words, separation and nonexistence is not a threat, as our object of love is Eternal. This calls to mind the Quranic verse *All that lives on earth or in the heavens is bound to pass away: but forever will abide your Sustainer's countenance, full of majesty and glory.* (Quran, 55:26–27), on which Nursi reflects at length elsewhere, in the 'Third Flash' of *Flashes*. He explains in detail that human longing for eternity is actually our longing for the eternal One and His beautiful qualities. And, it is through being a conscious mirror to the Eternal One that human beings have access to a sort of endurance and eternity.

within that tiny thing. You focus with the strongest feelings on a tiny memory or recollection and lose yourself therein.

Moreover, you are also gifted with such spiritual and subtle faculties that some of them can swallow the whole universe and still not be satisfied while some of them can be burdened by a tiny speck. Just like the eye cannot bear a single hair while the head can carry heavy weights, some human feelings are so delicate and fragile that they cannot withstand the slightest consequences of heedlessness and misguidance. In such situations, they can even choke and die.

Since this is so, be mindful lest you get drowned in a mouthful, an utterance, a flash of light, a hint, or a peck. Do not allow your precious emotions, which could engulf the entire world, to be lost in a tiny thing. For, there are very small things that can swallow up very major things. See, for instance, how a small mirror takes in the sky with its stars. Or how the tiny memory area of your brain contains much of your deeds and many of your life memories. Likewise, there are many small particular things that can 'swallow up' huge things. So, be careful not to lose perspective and drown in insignificant matters.

Fourth Indication: Seeing Your World as it is

The life of this world is but play and diversion: but if you believe and are conscious of Him, He will grant you your rewards. And, He does not ask for your possessions. (Q. 47:36) [7]

You will see the mountains and think that they are firmly fixed, but they float away like clouds: [this is] the work of God who has perfected all things. (Q. 27:88)

O human being, so attached to the fleeting world and unmindful of the Eternal One! Know that your world, which you imagine to be so vast, is narrow like a grave. However, the walls of this narrow grave

---

[7] Similarly, Q. 6:32 notes *And the life of this world is nothing but play and diversion; and the abode of the hereafter is by far the better for all who are conscious of God. Will you not, then, use your reason?* See also, Q. 10:24, 13:26, 18:28, 18:104, 20:131, 28:60, 29:64, 31:33, etc.

are made up of glass, and as the glass walls reflect on each other, you imagine your narrow space to be as big as a city. Indeed, your past and your future reflect within each other and your present moment seems expansive to you. In reality, the present is only a fleeting, passing moment, and both the past and the future are nonexistent. You confuse reality with imagination, and assume a nonexistent world to be present with you.

Imagine a fast-moving line; it looks like a surface when it is actually just a line. In the same way, the reality of your existence is as thin as a line, yet, because of your forgetfulness, illusion, and imagination your world seems vast to you and its walls seem far off...However, when you are shaken by an adversity, you hit at once the walls that seemed so distant, and so you wake up from your illusion. Then, you realize that your vast world is in fact narrower than a grave and more restrictive than a narrow lane. Your lifespan passes quicker than lightening, and your life flows faster than a river.

Now, since transience is the nature of worldly life, physical existence and animal life, it is wiser for you to stop restricting yourself with animality and corporeality, and enter the higher level of the heart and spirit. You will find a life much broader than the vast world you used to imagine. You will find a realm of light. The key to this world of light is in the sacred phrase, 'there is no god except God,' which reveals the secrets of knowing God (ma'rifatullah) and the oneness of God (waḥdāniyya). So, let your heart speak it and let your spirit flourish with it.

7

GRATITUDE IS AWARENESS: RECEIVING BLESSINGS ONLY IN GOD'S NAME

Worship God [alone], and be among those who are grateful (Q. 39:66)

Verily, We have shown him [human being] the way: to be either grateful or ungrateful. (Q. 76:3)

[Satan said]: Then I shall most certainly fall upon them [human beings] from their front and from their back, and from their right and from their left: and You will not find most of them grateful. (Q. 7:17)

Whatever good happens to you is from God... (Q. 4:79)

As indicated in the Quranic passages above, *tawhid* and gratitude are often linked in the Quran. Prophet Abraham, a paragon of *tawhid* in the Quran, is described as being always *grateful for the blessings granted by Him.* (Q. 16:121).[1] In the selection below, Nursi discusses

---

[1] In another Quranic passage, Abraham says: *Have you considered what you worship, you and your forefathers? Verily, they are enemies unto me, save the Sustainer of all the worlds, who has created me and is the One who guides me, and is the One who feeds me and gives me to drink, and when I fall ill, He is the One who heals me, and who causes me to die and then gives*

how gratitude to God and *tawhid* are connected by inviting the readers to reconsider their understanding of causality. In order to direct our gratitude to the deserving recipient, people need to recognize the true provider of the blessings they enjoy. By giving examples from nature and human relationships, Nursi suggests that all the goodness and blessing comes from God alone.

Nursi first explains a common error: we often mistake 'seeming causes' for the real creators of the results, and so we direct our gratitude to them. For instance, we may think a particular chemical solution causes our well-being or a particular person is the source of our sustenance. Consequently, we feel grateful to them as if they were the providers of health or sustenance. In reality, Nursi argues, they are only channels to the power and compassion of the Creator. To explain, Nursi offers a reasoning that can be outlined in two steps as follows.

First, Nursi distinguishes between 'conjunction' (*iqtirān*) and 'causation' ('*illiyya*). That is, just because two things occur concurrently over and over does not mean that one makes the other. This is a subtle point that is essential to witnessing *tawhid*. For those who are not familiar with classical Islamic theology, the following example from the classical Islamic theologian Ghazali may be of use. Ghazali offers a medieval scenario to clarify the distinction between conjunction and causation: '(Think of) a person taken to be beheaded, yet when the king sent a decree annulling and dismissing the process, he began to concentrate on the ink, the paper and the pen which were involved in the decree staying [his execution] saying: 'Were it not for the pen, I would not have been released.' It is as if he thought his salvation had come from the pen and not from the one moving the pen, yet this would be the height of ignorance.' Because his deliverance comes *with* the pen and paper, the prisoner thinks they *caused* his salvation. Yet, just because the two things appear together (decree and salvation) and disappear together (if the decree was not there, the man would not be saved) does not mean the decree *caused* his

---

me life—and who, I hope will forgive me my faults on Judgment Day! (Q. 26:75–82)

salvation. In reality, the decree—the pen, paper, ink—cannot be the real cause of the person's deliverance, since it does not display the appropriate qualities to cause such a result: it has no knowledge, volition and authority, to save the prisoner's life. The decree is just a seeming cause. The real cause of the man's salvation is the king, in whose hand the pen is just an instrument. Likewise, Ghazali says, 'the sun, moon, and stars, as well as rain, clouds and earth, along with all living and non-living things, are but instruments in the grasp of the divine power (*qudra*), as a pen subservient to the hand of an author.'[2] The gratitude, therefore, should be directed to God, not to the seeming causes. For another—more contemporary—example, one may consider a light bulb. If there is no bulb, there is no light in the room. And when we put the bulb, there is light. This constant conjunction between the bulb and light, however, does not prove that the light bulb *creates* electricity and light.[3]

Nursi explains this distinction between 'conjunction' and 'causation' in the excerpt below by using another example: a garden flourishing with water. He notes that the fact that the garden dries up when I do not open the water canal and that it flourishes when I do open the canal is not sufficient evidence for me to conclude that my action *causes* the flourishing of the garden. Why not? He brings into attention another fact: the garden dries up in the *absence* of one thing, but it flourishes in the *presence* of many things, such as air, bacteria in soil, sunlight, minerals, gravity, and so forth. Hence, 'argument from absence' can be misleading.[4] My *inaction* may be squarely blamed for the *absence* of the result, but my *action* alone cannot be taken to have *created* the result. Nursi's next step is to note that if such 'argument from absence' can be misleading, then the simple fact that a garden *stops* flourishing in the *absence* of a *number of things* is also not sufficient to prove that these natural factors col-

---

[2] Ghazali, *Faith in Divine Unity*, 17.

[3] Bouguenaya, *Genuine Tawhid*, 123.

[4] What we term as 'the argument from absence' is identifying A as the cause of B simply because of the appearance of A & B together and the absence of B in the absence of A.

lectively produce the garden. Actually, the presence of all these natural factors (such as a certain range of temperature and air pressure, sunlight, air, soil, water, seeds, bacteria, movements of the earth and sun, and so forth) serve only as a background for the real cause or agent—namely, divine will and power—to produce the result. The evidence comes from the mismatch between the attributes of seeming causes and effects. As Nursi argues elsewhere, 'to attribute a well-ordered and well-balanced being which has unity such as [a living being] to the jumbled hands of innumerable, lifeless, ignorant, aggressive, unconscious, chaotic, blind and deaf natural causes, the blindness and deafness of which increase with their coming together and intermingling among the ways of numberless possibilities, is as unreasonable as accepting innumerable impossibilities all at once.'[5] In other words, the attributes of the seeming causes, such as soil, water, and sunlight, fall short of bearing responsibility for a well-ordered and well-balanced unified being, such as a garden or a living being. That is, the seeming causes, even when they are considered as a *collective*, clearly do not display the knowledge, contrivance, power, mercy, or life displayed by their effects. Unfortunately, many people overlook this, Nursi regrets, and make the mistake of equating conjunction and causation. They thus *direct* their *gratitude* to 'seeming causes' instead of the real cause, the Creator.

In the treatise on *bismillah*, excerpted earlier in this book, Nursi argued that all beings, the whole universe, is actually acting in the name of a One with infinite power and wisdom, and he encouraged his audience to act in mindfulness of this reality. In this selection, he further elaborates on the importance of such awareness in the context of receiving blessings. He also extends such living in awareness of God to human relationships as well, noting some of its special challenges. Since human beings are conscious, it may be tempting to ascribe causal powers to human beings, as if they are the creators of benefits received through them. Moreover, unlike unconscious things, human beings have a choice on whether they give (or receive) in God's name or not. Addressing such circumstances as well, this

---

[5] Nursi, *Flashes*, 236 (modified translation).

text is as an invitation to climb up the ladder of acting in God's name.

***

RECEIVING GOD'S BLESSINGS WITH AWARENESS[6]

When a blessing (*ni'ma*) comes to you through 'seeming causes' (*al-asbāb al-ẓāhiriyya*), do not receive that blessing in its name, as if the blessing were really from it. Rather take it in the name of the Real Giver, God, the Sole Creator and Sustainer of all.

Beings without self-consciousness or free choice, like plants and animals, already offer all they give in God's name. [Through their being devoid of knowledge, power, and will, they act as mirrors to divine knowledge, power and will.] This way, they proclaim *bismillah* through their tongue of disposition (*lisān al-ḥāl*).[7] Since they give in God's name, you too receive what they give in His name, *bismillah*. On the other hand, if a blessing comes to you through a conscious being with free choice, then accept it only if the person gives it in God's name. If that person, who is just the means through which God's blessing comes to you, does not mention God's name, then do not take it. It is stated in the Quran '*and, do not eat of that over which God's name has not been pronounced.*' (Quran, 6:121). In addition to its obvious meaning,[8] this verse implies that one should not sustain oneself with that which does not remind of the Real Giver and is not given in His name. In sum, both the one who gives and the one who receives should invoke God's name.

---

[6] Nursi, *Lem'alar*, '17. Lema, 13. Nota 4. Mesele' [*Flashes*, 17th Flash, 13th Note, 4th Point], RNK I: 653–654. (The title added by the translators.)

[7] In other words, unconscious beings declare in the *way* they come into being and act: 'I cannot be the source of my existence and the power and blessings I display.' For details, see the first chapter on *bismillah*.

[8] By the 'obvious meaning' Nursi refers to the fact that this verse is commonly interpreted as an injunction to abstain from meat not harvested or sacrificed in God's name. It is noteworthy that there is actually no reference to meat in this passage, and hence Nursi's broader interpretation fits the literal meaning of the text as well.

If you are in a difficult situation in which you are really in need of what someone is offering but that person does not invoke God's name, then at least accept it in God's name. Say *bismillah* ('in the name of God'), and recognize the Most Merciful as the real giver behind that person, and receive the blessing with gratitude to Him. That is, take a moment to acknowledge the bestowal (*in'ām*) present within the gift. As you notice the act of bestowal, be aware of the Real Bestower (*al-Mun'im al-Haqīqī*). Such awareness itself constitutes gratitude to the Real Bestower. Then, if you like, pray for the person through whom God's blessing has reached you.

Heedless people are confused by the conjunction (*iqtirān*) of things. They assume that if two things appear together, it must be that one is causing and producing the other. This erroneous perception is reinforced by the fact that when the supposed cause is removed, the blessing that came with it disappears, leading people to mistakenly infer that the supposed cause must have created the blessing. With this misunderstanding, they direct their love and gratitude toward the supposed cause rather than to the Real Giver of blessings.

It is a big and common mistake to equate the cause of the *absence* of a blessing with the cause of its *presence*. This reasoning [that is, 'if it were not for A, there would not have been B, therefore A made B'] is fallacious because the *existence* of a blessing [e.g. A] is connected with many conditions [e.g. B1+ B2+ B3+ etc.] and preceding circumstances (*muqaddimāt*, lit. 'forerunners' or 'introductions'). In contrast, the *absence* of a blessing happens simply with the absence of one thing [e.g. B1]. Let us give an example to clarify.

When you do not turn on the switch of an irrigation system, you are the cause of the land drying up and the loss of all its harvest. This fact does *not* mean that when you do turn on the irrigation system, you are the cause of its bountiful harvest. For there are many factors that must be brought together for a land to yield its crop, [e.g. air, soil, sunshine, seeds, bacteria that enrich the soil through their role in chemical reactions, and so on,] while the absence of only one factor [such as water] can result in losing the crop.

Moreover, even when all of the factors are present, they remain merely the means to, and *not* the cause of, that harvest. The true cause that brings the blessings into being can only be the power and will of the Sustainer of all things. I hope you see now how fallacious the reasoning of the unmindful (*ghāfil*) who do not see beyond the apparent conjunction of things and thus they cannot see beyond the seeming causes.

Indeed, the conjunction of things does not necessarily mean one causes the other to come into existence. Conjunction and causation are completely different. A blessing comes to you. Let's assume that the blessing appears along with a friend's kind intention toward you. Your friend's intention is not a cause for that blessing; it doesn't create it. Your friend's intention cannot bring the blessing into being; it is just conjoined to it. The real cause of the blessing coming to you is God's mercy. Of course, if that friend did not intend to give, the blessing may not have reached you, in which case he would have been the cause of the absence of that blessing. And yet, as we explained above, this does not mean that he is therefore the cause of that blessing. Rather, your friend's kind intention to give represents only one of the many conditions of existence for that blessing.[9]

In this vein, some of the gifted disciples of the *Risale-i Nur*, such as Husrev and Refet, had felt overly indebted to me as their teacher. In that regard, they confused conjunction with causation. They thought: 'If our teacher had not come here and taught us, we would not have learned these great lessons of the Quran. Therefore, he is the cause of our benefiting from these precious lessons.' Yet in reality what has happened is a mere conjunction of two blessings from God: God has kindly blessed them with precious Quranic lessons and He has kindly blessed me with the gift of articulating the

---

[9] For example, if I met my best friend Nora through Maryam, I may think 'if Maryam had not introduced me to Nora, I would not have ever known her, and we would not have developed a friendship. Therefore, Maryam must be the cause of my close friendship with Nora.' It may be true that without Maryam's introduction, I would not have met Nora *through her*, it does not necessarily mean that I would not have met Nora otherwise. Moreover, Maryam cannot be responsible for the close friendship and understanding between us simply because she introduced us. She may not even be aware of my eventual friendship with Nora. How then can she be credited for something that she may not even be aware of?

precious teachings of the Quran. Therefore, my friends, know that God's compassion is the real cause (*'illa*) of both blessings.

I also made a similar mistake of confusing conjunction with causation in my relationship to you, my dear brothers and sisters. I have felt extremely indebted to you for your support of this service of faith, in your transcribing of the *Risale-i Nur*.[10] I was saying to myself: 'If they were not with me, how could I, a weak and half-illiterate person,[11] serve the Quran?' Then, I realized that God first blessed you with the sacred gift of supporting this service to the Quran and then blessed me with the gift of a successful service. These two blessings are conjoined but they are not each other's cause. That is why, instead of thanking you, I am happy for you.[12] And so you too instead of feeling obliged to me, be glad for me, pray for me and for blessings.

Thus, this piece shows how there are many degrees in lack of awareness (*ghafla*).

---

[10] The *Risale-i Nur* was originally handwritten and copied by hand under difficult circumstances.

[11] The author his referring to his inability to read the new Turkish script based on Latin alphabet, which in 1924 officially replaced the Ottoman script based on Arabic alphabet.

[12] What is translated here as 'I am happy for you' perhaps more literally can be translated as 'I congratulate you.' (Tk. 'tebrik ederim,' Ar. 'mabrūk.') In English, 'congratulations' is most often used when someone has 'achieved' something or 'done a good job'—in some ways it is almost the epitome of recognizing someone as responsible for their own success. Whereas here in this context, it is used when someone is gifted with something. The closest use in English to this context would be in the case congratulating a parent with the birth of a new baby.

8

BELIEF: LIGHT AND STRENGTH

This selection starts with a Quranic passage that predicates human perfection on belief (*īmān*) in God and doing righteous deeds (*ṣāliḥāt*). Nursi proceeds to explain, in five sections, how belief has the potential to transform human life and how it contributes to the flourishing of humanity. We have excerpted the first four sections here, saving the fifth one for the next chapter.

The first section explains how belief elevates human beings by connecting them to their Glorious Maker and raises their value by making them worthy of eternal paradise. The second section takes its cue from Quranic passages on the 'light' (*nūr*) of God and explains how belief enlightens our past, present, and future. The third section expounds the connection between belief and trusting in God (*ta-wakkul*). It highlights the relief and empowerment that comes with belief in one God as the believers entrust their burdens to their all-powerful and all-compassionate sustainer. The fourth section elucidates a special feature of human beings among all creatures: their ability to recognize their intense neediness, weakness and vulnerability. Belief in God and asking for help from God transforms human poverty into privilege and honor because they connect the human being to the source of infinite power, compassion and generosity.

Nursi's discussion of belief in the context of human nature is reminiscent of the Islamic concept of *fiṭra* or primordial human nature. According to the Quran, the human being has been molded with a nature inclined towards truth and recognizing *tawhid*. (Q. 30:30) Besides, a famous prophetic tradition attributed to Prophet Muhammad states that every human being is born with this innate nature inclined to truth, goodness and surrender to God (*islām*). While many contemporary Muslim scholars have invoked the concept of *fiṭra*—saying that belief in one God is intrinsic to human nature—, few have explained *how so*. Therefore, it is noteworthy that Nursi explains how belief in God is related to the fulfillment of human nature in various advantageous and important ways.

***

ON BELIEF AND HUMAN NATURE[1]

In the Name of God, the Merciful, the Compassionate.

Indeed, We have created the human being in the most excellent state, then sent him down to the lowest of the low, except those who believe and do good deeds.

—Quran, 95:4–6.

In what follows, we shall explain five of the numerous virtues of belief (*īmān*).

First Point: Belief Honors the Human Being

With the light of belief, the human being ascends to the highest of the high and acquires a value that makes him worthy of Paradise. In contrast, with the darkness of unbelief, he falls down to the lowest of the low, to a Hell-like state. For, belief *is* connection. Belief connects the human being to their Glorious Maker. Indeed, the human being is an artwork of God filled with inscriptions of the Most Beautiful Names (*al-asmā al-ḥusna*) of God. Through belief, all the divine artistry in him becomes visible. And, with that wonderful divine art, the human being acquires great value. In contrast, disbelief severs such a connection to the Glorious Maker. Thereby, the Divine artistry present in the human being is concealed. Thereby, the human being's

---

[1] Nursi, *Sözler*, '23. Söz, Birinci Makam' (*Words*, '23rd Word, First Station'), RNK 1: 132–134. The verse is in the original. The title and the following subtitles for each section has been added by the translators.

worth is reduced to the worth of his physical being or flesh. And the value of such a passing and ephemeral animal life is futile and worthless.

Let us explain how belief elevates the worth of a human being and how disbelief reduces human worth by using an analogy from everyday life. Let us take a work of art, say a painting, and think about the worth of the *material* used and the worth of the *art* it bears. Sometimes the art and the material used for it are of the same value. Sometimes the material used is more valuable than the artistry itself. And sometimes it happens that a very cheap material worth five cents carries art worth thousands of dollars. In fact, it even happens that an antique work made from very cheap material is worth a million dollars. Now think of such a valuable antique work of art. When it is taken to a high antique market and its relation to a talented famous artist is disclosed, the item will be appraised for a very high price. That is, the value of the item will be determined by the greatness of the artist and the value of his art. However, if you take the very same artwork to scrap-dealers, it would be appraised for its raw material only and sold for a couple of cents.[2]

Now, the human being is such a precious antique work of art of Almighty God. Indeed, the human being is a subtle and fine miracle of Divine power because he has been created as a recipient of all the manifestations of God's various Most Beautiful Names (*al-asmā al-ḥusna*). Indeed, the human being has been adorned with *all* the inscriptions that reflect and mirror God's Most Beautiful Names. He has been created as a miniature sample of the entire universe (*mithāl musaghghar*).

When the light of belief enters a human being, all these meaningful inscriptions of the Most Beautiful Names upon him become visible. As a believer, he will 'read' these inscriptions consciously. Moreover, through the connection of belief, he will elicit others to

---

[2] An alternative example would be the material of a computer chip and its material. The value of the computer is high when its superior programming is considered, while its value will be very low if its chip is neglected and merely its material is considered.

'read' these inscriptions of the Beautiful Names of God. That is, he will convey meanings such as 'I am the art and creation of the *Glorious Artist. I display His mercy and generosity...*' Thus, the art of his Sustainer on him will become visible through belief as a result of being a mirror to the Eternally Self-Sufficient One on Whom Everything Depends (*al-ṣamad*). And his value is gauged in accordance to that amazing art he displays. In this regard, through such a remarkable connection to God, an insignificant human being acquires a value above all creatures, and becomes an honored addressee of God and a guest of the Sustainer that becomes worthy of Paradise.[3]

In contrast, if disbelief enters the human being such connection to God is cut off and subsequently, all the meaningful inscriptions and adornments of the Beautiful Names of God are left in the dark and become invisible. For, if you forget the Artist, then the intangible meanings pertaining to the Artist become incomprehensible; most of the meaningful elevated art and spiritual sublime inscriptions become hidden. What remains as perceived through the senses also dissipates because it is attributed to lowly seeming causes, to nature, and blind chance. While each inscription and adornment is like a shining diamond, with disbelief they are reduced to dull pieces of glass. The value of the human being is thus reduced to his physical being. As we mentioned earlier, such physical existence yields only a limited life as a most wretched, most vulnerable and most miserable living being, after which human being passes away and decays. See how disbelief destroys human nature and transforms it from a diamond into coal.

---

[3] 'Becoming worthy of paradise' can be best understood in the context of Nursi's view that hell and paradise are direct consequences of choices of belief or unbelief *here* and *now*. According to Nursi, belief is itself joyful and carries the 'seed' of eternal happiness. And, unbelief is painful and carries the 'seed' of hell. (See, for instance, *Sozler*, '28. Soz, 'Cennet Sözüne Küçük Bir Zeyl' [*Words*, '28th Word, 'A Small Addendum to the Word on Paradise,'] RNK 1:224. Such understanding is based on the Quran, which repeatedly notes that human beings shall 'taste' the results of their choices of belief or unbelief both in this world and in hereafter.

Second Point: Belief Illuminates the Universe

Belief is a light that illuminates the human being and reveals the beautiful messages that are inscribed on them from the Self-Sufficient One on whom everything depends (*al-ṣamad*). So too, it illuminates the universe. Belief saves the past and the future from darkness. This mystery is alluded to in the following Quranic verse, *God is the ally of those who believe, He brings them out of depths of darkness into light.* (Q. 2:257).[4] Through the use of a parable, I shall explain how belief indeed takes us from darkness into the light.

In a vision, I saw two high mountains, connected by an astonishing bridge. I was standing on that bridge, under which was a very deep river. The entire world around me was shrouded in darkness. I looked to my right, and saw within the depths of darkness an enormous graveyard, a mass grave. Then I looked to my left, and it seemed that huge storms and hurricanes were building up within the darkness. I looked below the bridge, and it looked like there was a huge abyss underneath. In the midst of all this scary darkness, all I had was a flashlight. When I turned it on and looked around, the situation became even worse: I saw terrible monsters, lions, and dragons all around the bridge. I exclaimed, 'I wish I did not have this torch and did not see all this terrifying stuff!' Wherever I directed my flashlight, I saw more horrors. I said to myself, 'This flashlight is trouble!'

I became so angry at the flashlight that I smashed it on the ground. As soon as it broke, it is as if I turned on a light switch for the entire world: all the darkness disappeared. Everything filled up with light, which revealed the truth of things around me. I realized that what seemed to be a bridge over an abyss was actually a well-built road on a valley. What I thought was a huge mass grave on my right side turned out to be a beautiful green garden where meaningful and joyful gatherings of worship and service are held under the leadership of enlightened people. On my left, what I thought were tumultuous and stormy abysses and heights, turned out to be splendid banquets and beautiful scenery, barely visible behind lovely and

---

[4] See also Quran 5:16, 14:1, 33:43; 57:9; 65:11.

impressive mountains. And, I realized that what seemed to be terrifying monsters on the bridge were actually domestic familiar animals such as cows, sheep, goats, and so on. I said, 'Thanks and praise is due to God for the light of belief,' and recited the Quranic passage *God is the ally of those who believe: He brings them out of the depths of darkness and into the light* (Q. 2:257) and woke up from my vision.

Now, the two mountains in the vision symbolize the start and the end of life, one being the entrance to this world and the other being the entrance to the intermediate world (*'ālam al-barzakh*).[5] The right side in the vision represents the past and the left side represents the future. And, what seemed to be monsters in the vision are the strange events and beings in this world. The flashlight symbolizes the arrogant human ego, which rejects the heavenly message brought by the prophets (*al-waḥy al-samāwī*) and pretends to know the truth on its own. The person who puts his trust in his ego and falls into the darkness of heedlessness and misguidance is represented by my first situation in the vision. The flashlight represents his inadequate information and misguided approach, which shows the past as a big graveyard, plunged in the darkness of non-existence. This flashlight also shows the future as tumultuous and scary, and as subject to the tortures of blind chance. Moreover, it depicts events and beings that are under the care of a Merciful and Wise One as harmful monsters. Consequently, this person experiences the situation described in the verse: *as for the disbelievers, their allies are false gods who take them from light to the depths of darkness.* (Q. 2:257)

When God's guidance comes, belief enters into the heart, the arrogance of the ego is broken and it heeds the book of God (*kitāb allāh*). This is what my second state in the vision represents. The entire universe lights up, being filled with the light of God. The universe declares the Quranic verse, *God is the light of the heavens and*

---

[5] The Intermediate World, or *'ālam al-barzakh,* the refers to the 'in-between' or the transition world between this life and the next. It is traditionally understood to be the realm of the grave, where people have an existence after this life and before being raised on Judgment Day.

the earth. (Q. 24:35) This light reveals that the past is not a huge, scary graveyard plunged into non-existence. Rather, as the heart now perceives it, the past is the dwelling place where purified spirits of all eras exist. Various communities, each gathered under the guidance of a prophet or a friend of God, having completed their life duties, glorify God and ascend onto high stations and pass onto the future. Similarly, when the person enlightened with the light of belief looks to the left, onto the future, he senses that beyond the major transformations of afterlife and the intermediate realm, there are wonderful feasts of the Compassionate One set up in palaces of joy. The person knows that everything, including events such as storms, earthquakes, and diseases, is subservient to God's will. He sees that many outwardly harsh events are inwardly full of subtle wisdom. He realizes that death is the beginning of an eternal life and the grave is the door to eternal happiness. You can interpret the remainder of the vision and how it applies to reality.

Third Point: Belief Empowers Human Being

Belief is both light and power. Indeed, a person who has attained to genuine belief can be saved from the pressures of events in life, in accordance with the level of his belief. Saying, 'I place my trust in God' (*tawakkaltu 'ala allāh*), a genuine believer can journey with perfect peace in the ship of life, sailing amidst the huge waves of events. He entrusts all his burdens to the Absolute Powerful One and journeys through this world with ease, then rests in the Intermediate World. Then, he flies to paradise to enjoy unending happiness. In contrast, if he does not place his trust in God, instead of flying, he takes up the burdens of the world and he is pulled down to the lowest of the low (*asfal al-sāfilīn*) [Q. 95:5].

Indeed, genuine belief requires *tawhid*, which necessitates surrender (*islām*), and surrender necessitates trust (*tawakkul*), and trust, in turn, yields happiness in this world and in the next. Now, please do not misunderstand the meaning of putting your trust in God. Trust in God does not mean giving up recourse to seeming causes. Rather, it is to utilize seeming causes with the understanding that these causes are merely 'veils' to Divine power. In other words, entrusting your affairs to God means that you have recourse to seeming causes as a way of requesting your needs from God, as a *prayer* through action (du'ā fi'li). Consequently, you seek the outcome from God alone and you acknowledge the results as being His gifts, and therefore you offer thanks to God alone.

Here is a parable that clarifies the difference between the one who puts his trust in God and the one who does not. Once upon a time, two men with heavy loads on their back purchased their tickets and boarded a big ship. One of them released all his burdens on the deck as soon as he got on the ship and sat on top of them to look after them. The other man, who was both foolish and arrogant, kept his loads on his back, and on his head, and refused to put them on the floor. People said to him, 'Just put your heavy burdens down, and be at ease.' He replied, 'No way! I will not put them down! They may get damaged. I am strong; I will carry my belongings myself.' People said again, 'Listen, this strong ship is carrying all of us together with our loads, including you and your luggage. The ship is much stronger than you are and can protect your load. If you keep your burdens on, you will get tired and weak, and perhaps you will even get dizzy and fall into the sea. Your back is weakening, and your head is tiring; you will not be able to continue carrying your burdens for long; you will collapse. And if the captain of the ship sees you, he will either think you are insane and disqualify you from being on the ship, or he will think you are viciously belittling the ship, and he will order punishment for you. And see how ridiculous you look in front of everyone. Any careful person can see the weakness within your pretension of strength and your helplessness within your arrogance. Your hypocrisy and wretchedness written all over your pretense. Everyone can see it. Look, everyone is laughing at you...' When he heard all this, the man came to his senses. He put down his load, and said 'Thank you so much! I am saved from all the trouble and from punishment and ridicule!'

O human being who does not put his trust in God! Come to your senses like the man in the story, and trust God. And, you will be saved from begging before the entire universe, from trembling with fear before all the challenges of life and you will be delivered from conceitedness and pretending to be in control. You will be saved from ridicule, and from the pressures of a constrained life in this world and from regrets in the afterlife.

Fourth Point: Belief Nurtures True Humanity

Belief makes you a true human being. Indeed, it makes you a noble sovereign. Therefore, a human being's real aspiration is belief and supplication (*du'ā*). In contrast, disbelief turns human beings into helpless animals.

There are many evidences supporting the truth that true humanity is attained through belief. A clear and decisive evidence lies in the difference between the way human beings and animals come into the world. When an animal comes into the world, it comes with perfected abilities for its life. It is as though it has developed its capacities in another world, before arriving here. Indeed, an animal quickly learns the necessities of its life within a couple of hours, days or months. In a very short period of time, it becomes appropriately oriented to its environment and starts functioning efficiently. A sparrow or bee acquires—it is inspired to acquire—[6] necessary life skills for its duties within couple weeks whereas it takes at least two decades for a human being to get to a similar level of command over their life.

This fact shows that the main task of an animal is not to develop through learning and acquiring knowledge, nor is it to seek help and pray through disclosing its neediness, weakness and vulnerability. Rather, the purpose of an animal is to work according to its abilities. It is to perform a particular function—as it is commanded and inspired by God—and thus offer worship through action (*'ubūdiyya fi'liyya*).

In contrast, when human beings come to the world, they are in need of learning everything and they are completely ignorant of the rules of life. They cannot learn all about life even after twenty years. Indeed, their need to learn continues their entire life. Also, a human being is born in such a weak and needy condition that even learning

---

[6] By adding this clarification, Nursi underscores that an animal gaining command over its life is not happening randomly or its own, rather it is made possible by Divine knowledge and power. Nursi is implicitly referring to the Quranic reference to a bee being inspired to make honey (Q. 16:68–69).

to walk takes a year or two. Only around the age of fifteen is a human being able to discern between harm and benefit, and only with the help of support from society are they able to manage in life, fulfilling their needs and avoiding dangers.

All these facts about human development show that human nature is wired for growth through learning and worshipfulness through supplication and asking for help (*al-'ubūdiyya bi'l du'ā*). In other words, human duty is to seek answers to questions such as 'Through whose compassion am I being taken care of so wisely? How am I being nourished so delicately? Whose blessings am I receiving?' Through recognizing the answers to these questions, the duty and calling of human beings is to turn to the One Who Fulfills All Needs (*qāḍi al-ḥājāt*) and supplicate Him through her vulnerability, weakness and need. Indeed, while the human being has innumerable needs, she cannot take care of even one of them on their own. Hence, her natural calling is to consciously ask for help and supplicate in regards to their various needs. In other words, the human beings are meant to rise up to the heights of worship with the wings of weakness (*'ajz*) and poverty, (*faqr,*) i.e. through recognizing and embracing their helplessness and complete dependence on their Creator.

Therefore, it is understood that the human being has been sent to this world to grow and develop through knowledge and supplication (*du'ā*). All human nature and capacities depend on knowledge. And at the heart of all genuine disciplines and knowledge lies knowing God, which is the basis, resource, light and spirit of all genuine knowledge. And at the heart of knowing God is the belief in God.

Besides, given that human beings are extremely weak while being exposed to endless troubles and challenges, and given that they are extremely poor despite their endless needs and yearnings, it is only befitting that their innate calling and goal is belief (*īmān*) accompanied by supplication (*du'ā*). Supplication is the essence of worship (*'ubūdiyya*). Think of a baby who cries for something she cannot reach. She is in effect calling for help (*du'ā*) using the 'tongue' of her weakness, either through action or verbally, and thereby she attains what she asks for.⁷

Similarly, among all living creatures, human beings are like delicate and pampered children. A human being should either cry out for help through his weakness and inability (*'ajz*) or pray through his poverty and neediness (*faqr*) at the court of the Most Merciful and Compassionate. So that he will attain their wish or express their gratitude for things being subjugated to their needs. In contrast, if the human being claims, 'I have subjugated all these strange things in the universe, which are impossible to control and are thousand times more powerful than myself, to my needs, and I control things with my own thinking and planning,'⁸ he is being like a silly and naughty child who cannot even protect himself from a tiny fly but pretends that he actually controls his parents and others that assist him. Such an attitude of ungratefulness is completely against human nature and thus leads the person to experience much suffering, which leads to hell.

---

⁷ In other words, we witness that the baby is unable to meet her need and her need is met after she cries. This shows the baby's cry is like a request or prayer. The child is 'speaking' through her weakness, her inability to meet her own need. Through her crying, she is in effect 'asking' or 'praying' for her need to be fulfilled.

⁸ Nursi is probably referring to technology here. While many people tend to be proud of technology as a human achievement, it is actually a gift given to human beings due to their neediness.

9
CALLING UNTO ONE GOD: PRAYER

This selection is the 'fifth point' of the '23ʳᵈ Word,' whose first 'four points' have been excerpted in Chapter 8. Having explained how belief in God (*īmān*) honors and elevates human being in the preceding 'points,' Nursi now turns to the culmination of belief in God: supplication and prayer. Taking cue from a number of Quranic passages, Nursi explains the significance of prayer and worship for human life. In translating this selection, we rendered *du'ā* as 'prayer,' rather than 'supplication' so as to highlight that the text is relevant broadly, applying not only to supplicatory prayer but prayer in general.

It may be recalled that Nursi prefaced '23ʳᵈ Word' with Q. 95:4–6 according to which only *those who believe and do good deeds* avoid descending to the *lowest of the low* and retain the excellent pattern of humanity, *aḥsan al-taqwīm*. Having explored human excellence in four points—as being conscious of one's neediness, seeing the embroideries of the Most Beautiful Names of God in oneself and the world, and turning to the One in surrender and trust—Nursi now reflects on the significance of supplication or prayer as the culmination of human virtue. The section suggests that 'prayerfulness' or 'worshipfulness' is an essential feature of the 'good deeds' mentioned in the Quran (*al-'amal al-ṣāliḥāt*). Indeed, even an act of kindness may be a 'good' deed or not, depending on whether it is done in the name of one God or for the sake of selfish interests of the ego. For instance, giving in charity is 'good deed' from Quranic perspective only if it is given with awareness of *tawhid*, that wealth and compassion is from God. It is not a righteous deed if it is given with the illusion of *shirk*, with arrogance and boasting (Q. 2:261–267).

***

CALLING UNTO ONE GOD[1]

Belief (*īmān*) certainly requires supplication and prayer (*du'ā*). And, human nature (*fiṭra*) strongly yearns for prayer. Also, God Almighty declares in the Quran, *Say [unto those who believe]: 'No weight or value would my Sustainer attach to you were it not for your prayer!'* (Q. 25:77) God also commands us, *Call unto Me, I shall respond to you!*(Q. 40:60)

Now, you may ask: 'We frequently offer prayers, but they are not accepted. While the verse is general, it states that every prayer is answered. How is that so?'

The reply is that answering and accepting are two different things. Each prayer *is answered*, but for it to be *accepted* and for you to get exactly what you asked for depends on God's wisdom. For instance, think of a child calling unto his doctor: 'Doctor! Doctor!' The doctor responds by saying, 'Sure, here am I. What do you need?' The child, who was prescribed a sweet and colorful pill previously, asks to get it again: 'Please give me that medicine!' The doctor will either give him exactly what he asks for or something better and more beneficial for him. Or knowing that it is harmful for his illness, she may give him nothing. Therefore, even when she decides to prescribe no medicine, she *is* answering him.

Similarly, since Almighty God is the Absolute Wise, (*al-ḥakīm al-muṭlaq*), All-Present and All-Seeing, He responds to the prayers of His worshipers. Through His presence and response, He transforms their desolation of loneliness and solitude into familiarity. Let's keep in mind that as He responds to all prayers, He does so not in accordance with our capricious demands and wishful thinking, but in ac-

---

[1] Nursi, *Sözler*, '23. Söz, Birinci Makam, Beşinci Nokta' (*Words*, '23rd Word, First Station, Fifth Point'), RNK 1:134–135. Title added.

cordance with His Divine wisdom. He gives either what is asked for, or what is better than it, or He gives nothing at all.

Besides, prayer is worship. The consequences of worship pertain to eternity. While our earthly needs and wishes mark the times for such prayer and worship, they cannot be the real thrust and aim of our worship.

For instance, supplication and *ṣalāt* (ritual prayer) for rain is an act of worship. Just as the setting of the sun marks the time for sunset ritual prayer (*ṣalāt al-maghrib*), the lack of rain marks the time for rain ritual prayer (*ṣalāt al-istisqā'*). The ritual prayer for rain is *not* for bringing the rain per se. Rather it is an act of worshipping God at a time of drought, admitting our neediness, and articulating our dependence on God. If your intention in the ritual prayer of rain is solely focused on getting rain, then your ritual prayer is not sincere and genuine worship.[2] Therefore, it is not worthy of acceptance.

Similarly, the eclipses of the sun and the moon mark the time for two special prayers, known as 'ritual prayers at eclipse' (*ṣalāt al-kusuf* and *ṣalāt al-khusuf*). During these eclipses the night and day, which are two bright signs of God, become temporarily veiled. This veiling reveals the grandeur and majesty of God in a new way, and the ritual prayers offered at this time are a way of recognizing God's grandeur and majesty. The eclipse ritual prayers are not so that the eclipse is lifted—after all, the duration of eclipse is already set and computed by astronomers in advance.

Likewise, drought is the time for the rain prayer. Similarly, when you encounter challenges and you are afflicted with various trials, it means it is time for certain prayers. During these trying times, you realize your weakness and seek refuge in the Absolute Powerful One. If the troubles do not cease despite a lot of prayers, do not say: 'my prayers were not accepted.' Rather, understand that the time for the prayer is not over yet. If God lifts the affliction with

---

[2] It is insincere and inauthentic in that with such attitude, the believer is simply seeking to get his 'shopping list' done, rather than intending to connect with God.

His benevolence and generosity, then light upon light, and the time of the prayer is done.

In sum, prayer is a mystery (*sirr*) of worship. And, worship must be purely for the sake of God. Admitting and articulating our weakness, we should seek refuge in God with prayer. We should not meddle with His nurturing care. We should trust His Providence and wisdom, and not deny His compassion.

In fact, as the Quranic verses attest, the reality of existence is that all beings are in a state of worship, each offering a special glorification, a particular act of worship, and bowing down before their Creator.[3] Thus, what rises up from the entire universe to the Divine court is prayer. Such prayers take various forms:

- The prayers that all plants and animals offer through their *innate potential* (*lisān al-isti'dād*):

Through its potentials, each plant and animal asks to take an appropriate form and to reflect His beautiful names. In other words, through their very being and existence creatures are asking God (*fayyāḍ mutlāq*) to make them flourish and thus to become like mirrors to His beautiful names. [That is, their potentials are forms of prayers directed to the One who can actualize them. For, obviously, the various potentials of plants and animals are realized through Divine power and wisdom, not through their own making.][4]

- The prayers that all living beings offer through the 'tongue' of *innate need* (*lisān al-ḥāja al-fiṭriyya*):

It is their prayer for all their essential needs that are beyond their reach. Through the 'tongue' of their innate needs, they request the continuation of their lives from the Absolutely Generous One.

- Another form of prayer is performed through the tongue of *distress* (*lisān al-iḍṭirar*).

---

[3] For instance, *are you not aware that it is God whose limitless glory all that is in the heavens and on earth extol, even the birds as they spread out their wings? Each knows indeed how to pray unto Him and to glorify Him; and God has full knowledge of all that they do.* (Q. 24:4)

[4] For Nursi's explanation of how plants and animals are not acting with their own power, see the first chapter on *bismillah*.

It is when a soul is in a situation of intense distress and exigency seeks refuge in their unknown Guardian, that is, when they turn to their Merciful Sustainer. These three types of prayers—of innate potential, innate need and distress—are always accepted, unless there is a contrary situation.

The fourth type of prayer, the one that is most well-known, is our prayer and it consists of two types. One is offered through our actions and our states of being, and the other through our hearts and tongues.

For instance, having recourse to seeming causes is a prayer through action (*du'ā fi'lī*). The gathering of seeming causes is not for creating the result. Rather, it is to request the result from the Almighty Creator through assuming an acceptable position and praying through the 'tongue' of our situation (*lisān al-ḥāl*). When a farmer ploughs a field, it is an act of prayer: the act of ploughing is an act of knocking on the door of divine mercy. This type of prayer through action is most often accepted because it is directed at the name and title of the Absolutely Generous One.

The second type of prayer is through the heart and tongue. It is to ask for certain wishes that we are unable to obtain. The most important aspect, the most beautiful purpose and the sweetest result of this prayer are the following: the person who is praying realizes that there is someone who hears his deepest wishes in his heart, who is able to do anything, who is able to fulfill all his wishes. He feels that there is someone who has compassion for his weakness and his poverty.

Now, o weak and poor human being! Never give up prayer; it is the key to the treasure of mercy and means to endless power. Hold on to it, rise up to the peaks of humanity, to the highest of the high (*'ala 'illiyin al-insaniyya*)! Like a king, include the prayers of the entire universe in your prayer. As a comprehensive worshiper (*'abd*) and a representative of the universe say: 'You alone *we* worship,' (Quran, 1:5) and become a paragon of the universe.

10

SIGNS OF GOD IN REGULARITY AND DIVERSITY

The seven heavens and the earth and everyone in them glorify Him. There is not a single thing that does not celebrate His praise, though you do not understand their praise: He is most forbearing, most forgiving.

—Quran, 17:44

The selection below starts with a verse traditionally known as the verse of the 'five unknowns,' *al-mughayyabāt al-khamsa* (Q. 31:34) The verse is commonly interpreted to mean that only God knows the five things mentioned in it: when doomsday will occur, when it will rain, what is in a woman's womb, what will happen to one tomorrow, and where one will die.

In the selection, Nursi responds to a question, which states that the verse contradicts technological developments that enable us to forecast the weather and to scan an embryo in the womb. The text proceeds to explains how there is no tension between the message of the verse and contemporary technology. Despite technological advances, our ability to anticipate the things mentioned in the verse, such as the rain, remains different from our prediction of other regular events, such as the sunrise. Unlike the sunrise, the rain does not have a set pattern for its occurrence.

It is noteworthy that the treatise reconciles the verse with contemporary advancement in technology, but it does not leave it at that. It goes further, offering another fine example of how to read the 'book of the universe' in the light of the Quran and vice versa.

Nursi shows that through the guidance of this Quranic sign/verse (*aya*), we can recognize the signs (*ayāt*) of God in creation. By attracting attention to these five things, and concluding with a reference to the Beautiful Names of God, the Quran is suggesting that the fact that certain things in creation unfold without a regular pattern is a sign to a deeper reality, as explained below.

As will be seen in the excerpt below, Nursi first notes how the verse attracts our attention to the fact that certain things in the universe happen without following a regular pattern. Indeed, there are mainly two types of occurrences in the universe: (1) the ones that come into existence according to a regular pattern, (2) the ones that come into existence without a regular pattern. He explains how both types of events serve as *signs* (*ayāt*) pointing to their Creator in different ways. *Regular* events in the universe point to God's power and wisdom and show that things do *not* happen randomly by chance.[1] At the same time, the *irregularity* and diversity in the world point to divine choice and free will, and purpose. (It may be noted that even individually irregular events often follow regular probabilistic patterns, as in the quantum level, which again points to the Creator's will and wisdom.)

As Nursi elaborates elsewhere,

> The All-Powerful & All-Knowing One (*al-qadīr al-'alīm*), the All-Wise Maker (*al-ṣāni' al-ḥakīm*), shows His power and His wisdom and that chance can in no way interfere in His works through the order and regularity with which he governs the

---

[1] Nursi interprets the *regularity* of events and the seeming causes connected to them as *mirrors* to Divine activity. That is, along with seeming causes involved, regularity of the connection between seeming causes and their results, reveal that things are not happening randomly. They indicate to those who are willing to reflect, the existence of an unseen maker who has control over all things. As for others who are not open to acknowledging the Creator, the seeming causes and regularities in nature become like a *veil* concealing Divine power and will. Nursi explains the wisdom of the 'veil of seeming causes' in the creation in the 22nd Word, translated in the last chapter of this volume.

world. Such order and regularity manifests in the form of laws
[in nature.] At the same time, through exceptions to the laws,
the breaks in established patterns,[2] changes in appearances, differences in individual characteristics, and changes in the emergence [of blessings], He shows His volition, will, choice, and
that He is an agent with choice, and He is under no restrictions
whatsoever.[3]

Using the example of a baby in the womb, Nursi further explains
how regularity and uniformity complement the irregularity and
uniqueness of phenomena in the world. Together, they point to the
one God's wisdom and will. On the one hand, there is a uniform
aspect, a regular pattern to the growth of a fetus, on the basis of
which we reliably predict that a human fetus will share basic features
with other fellow human beings. On the other hand, there is a non-
uniform aspect to each fetus, such as her specific personality and
unique potentials. These special aspects of the fetus cannot be
known in advance. In fact, Nursi suggests that it is not even possible
to anticipate the facial features of the child since each person's features are unique. He considers the human face as a fascinating 'signature' of the Divine Uniqueness. Indeed, while the essential features
of the human faces are similar, each face carries a distinguishing mark
unique to each person, revealing both the wisdom and the free
choice of its Maker. In sum, the selection explains how irregular
events in the universe disclose Divine choice and will. Hence, as alluded to in the Quranic passage, the timings of rainfall, the particular
life journey of a human being, the hidden potential of a baby in the
womb, or the life span of each individual—all highlight the will and
choice of their Maker, and show us that His mercy and power are not
bound by any restriction.

In this text, Nursi also highlights that the uniqueness of events
and individual cases is among the signs to *aḥadiyya*. While the terms
aḥadiyya (unicity) and *waḥidiyya* (oneness) both come from the
same root *w-ḥ-d*, there is a nuance between the two, as has been not-

---

[2] (Ar. *kharq al-'ādah*; Tk. *hark-ı adet*, literally, 'breaking of custom.')
[3] Nursi, *Words*, 217 (modifed translation); Nursi, *Sözler*, RNK 1:76.

ed by a number of Muslim theologians and spiritual masters. Nursi employs *aḥadiyya* to denote that a *single thing* testifies the existence of the Creator of all things and that most of the Divine names are manifested in each thing. He uses *wāḥidiyya* to express the Creator of *all* is one. Nursi also notes that the former is the oneness of God reflected on the individual or microcosm and the latter is the stamp of unity on the universe or macrocosm.[4]

In this text, Nursi also notes how understanding the signs in the universe have direct implications for our lives. Our inability to find out a precise pattern for certain events makes us notice the Divine will and choice manifested in them. As we notice divine will and choice behind them, we tend to become more mindful and more appreciative of them. Eventually, we become aware that not only relatively unpredictable phenomena, such as existence, life and rain, but *all* things are under the control of the divine will-- including things that we often take for granted because of their regularity. In other words, by creating exceptions to order and non-regular phenomena, the Creator 'draws back the 'curtain' of monotonous order and teaches us that *everything* at *every* moment, in *each* task and in

---

[4] 'For the macrocosm is like the microcosm: both are fashioned by His power, inscribed by His pen; He creates the macrocosm as a place of prostration, while He gives existence to the microcosm so that it is prostrating; He brings the former into being as a property, while He gives existence to the latter as owned and needy for the property; His art in the former displays it as a book, while His coloring in the latter shines through speech; His power in the former reveals His majesty, while His mercy in the latter arrays His bounty; His majesty in the former testifies that He is One (*al-wāḥid*), while His bounty in the latter proclaims that He is Single, Undivided (*al-aḥad*); His stamp on the former is on all things, universal and particular, whether at rest or in motion, while His seal on the latter is on the body and on the limbs, and on their cells and particles.' Nursi, '*Letters,* 20th Letter, Second Station,' 275 (also in Nursi, *Flashes,* '29th Flash, Third Chapter, First Degree'). For a discussion of these terms by Nursi see Turner, *The Qur'an Revealed,* 30–31. For a helpful explanation of the difference between oneness (*wāḥidiyya*) and unicity (*aḥadiyya*) with examples, also see Turner, *Islam: The Basics,* 111–112.

every single thing, is in need of Him and is totally dependent on His sustaining (*rubūbiyya*).'[5] According to Nursi, our Sustainer wakes us up 'from heedlessness and forgetfulness (*ghafla*) and redirects our attention from seeming causes (*asbāb*) to the Causer of All Causes (*musabbib al-asbāb*.)'[6] This selection, then, offers a Quranic way of perceiving the world in its regularity and diversity, and of responding to this reality in awareness of, and with gratitude to, the One.

***

ON THE FIVE UNKNOWNS[7]

Truly, with God alone rests the knowledge of the Hour, and it is He who sends down the rain; and He knows what is in the wombs. No soul knows what it will earn tomorrow, and no soul knows in what land it will die. Truly, it is God who is all-knowing, all-aware. (Quran 31:34)

Question:[8] Some atheists criticized the above verse, by questioning its references to the timing of rain and the status of the baby in the mother's womb. They said, 'We now have tools to forecast rain successfully, therefore people also know when it will rain. In addition, using X-ray technology we are now able to predict the gender of a baby before it is born. Hence, it is possible to know these things which this verse describes as known to God only.'

In response to this, let us note the fact that the timing of rain does not follow a regular pattern; it is directly connected to Divine will in a special way. It is tied to a special decree from Divine Mercy.

---

[5] Emphasis added. Nursi, *Sözler*, '16. Söz, Küçük bir Zeyl' [*Words*, 16th Word, 'A Small Addendum'], RNK 1:76.

[6] Ibid.

[7] *Lem'alar*, '16. Le'ma, Mugayyebatı Hamseye Dair,' [*Flashes*, '16th Flash, On the Five Unknowns'], RNK 1: 640–641.

[8] This text is part of a letter which Nursi wrote in response to a question from two of his disciples. We skipped the greetings in the beginning of the letter.

Now, what is the wisdom behind such special dispensation for certain things? We shall explain some of that wisdom as follows.

There are four qualities in the universe that are transparent and reflect Divine power and special Divine will, with no veils or intermediaries. These are: existence, life, light (*nūr*) and mercy (*raḥma*). In other created beings, 'seeming causes' are present, they are like veils to the acts of Divine power. Similarly, to some extent, regular patterns and laws in nature veil Divine will and choice. In contrast, there are no such veils placed on existence, life, light and mercy. In these four cases, the wisdom of placing veils does not apply, as will be explained later.

Now, in regards to the timing of rain, let us remember that the most important truth in existence is mercy and life. And life springs from rain, which is like an axis around which Divine mercy revolves. Indeed, rain, that is water, is mercy. Therefore, there are no intermediaries that veil the mercy reflected within rain. Regularity and set patterns do not conceal the 'special' Divine will (*al-mashia al-ilahiyya al-khāssa*) pertaining to rain. The absence of such veils encourages *everyone* to appreciate rain[9] and *all* things[10] and ask and supplicate for them.

Now, contrast the timing of rain with the timing of sunrise. There are so many benefits associated with the rising of the sun, as you know. Yet, because the timing of sunrise has a regular and predictable pattern, people commonly do not pray for the sun to rise, and they do not offer thanks when it does rise. Besides, since we can predict the sunrise on the basis of scientific calculations, we do not regard the timing of sunrise as a matter pertaining to the unseen (*ghayb*). In contrast, since the particularities of rain do not display a set pattern, people often ask and pray for rain. And, since we are unable to discover a regular pattern for rain times, people often perceive

---

[9] If the timing of rain were tied to a regular pattern, then people would take that pattern for granted, and stop appreciating rain and praying for it.

[10] The reference to 'all things,' instead of just rain, is noteworthy here. See the introductory note for further explanation of how 'irregularity' of certain phenomena call to mind the divine will and choice in regular events as well.

rain as a special blessing sent directly from the Treasure of Divine Mercy. That is why the above verse includes the time of rain among the 'five unknowns' (*mughayyabat al-khamsa*).

As for the forecast of rain in observatories, it is not because we discovered a regular pattern for the timing of rain. Therefore, the verse's reference to it as a special act of Divine mercy remains valid. Rather, our forecast is based on the symptoms of approaching rain, which has emerged out of the World of Unseen (*ghayb*) and is about to enter the World of the Seen (*ʿālam al-shahāda*).[11] It is only then that those symptoms become detectable by our weather forecasting tools. It is like sensing, or having a premonition of, a very secret plan when it is actualized or when it is about to be so...Such knowing is not knowing the Unseen or the not-yet-existent. Rather it is to know what has been already brought or what is being brought into existence. Because of my rheumatoid arthritis, even I can foretell the rain sometimes a day before it comes because I can feel the humidity in the air increasing as it approaches.

In other words, rain has preliminaries and symptoms that precede its coming, such as humidity. Scientists predict rain on the basis of such preliminaries and indications that follow a regular pattern. However, only the One who knows the unseen knows the timing of rain whose preliminaries have not yet showed up in our sphere of experience because it has not yet been sent out of the unseen world with 'special' Divine will and mercy.

In regards to the baby in the womb, knowing the gender of a baby in the womb does not contradict the Quranic verse's statement that *God knows what is in the womb*. Indeed, the verse does not just refer to the gender of the baby. Rather, it also refers to knowing her unique capacities that will eventually flourish in her particular appointed course of life. These are only known by the One who knows

---

[11] The term *ghayb* is used in the Quran to denote that which is beyond human perception and known to God only, as in Q. 6:59 *For, with Him are the keys to 'the things that are beyond the reach of a created being's perception'* (ghayb): *none knows them but He.*

the future that pertains to the Unseen (*ghayb*)...Even the baby's unique facial features, and how they change over time, which is an awesome signature of the Unique One on whom everything depends (*al-Ṣamad*), cannot be anticipated beforehand...

In the beginning, we had stated that existence, life, and mercy are the most important truths in the universe and that they hold a most significant position. That is why the comprehensive truth of life is directly linked to the special will, special mercy and special volition of God in all its details and finesse. The wisdom behind such a transparent manifestation of Divine will and mercy in the case of life is as follows.

With all its faculties, life is a means for gratitude, worship, and praise. Therefore, the phenomenon of life has not been veiled, unlike most other phenomena. That is, life has not been veiled with regularity and uniformity, which veil special divine will, and seeming causes, which veil special divine mercy. Let us further explain by reflecting on a fetus how regularity and non-regularity are both signs of God.

A baby in the womb is a sign to God in two ways.

First: The fetus reflects the oneness (*waḥdāniyya*), unicity (*aḥadiyya*) and power (*ṣamadāniyya*) of her Creator. Her basic structure, face, organs and faculties conform with the *regularity* seen in the human species. Through this similarity and correspondence with other human beings, the fetus in the womb conveys the following meaning: 'Whoever fashions my face and organs is the same one who fashions all other human beings, and He is the maker of all living beings.' Such a testimony of the fetus to her Maker is *not* a matter of the unseen. For she conforms to a regular pattern and uniformity, and is in agreement with her species. We can know this aspect of the baby in advance, even if the fetus is currently hidden from our sight in the womb.

Second: The fetus testifies to the *choice, will, and 'special' mercy* of her Maker through her *special* capacity and her *unique* facial features. That is, the particularity and unique characteristics of the fetus in the womb show the free choice of her Maker, and that He is under no restriction whatsoever. However, such a testimony of the fetus comes from the unseen (*ghayb*). That is, other than the Eternal Knower, no one can anticipate or foresee this aspect of the baby before it becomes manifest in the world. Visualizing the fetus in the womb via scanning techniques does not reveal this unknown aspect.

In sum, the physical and nonphysical features of the fetus testify to both divine oneness (*waḥdāniyya*) and divine choice and will (*ikhtiyar wa irada ilahiyya*).

I could write this much for now. God willing, I hope to be able to write more on the 'five unknowns' later.

The Eternal One, He is the Eternal One.

Said Nursi

II
JOYFUL AND RADIANT CONSEQUENCES OF
TA WHID

This selection offers a deeper and denser reflection on how the perspective of *tawhid* reveals Divine beauty and splendor reflected in the universe and in human nature. It shows how *tawhid* is deeply enjoyable as it reveals the beauty and sweetness of Divine sustaining (*rububiyya*). Nursi shares a personal note at the end of each 'fruit' of *tawhid*, in order to portray how challenges of life may bring one to the threshold of tasting these fruits of *tawhid*. And, once a person tastes these delicious fruits of *tawhid*, they inevitably fall in love with the Divine Essence (*al-dhat*) that creates and sustains human beings and the universe. It is particularly meaningful that Nursi composed this treatise while he was detained in prison under very difficult circumstances.

This text is yet another example of living with the Quran. We see once more that the central Quranic theme of *tawhid* is achieved by looking at the world as well as by tuning into the human soul. In such a spiritual journey, an intense love and yearning for the One who fashions and sustains the universe emerges. This treatise is an illustration of how the Quran connects belief with profound love, awe, and peace *whereas those who have believed love God more than all else* (Q. 2:165), *Believers are only they whose hearts tremble with awe whenever God is mentioned* (Q. 8:2; see also 22:35); and *Truly, they who are close to God - no fear need they have, and neither shall they grieve* (Q. 10:62).

Nursi encourages the reader to study the treatise with special care and attention, given its precious potential to reflect the radiance of *tawhid*. In order to facilitate the reading, we have occasionally added brief explanations to the text. Since we thought such insertions go beyond paraphrasing, we placed such explanatory additions in square brackets.

***

JOYOUS AND BEAUTIFUL CONSEQUENCES OF TAWHID[1]

Note: This chapter was composed sixteen years ago [in 1936] when I was left alone in Eskisehir Prison after my friends had been released. It was written in a rush, in very difficult, uncomfortable and stressful circumstances. Despite its disorganized style and my shortcomings in composing it, today as I was editing it, I found it extremely important, powerful and precious regarding belief (*īmān*) and the oneness of God (*tawhid*).

> *Know, then, that there is no god except God.*

> —Quran 47:19

Inspired by this awesome Quranic verse and by a famous prophetic oath, I perceived three exquisite, lovely and delicate fruits of oneness of God (*tawhid*) and their three requisites and three proofs.

When the Messenger of God, peace be upon him, used to make a solemn statement, he repeatedly and most frequently used the phrase: 'By Him in whose hand is Muhammad's soul' (*walladhī nafsu muhammadin bi yadihi*). This phrase indicates that even the broadest circle of existence, the furthest branch and fruit of the 'tree' of the universe exists by the power and will of the Single and Unique One (*dhat wāḥid aḥad*). Indeed, if Muhammad—peace and blessings be upon him—the most exceptional and chosen being in creation, does not own his self, and is not free in what he does, if he is fully dependent on Someone else's will, then nothing and no one escapes the power and will of the One. Nothing, no action, no situa-

---

[1] Nursi, *Şualar*, 'İkinci Şuanın Birinci Makamı,' [*Rays, 'First Station of Second Ray'*] RNK I: 848–854. We added the title.

tion, whether particular or universal can be outside that comprehensive will and power.

This very meaningful oath of the Prophet, peace be upon him, is an expression of the glorious and comprehensive oneness of sustainership (*tawhid al-rububiyya*). Since elsewhere in the *Risale-i Nur* hundreds of clear evidences for this oneness (*tawhid*) have been elucidated, for now we shall only offer some indications to this significant truth of belief...[2]

In the first station, I shall very briefly present three universal (*kulli*) fruits out of the many very subtle, lovely, precious, and luminous 'fruits' of the truth of the oneness of God, *tawhid*. I shall also indicate what moved my heart to these three universal fruits of the oneness of God...

First Fruit of the First Station: *Tawhid* Reveals Divine Beauty and Perfection

Divine beauty and the perfection of sustainership (*rububiyya*) are revealed within affirming the oneness of God (*tawhid*), through which Divine oneness (*wahda*) is seen. If there is no oneness (*wahda*), then that eternal treasure becomes hidden.

Indeed, limitless Divine beauty and perfection, endless magnificence and splendor of the Sustainer, the countless splendid gifts of the Merciful, and the infinite perfection of the beauty of the Eternally Self-Sufficient upon whom everything depends (*al-ṣamad*) become visible only in the mirror of oneness (*wahda*) and the manifestations of the Most Beautiful Names. This is because oneness is like a focal point that combines the various reflections of the Most Beautiful Names (*al-asmā al ḥusna*) that shine on the 'faces' of particulars at the edge of the tree of creation.

For instance, let us consider the particular event of breast milk and how it is created. A helpless and unaware infant receives what

---

[2] We skipped a paragraph here and below, in which Nursi explains that the treatise contains three levels ('stations'). In this selection, we have only translated the first one. For translation of the entire chapter, see Vahide's translation: *Rays*, 'Second Ray,' 13–50.

she needs in the form of pure and wholesome milk. What is more, this milk is sent from an unexpected place [see Q. 65:3],[3] from amidst blood and excrement [see Q. 16:66].[4] When we look at this particular event from the perspective of Divine oneness (*tawhid*), we immediately realize that it is connected to a comprehensive and universal reality: the utterly wonderful and compassionate feeding of *all* infants through their mothers shows the eternal beauty of the compassion of the Compassionate One (*rahmān*) in all its splendor. However, if we were to look at the same particular event of an infant being breastfed without taking the reality of *tawhid* into consideration, that beauty would be concealed; and, that particular event of feeding an infant would be explained away by invoking unconscious causes, nature and blind chance.[5] The event would thus completely lose its value and even its essence would be distorted.

Also, for instance, when considered from the perspective of *tawhid*, being healed from a terrible illness appears to be tied to a universal reality of bestowing healing on all the sick all over the world, with remedies and medicines from the huge 'pharmacy' of the world. Thus, the beautiful compassion of the Absolutely Merciful One (*al-rahīm al-mutlaq*) and the beauty of Divine mercy (*rahimiya*) will become visible with its universality and splendor. However, if it is not considered from the perspective of *tawhid*, it will not be possible to see how a particular instance of recovering from serious illness occurs knowingly, intentionally, and with wisdom. Instead, it

---

[3] This phrase calls to mind the Quranic phrase saying that God shall *provide from an unexpected source* (Quran, 65:3).

[4] In other words, the milk is produced in the body in such a way that nutrients are distilled from the blood and also purified from excrements that are discarded. The text is again indirectly referring to a Quranic verse: *And, surely, in the cattle [too] there is a lesson for you: We give you to drink of that which is within their bellies, between that which is to be eliminated and blood: milk pure and pleasant to those who drink it.* (Q. 16:66)

[5] In other words, since these unconscious causes—such as hormones, breast tissue and brain—are incapable of having compassion and purpose, we will overlook the incredible universal mercy and purposefulness manifested in each case.

is explained away with lifeless medicines and blind and unconscious nature. Thus, its reality will be distorted and it will lose its wisdom and value.

In connection with this example, let us also note a well-known blessing (*salawāt*) on the Prophet. This is an invocation commonly recited after the daily prayers, especially by followers of the Shafiʿī School:[6]

> O God, bestow blessings on our master Muhammad and on his family, *to the number of all illnesses and all cures,* and bless him and all of them and grant them endless peace.

This is a very important invocation. Human beings have been created for the purpose of turning to their Creator at all times, through asking for help, praising and thanking. They have been endowed with a comprehensive nature and needs that connect them to so many things and thereby with opportunities to ask for help, to thank and to praise. Sickness is a most powerful motivation that prompts people to turn to God and seek help from Him. Similarly, getting well and recovering health is among the most exquisite blessings in life that inspire gratitude and praise. That is why this blessing on the Prophet, peace be upon him, is so meaningful and so eminent. Sometimes when reciting the part 'to the number of all illnesses and all cures,' I perceive the entire world like an efficient hospital. I feel the clear existence and comprehensive compassion of a True Healer, who heals all physical and spiritual sicknesses and provides for all needs.

[In order to further understand how the *tawhid* perspective reveals the eternal beauty of the Creator manifesting in the world], let's reflect on the following example. Consider someone who has experienced the terrifying pain of misguidance and then has been

---

[6] Shafiʿī School, founded by Imam al-Shafii' (d. 204 AH/ 820 CE) is one of the main schools of Islamic law and ethics. The main schools of Islamic practice that remained in use share much in common. Muslim scholars tend to consider differences between them as legitimate in that each school represents a sincere attempt to interpret the Quran and the Prophetic legacy according to carefully derived principles.

granted belief in God and guidance. From the perspective of *tawhid*, that particular, transient, and powerless person becomes an addressee of the True Object of Worship, the Creator and Sovereign of the whole universe. Through belief, he is gifted eternal happiness and a wonderful and extensive eternal property and an everlasting world along with all other believers, each according to their level. This generous favor and bestowal reveals the splendor of the eternal beauty of a generous and munificent one. One flash of that everlasting beauty draws all believers close to Him, and makes a special class among them in love with Him.

In contrast, if it is not considered from the perspective of *tawhid*, then the beauty of that particular granting of belief will dissipate. That particular event of becoming a believer would be explained away, by being attributed either to the person herself—as in the wishful and self-centered approach of the Mu'tazilites[7]—or to some seeming causes. Consequently, that diamond of Divine mercy, which is worth no less than Paradise, would lose the shine of the sacred beauty reflected on it; it would be reduced to a mere piece of glass.

As illustrated in the three examples above, from the *tawhid* perspective it is possible to see, understand and realize how innumerable

---

[7] Here Nursi is referring to the Mutazilite view on the creation of human actions. According to this view, human beings are the creators of their voluntary acts and their consequences. The Ash'arite and Maturidi schools of thought reject such view as problematic. Instead, they argue that a person freely *chooses* between possible options and God *creates* the act she chose and its consequences. To apply to the example above: while it is the human being who chooses to believe, it is God who creates belief as result of his choice, with all its beautiful consequences of enlightenment and eternal happiness. Nursi agrees with this mainstream view that became adopted by the majority, and disagrees with Mutazilite view that would suggest that human being who chooses belief is also the creator of belief and its consequences. For a discussion of human freewill and Divine will and power in the context of classical Islamic theology and Nursi's approach, see Yazicioglu, 'A Graceful Reconciliation: Said Nursi on Free Will and Destiny,' 129–145.

kinds and varieties of the Sustainer's perfection and of His Divine beauty are reflected in particular situations of particular beings within the realm of 'multiplicity.'[8] Through *tawhid*, Divine beauty and perfection become visible to the heart and perceptible to the spirit. That is why all those close to God (*awliya allah*) and the purified ones (*asfiya*), find enjoyment and delightful spiritual nourishment in remembering and repeating the affirmation of *tawhid*, *la ilaha illallah* ('there is no god except God').

Moreover, the grandeur, majesty and absolute sovereignty of the sustainership of the Self-Sufficient One on whom everything depends, (*al-rububiyya al-samadaniya*) is realized through this statement of *tawhid*. That is why the Noble Messenger, peace be upon him, has declared: 'The most virtuous and precious statement that I and all the prophets before me have said is: there is no god except God (*la ilaha illallah*).'

Indeed, a small gift, blessing or sustenance, such as a fruit, a flower, or a ray of light is like a small mirror [of God's beauty.] Through the mystery of *tawhid*, however, that small mirror becomes connected to all its peers, and its whole species and becomes a huge mirror, which reflects a unique type of Divine beauty. Moreover, through its passing beauty, it reveals that the reflected Divine beauty is permanent...[9]

Otherwise, if there were no *tawhid* perspective, that particular fruit or gift would remain all by itself. It would not show the sacred Divine beauty and perfection. And even the particular and limited

---

[8] For the explanation of multiplicity, see the last footnote in Chapter 3.

[9] The author has the following sentence here, which we skipped: 'As Mawlana Jalal al-din al-Rumi said, it becomes a mirror of Divine beauty: "The imagination which is the snare of saints, is the reflection of the fair ones God's garden." '(Mathnawi, Book I, 72, quoted by Nursi in Persian). In Mawlana Rumi's discourse, the imaginal world of the friends of God (*awliya*) is a 'trap' laid before them from the lovely beings of the divine realm. Thus, 'God's garden' [Pers. *bustan-e khoda*] is a metaphor for the Divine realm, and the trap [Per. *daam*] is what the beautiful moon-faced ones of the Divine realm use to bring the friends even closer to the Divine. (Thanks to Dr. Omid Safi for clarifying this point.)

shine on it, eventually dissipates and disappears. While being really a diamond, it is reduced to a cheap piece of glass.

[Just as the mystery of *tawhid* connects particulars to the universal beauty and reveals the sacred beauty reflecting on the creation, it also reveals the universal beauty reflected within particular living beings.] Through the mystery of tawhid, a Divine *personality* (*shakhsiya ilahiya*), a *unicity* of sustainership (*ahadiyya rabbaniyya*), an incorporeal *countenance* of the Merciful stemming from the seven Divine attributes, and a *concentration* of the Divine names become manifest in living beings, which are like the 'fruits' of the tree of creation.[10] Living beings become focal points for the Most Beautiful Names of God (*al-asmā al-ḥusna*), and a manifestation of specification and particularization of the Divine Essence (*dhāt*) who is the addressee of *thee alone we worship and from thee alone we seek help* (Quran 1:5) becomes manifest.

---

[10] In Islamic theology, the names and attributes of God have been classified in a number of different ways so as to understand and express them better. The 'Seven Divine Attributes' stem from a common classification that was developed in the later classical period (12th century onward) on the basis of earlier classifications. The attributes of God are thus often classified into two main categories. The first category is called Attributes of Negation (*al-ṣifāt al-salbiyya*). This category includes attributes that highlight the infinite difference between the created and Creator, which are best expressed in the form of negation. They are usually listed as six: existence (*wujūd* i.e. the One whose non-existence is impossible), pre-existence (*qidam* i.e. the One who has no beginning), eternity (*baqā* i.e. the One who has no end), oneness (*waḥdāniyya* i.e. the One who has no partners), 'difference from creatures' (*mukhalafatu li al-ḥawādith*, i.e. the One is not similar to created things), and self-subsistence (*al-qiyām bi nafsihi*, i.e. the One who does not need anything for His existence.) The second main category is called Attributes of Affirmation (*al-ṣifat al-thubuṭiyya*) that highlight attributes whose glimpses of manifestation are reflected in creation and are expressed in the form of affirmation. They usually contain seven attributes of God: life, knowledge, hearing, seeing, will, power, and speech. This latter category is what Nursi means by 'seven attributes'. What is most noteworthy in Nursi's text is that through contemplating the creation (as seen in the rest of the paragraph) that one can confirm these attributes.

Otherwise, the manifestation of that personality, that unicity, that countenance, and that specification would expand to the entire universe, and become scattered and concealed from most people, except from those who possess huge and comprehensive hearts. Indeed, the splendor of Divine grandeur is like a veil and therefore not all hearts can discern it.[11]

Moreover, particular living beings clearly show that their Maker sees, knows, hears, and does as He wills. Thus, the believing heart can perceive behind the artistic making of those living beings a spiritual personality of an all-seeing, all-hearing, all-knowing, all-powerful Divine Essence (*dhāt*) Who possesses the will to do as He chooses. Through the light of *tawhid* and belief, such spiritual personality and sacred specification becomes very clearly visible, particularly in the creation of human beings. Indeed, attributes, such as knowledge, power, life, hearing, seeing and so on, which are the basis of the particularization of the unicity (*tashakhkhus al-aḥadiyya*) are all found in human beings. These human faculties indicate the Divine attributes of seeing, hearing, and so on. For, whoever makes your eyes, must be able to see them and also see what they see. It is like an optical manufacturer who knows what glasses would suit a person, and he makes them accordingly. Similarly, the One who gifted you with ears certainly knows and hears what those ears hear, and accordingly He creates them and bestows them upon you. You can apply the same reasoning to the other attributes of God [manifested in human beings] such as knowledge, power, life, and so on...

Moreover, human beings carry 'inscriptions' and manifestations pointing to the various beautiful names of God. Through them, human beings bear witness to such sacred meanings.

Furthermore, human beings also reveal God through their weakness. That is, through their inherent weakness, vulnerability, poverty and ignorance, human beings bear witness to qualities such

---

[11] Here, Nursi seems to be making implicit reference to the famous *hadith* mentioned in variant forms both in Abu Dawud and Muslim, according to which God said 'Pride is my cloak and Grandeur is my robe' (*al-kibriyā ridāī wa al-ʿaẓamatu izārī*).

as the power, knowledge, and will of the One who compassionately sustains and assists them.

Hence, through the mystery of Divine unity, countless beautiful Divine names (*al-asmā al-ḥusna*) concentrated in *living beings* become like clearly legible tiny missives in the four corners of the world of multiplicity as well as in the most scattered particulars. This is the reason why the Wise Maker multiplies these 'pages' of living beings. He especially creates many species of tiny creatures and spreads them all around.

How I encountered this First Fruit of tawhid

I was attracted to the truth of this first fruit of *tawhid* through a spiritual experience of tasting (*dhawq*). Once, due to excessive compassion and sympathy, I was feeling a lot of pain in my heart regarding living beings, especially the conscious beings, especially human beings and particularly the innocent oppressed and the afflicted. I was asking in my heart: 'Who hears the weeping of these weak and vulnerable afflicted? The universal laws operating in nature do not listen to them. Nor do the pervasive and unconscious natural elements hear them. Is there not anyone who has mercy on these poor beings and takes care of their particular needs?' My spirit was crying out at their calamities. My heart was also weeping: 'And, how about all those beautiful estates, precious goods, and these longing and grateful friends? Don't they have an owner, a supporter, a real friend who would attend to them, protect and assist them?'

The mystery of *tawhid* led me to a satisfactory, convincing response that satisfied and soothed my crying spirit and disturbed heart. Through the mystery of the Quran and the light of belief, I saw that *tawhid* meant that the Glorious One (*al-dhat dhu al-jalāl*), who is Merciful and Compassionate, offers special gifts and personalized help above and beyond the universal laws operating in the universe. He attends to those crying out at the pressure of universal laws and assault of events. The Glorious One has a direct connection to them and a special sustainership (*rubūbiyya*) for them. Hence, He takes care of everything directly and hears everyone's grief personally. He is the real owner, protector, and sustainer of every being. Thereby, through the light of belief and the mystery of the Quran, instead of incredible despair, I felt boundless joy. And each living being's worth increased dramatically in my eyes, since I became aware of their direct connection and belonging to such a Glorious Owner.

Indeed, everyone feels honored with their master's rank and fame.

Connection and belonging to the Glorious One unfold through the light of belief (*īmān*), and reveals how a tiny ant can defeat a Pharaoh with the power of that connection. And, through the honor of such connection to its Glorious Creator, an ant deserves to be prouder than a heedless Pharaoh, who imagines to own himself, and whose pride of his wealth and ancestors does not extend beyond the grave. Likewise, through the honor of its connection a fly can overtake a powerful king like Nimrod, whose pride devolved into punishment and shame at his deathbed.[12]

Indeed, there is great honor in being connected to the Glorious One and creatures are proud of being His artwork and creatures. That is why *shirk* (rejecting *tawhid*, and associating partners with God) is an insult to the creation.[13] Indeed, *shirk* is an enormous injustice to all creatures. That is why, the verse says, *Truly ascribing partners* (shirk) *is a tremendous wrongdoing* (Q. 31:13). *Shirk* is a crime that transgresses against the rights, honor and dignity of every created being. [It denies that they are honored creatures of a Glorious Creator and insults them as insignificant and worthless]. Only hell can purge such a major transgression.

Second Fruit of *Tawhid*

Just as the first fruit is related to the Most Sacred Divine Essence (*al-dhāt al-aqdas*) who is the Creator of the Universe, this second fruit is related to the essence (*dhāt*) and quiddity of the universe.

---

[12] Nursi seems to be taking these examples from the traditional exegetical stories about Pharaoh, the unnamed king in the Quranic narrative that opposed Prophet Moses (e.g. Q. 7:103), and Nimrod, who is identified as the king that opposed Prophet Abraham in Q. 2:258. It is said that Pharaoh's palace was destroyed by ants and Nimrod died as a result of a fly entering from his nose.

[13] Just as denying a great sovereign is an insult to his subjects who take pride in their affiliation with him.

Indeed, the perfection of the universe is realized through the mystery of oneness (*waḥda*). That is, through recognizing the oneness of God:

- The elevated duties of beings are understood,

- The purpose of creation of beings is accomplished,

- The value of creatures is recognized,

- The Divine purposes in the creation of the universe are realized,

- The wisdom behind the creation of living beings and conscious beings is revealed,

- The beautiful and smiling face of mercy and wisdom emerges from behind the seemingly angry and unhappy face of horrifying events in the world,

- It becomes known that although beings vanish, they leave in their stead enduring legacies and many existents, such as their results, identities, essences, souls and glorifications of God in the witnessed world (*'ālam al-shahāda*).

- It becomes clear that the universe in its entirety is a book of the One on Whom Everything Depends (*kitāb ṣamadāni*). It becomes manifest that beings throughout the universe are a miraculous collection of messages of the Glorious One (*maktubat subḥaniya*). All creatures with all their species are an incredible, orderly army of the Sustainer. Indeed, all creatures, from bacteria, to ants, to rhinos and eagles, to plants, are all faithful employees of the Eternal Sovereign.

- The riddle of difficult questions such as, 'Where is this flow of beings coming from? Where are they going? What are they doing here? What is the purpose of all this flow?' is solved.

Otherwise, all these lofty virtues of the universe would vanish; all these great and sacred truths (*ḥaqāiq*) would turn into their opposites.

That is why attributing partners to the One (*shirk*) and rejecting God constitute such a transgression against the virtues, important rights, and sacred truths of the universe. Hence, the universe resents those who identify with *shirk* and unbelief. The heavens and

the earth are upset with them, and bring down the people who re-
jected Noah, as well as the people of 'Ad, Thamud, and Pharaoh.
Even hell is outraged at people who insist on *shirk* and unbelief, as
alluded in the verse, it is *well-nigh bursting with fury.* (Q. 67:8)

Indeed, associating partners with God is a major insult and
transgression against the universe because it rejects their sacred duties
and the wisdom in their creation. Let us consider just one example
out of many. For instance, through the mystery of oneness (*waḥda*),
it becomes clear that the universe is such a huge embodied angel that
sings the glories of its Maker with billions of tongues! Each living
being together with each of its organs and cells are like a 'tongue,'
praising and hallowing the Maker in thousands of different ways!
Thus, the world is like an incredible created being that offers such an
amazing worship, in the manner of Angel Israfil (Raphael).[14] Moreover, through the mystery of *tawhid* it becomes apparent that this
universe is a fertile field that yields an abundant harvest for the
realms of the hereafter. The universe is also an amazing workshop
where the harvest from human deeds is supplied for the various
abodes of happiness in Paradise. It is like a multi-faceted video cam-
era, which constantly records images from this world to be shown to
the residents of the Highest Paradise. However, *shirk* rejects this elevated reality of the universe. It assumes this incredible, obedient,
lively and embodied angel to be a lifeless, spiritless, finite, purposeless, vanishing and meaningless entity. *Shirk* makes the universe appear as a chaotic result of unconscious random factors resulting from
deaf and blind nature.[15] Moreover, it turns the world into a place of

---

[14] In Islamic sources, Angel Israfil is considered as one of the four main angels. Israfil is mentioned in a *hadith* as the angel responsible for announcing
the coming of the Judgment Day by sounding the trumpet. While the name
is not mentioned in the Quran, there seem to be references to Israfil's duties
such as Judgment Day being announced, trumpet being sounded, etc. (See:
Q. 39: 68, 50: 41; 27:87; 54: 6–8).

[15] The author here is highlighting how natural factors, which are unconscious and ignorant, cannot be the creators of the orderly and wise results
associated with them. The terms 'deaf' and 'blind' in reference to nature is
an exposition of Quranic verses that reject partners attributed to God as in

mourning for those who have consciousness, and a depressing slaughterhouse for all living beings [because it denies enduring legacies of glorification and the eternal life, and regards death as final.]

Therefore, while *shirk* is just one act, it perpetuates many major transgressions. That is why the verse declares that *truly shirk is a tremendous wrongdoing* (31:13), and that is why it deserves endless suffering in hell. *Sirāj al-nūr*[16] contains more details on this 'Second Fruit,' so we will end the discussion here.

What Brought Me to This Second Fruit of Tawhid

It was a strange feeling and perception that brought me to this second fruit of *tawhid*. Once as I was contemplating during a spring season, I saw processions of beings and especially living beings appear one after the other in groups—a continuous flow and journeying on earth, disclosing endless samples of Resurrection (*hashr*) and of the Great Gathering (*nashr al-aʿzam*). I saw that these living beings, and especially the tiny ones, came into existence, remained for a brief time, and then died and disappeared from sight. This daunting activity and the death and separation it brought about seemed so sad to me. I felt intense pity and started weeping. My heart ached at the death of those lovely tiny creatures. My spirit was deeply disturbed and crying out. I said to myself: 'If this is the outcome of life, then living is worse than dying.'

Moreover, among plants and animals, extremely beautiful, lovely and precious living beings open up their eyes to this exhibition of the world just for a moment and then, within that same moment, they are extinguished and gone. My heart ached deeply as I observed this. I wanted to cry and complain awfully against fate, asking: 'Why are they coming and leaving so quickly?' After having been brought into existence—before our eyes—with such care, attention, artistry and being equipped, taken care of and arranged so well, they are

---

Q 7:195: *Have they perchance, feet on which they could walk? Or have they hands with which they could grasp? Or have they eyes with which they could see? Or have they ears with which they could hear?*

[16] Lit. 'lamp of light;' it is another title for *Risale-i Nur*.

shredded like worthless rags and thrown into darkness of nothingness. They are executed quickly with no benefit, purpose or result. To this, all my subtle feelings and emotions—which are in love with perfection, beauty and precious things—cried out 'Why no mercy to them? What a pity! How come this dizzying activity of transience and impermanence haunt these poor beings?' Seeing the painful circumstances of the façade of life events, strong objections against destiny was swelling up inside me.

At that moment of frustration and resentment toward fate, through the light of the Quran, and the mystery of belief, as well as the grace of the Merciful, *tawhid* came to my assistance. It enlightened all the darkness and transformed my sadness into joy. I said, 'Praise be to God for the light of belief!' For, through the light of belief, I saw the following:

Through the light of *tawhid*, each created being, especially each living being, has many purposes and universal benefits. Each living being, such as an adorned flower or a honeybee, is a meaningful and well-composed 'ode' of God. Countless conscious beings take delight in 'listening to' it.[17] Indeed, each living being is a miracle of Divine power. It declares the wisdom of the Creator and reveals the Artist's art to innumerable spectators, attracting their admiration.

[Furthermore, the purposes of living beings' existence pertain not only to their conscious spectators, but also to their Creator.] Indeed, the Majestic Creator wants to behold His art Himself, see His own beauty for Himself, and watch the manifestation of His names in the mirrors [of creatures]. To be exposed to the gaze of their Glorious Creator is an honor for living beings, and it is a major purpose of their existence.

Moreover, the endless infinite activity in the universe is necessitated by the manifestation of sustainership (*rubūbiyya*) and divine perfections (*al-kamālat al-ilāhiyya*). Thus, it is understood that an-

---

[17] In other words, each living being discloses precious messages regarding the Creator to the conscious beings that witness them.

other elevated duty of the creation is to reveal the *rubūbiyya* and divine perfections in five ways, as explained in '24th Letter.'[18]

Accordingly, after yielding such benefits and results, each living being leaves this world with joy, like someone graduating or retiring. They do not vanish like it seemed to me earlier. Rather, their reflection and nature remain preserved in countless memories and other 'preserving tablets' (*al-alwāḥ al-maḥfūẓa*), and if they are conscious their spirit is preserved.[19] The principles of that being's existence are also preserved in its seed or egg, so the creature in a sense lives into the future. As it passes from this world, each living being also leaves behind enduring meanings in the unseen world: i.e. the perfections and the beauty of the Beautiful Names of God, (*al-asmā al-ḥusna*) that it reflected. Hence, what I had perceived as unfair death and separation turned out to be simply a disappearance from sight in this world [after having accomplished crucial tasks and continuing to be preserved in so many ways].

In sum, the shining, strong, rooted and flawless instances of beauty found throughout the universe and in all species show that the ugly, harsh, disgusting and miserable appearance of the universe necessitated by *shirk* is certainly false. For, it is not possible for such terrible ugliness to be hidden behind this conspicuous veil of beauty that we see before our eyes. If that were the case, then that truthful beauty would have no truth or reality whatsoever. But it is *shirk* that has no truth or basis; its path leads to deceit. It is an impossible and absurd conjecture.

Since this experiential truth of belief has been explained elsewhere in the *Risale-i Nur*, we shall skip a detailed discussion here.

Third Fruit of Tawhid

The third fruit of *tawhid* pertains to human beings directly. Indeed, through the mystery of oneness (*waḥda*), human beings can attain the highest virtue within creation and become the most precious

---

[18] In Nursi's *Letters*, one of the major volumes of the *Risale-i Nur*.
[19] This phrase reminds of the Quranic reference to *al-lawh al-mahfuz*, see Chapter 6, fn. 109.

'fruit' of the universe. Moreover, through the secret of unity, human beings can become the most sensitive and most perfect among all creatures. Thereby, a human being becomes the happiest of all living beings, becoming the addressee and friend of the Creator of the Worlds.

In fact, all the virtues of humanity and high aspirations of humankind are tied to *tawhid* and are realized through the mystery of oneness (*wahda*). Otherwise, if there is no unity, a human being becomes the most unfortunate of all creation and the lowliest of all existents. Without *tawhid*, human being turns into the most helpless animal and the most despondent and depressed of all conscious beings. For, human being has a very interesting nature. He is utterly weak yet he is subject to endless challenges (lit. 'enemies'). He is so poor and yet he has innumerable needs. Moreover, human nature is equipped with so many varied capacities and feelings that human beings can experience thousands of different kinds of sorrows, and they can enjoy and desire thousands of different kinds of pleasures. Moreover, they have such aspirations and yearnings that anyone who does not have control over the entire universe cannot fulfill them. [That is why, it is only through the secret of *tawhid*, which connects them to the One who has control over everything, that human beings can be fulfilled and perfected.]

For instance, human beings have a very strong desire for eternity. Clearly, only the one who takes care of the universe as easily as taking care of a palace can fulfill this desire. Only such a one will be able to open a new realm of existence after closing the realm of this world—as easily as closing one room's door and opening another's. Like this desire for eternity, human beings have so many desires and worries related to so many things, which extend to eternity. The one who can fulfill all these desires can only be the one who can heal the two terrible wounds of humanity: powerlessness (*'ajz*) and neediness (*faqr*). And none other than the Unique One (*al-dhāt al-ahad*) who holds the entire universe in His hand can accomplish that.

Moreover, the human heart has such subtle, hidden, and specific wishes related to the peace and contentment and the human spirit has such great, comprehensive and universal purposes regarding its endurance and happiness that only the one who sees and cares about the subtlest and most hidden layers of the heart can fulfill. He is the one who hears the most secret and silent whisperings and answers them. And, only the one who has the power to the level of ruling over the heavens and the earth for universal purposes as if they are two obedient soldiers can fulfill human needs and desires.

Furthermore, all human capacities and organs gain remarkable worth through the secret of unity (*wahda*), and they lose their worth and value when perceived through *shirk* (association of partners with the One) and with unbelief (*kufr*). For instance, your most precious tool is your intellect. Through the mystery of *tawhid,* the intellect becomes a precious key unlocking incredible treasures [of wisdom] in the universe, and revealing eternal and sacred truths pertaining to the most beautiful divine names. If someone falls into *shirk* and *kufr*, then his intellect turns into a troublesome tool that gathers sorrows from the past and scary apprehension concerning the future. To give another example, let's take the human feeling of solidarity and compassion. If the mystery of *tawhid* does not enlighten it, then that feeling turns into a terrifying feeling of separation and sadness, which destroys human beings. A mother who is unaware of *tawhid* and has lost her beloved child knows the terrifying and crushing feeling that such compassion yields.

Similarly, the delightful feeling of love takes a completely different meaning depending on whether it is viewed from the *tawhid* or *shirk* perspective. Through *tawhid,* the sweet and precious feeling of love expands the tiny human being to embrace the entire universe. With such an open and comprehensive love, the human being becomes a delicate sovereign[20] dear to the entire universe. In contrast, if the human being were to fall into *shirk* and *kufr*, (may we be all pro-

---

[20] This use of the phrase 'delicate sovereign' to describe human status through *tawhid* is noteworthy. 'Sovereign' highlights the human capacity that enables him to be a leader for the entire creation. 'Delicate' emphasizes that such capacity is not his. The human being is vulnerable on his own and is completely dependent on God, like any other creature. Therefore, his ability to rule over the creation is not a reason for boasting. In fact, the human being is the potential sovereign of the universe precisely because he is one of the most needy and vulnerable creatures. Hence, instead of arrogance, gratitude and embracing the rest of creation is called for.

tected from it!), the same capacity to love becomes a source of unending pain that crushes his heart as all his beloveds seem to be drowning in the waves of separation and death, never to come back again. People do not sense these painful consequences of *shirk* because of the distractions, diversion and idle entertainment that numb the feelings.

In addition to the above three examples, you may reflect on other many human capacities and feelings. You shall see that oneness (*wahda*) and affirming divine unity (*tawhid*) is an amazing source for human virtues. We have expounded further on this elsewhere. Now, I shall just note what brought me to this third fruit of tawhid.

Once, I was at the top of a mountain, when I experienced a spiritual awakening that interrupted my heedlessness (*ghafla*). I saw death in all its nakedness and realized the tragedy of separation and transience. Like everyone else, I had innate love for eternity. Unexpectedly, it revolted against transience (*zawāl*) and resented the fact that all the virtuous and great people that I loved so much, such as the prophets, saints and purified ones, had died and vanished. As a consequence, my feelings of solidarity and compassion for other human beings also rose in protest against death. I searched for help in all directions. Alas, I could not find any solution, hope or consolation. The past seemed like a huge cemetery, utterly dead. And the future was totally dark. Wherever I turned, I saw horror, sadness and peril.

Suddenly, the mystery of *tawhid* came to my assistance. It lifted the veils and showed me the true nature of things. It said, 'Look!' And, I looked at the face of death that had been so scary and painful. I saw that in fact for people of belief (*ahl al-īmān*), death is a time for transfer to a better place. Death is the gate and the beginning of an eternal life. It means leaving the limited realm of this world behind and flying to the gardens of paradise. Death is a rendezvous to enter in the presence of the Merciful and get the reward for your service in this world. I understood with certainty that death is an invitation to the eternal abode of happiness and thus I started liking death.

Then, with the light of *tawhid*, I looked at transience (*fanā*) and ephemerality (*zawāl*). I realized that it is actually a delightful process of renewal. It is enjoyable like the changing of scenes in a movie theater [one scene goes and another scene replaces it]. To offer another metaphor, the transience of beings is as enjoyable as watching the flow of a river under the sun: water bubbles keep flowing as they sparkle with sunlight. I realized that things and beings in the world flow constantly, moving from the World of the Unseen (*'ālam al-ghayb*) into the World of the Seen (*'ālam al-shahāda*) thereby revealing and shining with the wonderful manifestations of the Most Beautiful Divine Names (*al-asmā al-ḥusna*). Indeed, the transience of things is a purposeful celebration of the beauty of sustainership (*rubūbiyya*). And, I knew with certainty that this is how beings (*mawjūdāt*) act as mirrors to eternal Divine beauty (*ḥusn*).

Then I looked all around again, into all 'six directions.' I saw that through the light of *tawhid*, all directions shined with intense brightness. I saw that the past is not a huge cemetery: rather it consists of thousands of light-filled assemblies and gatherings of friends, who have moved from the past into the future. Similarly, I saw the truth of all the remaining four aspects. I realized that in reality they do not yield anything except joy and gratitude. I have expounded elsewhere in the *Epistles of Light*, the details of and evidences for the perception and feeling that led me to this third fruit. I especially recommend the thirteen 'Hopes' in the 26th Flash, the Epistle for the Elderly, where it is explained thoroughly and eloquently. Thus, I have cut the long discussion very short here.

12

THE WORLD IS SPEAKING OF *TAWHID*: A PARABLE

How many signs there are in the heavens and on the earth.
Yet they pass them by [unthinkingly], and turn away from them!

—Quran, 12:105

The selection translated here is a long parable that Nursi offers in 'The First Station' of the 22nd Word. He unpacks the parable in the 'Second Station' of the 22nd Word, which can be found in the next chapter.

The entire 22nd Word is a fine example of Quranic reasoning in practice. Taking to heart the central Quranic teaching on the 'signs' (*ayāt*) of God, Nursi offers a detailed reflection on nature. The text is richly attentive to nature as an attestation of divine creativity and shows awareness of the theological and philosophical questions associated with interpreting the signs of God in the universe. Like much of the other texts in the *Risale-i Nur*, the treatise is meant to introduce the Quranic message and make it accessible to the common person. While Nursi does not assume prior theological training on the part of the reader, there is a crucial expectation: to reflect on the text carefully and with the willingness to relate it to one's life. To put it in Nursi's words, the treatise is not to be read it 'like a newspaper.'[1]

In the preface of the text—as will be seen below—Nursi quotes two Quranic verses on parables, suggesting that the parable follows the Quranic purposes for parables, which is to facilitate reflection on the signs of God in nature and to grasp their relevance to the human condition. The parable is about two men who find themselves transported to a new world and their attempt at making sense of the things there. The conversation between these two men represents an inner conversation within each human being, which also corresponds to opposing worldviews of belief and unbelief. One of the men in the parable is arrogant and rejects that there is an owner of the place; he represents the unbelieving potential within each person, the tendency to ignore or reject the signs of the One. The other man is humble and he talks about the abundant indications to the sovereign of this new place. He represents the believer who confirms *tawhid* based on the testimony of the signs in the world pointing to an unseen maker and making Him known.

The parable is set in a 'strange' world because Nursi wants to train the reader to look at the familiar world anew. (As was noted earlier in the introduction chapter, according to Nursi one of the aims of the Quran is to break through 'the veil of familiarity' in order to show the miracles of divine power all around.) So, while reading this parable, it may be helpful to visualize oneself in an unfamiliar world—perhaps even some alien planet—so as to appreciate the need for understanding and safety that the believing character in the parable keeps bringing up. At the same time, as Nursi reveals in many footnotes of the parable, the purpose of the parable is to induce the readers to reconsider their familiar world and contemplate it in order to discover its many hidden marvelous aspects. Thus, the readers are expected to be flexible in considering the parable in the sense that they need to be able to switch back and forth between the

---

[1] Nursi gives this advice in a letter to a disciple regarding another treatise, the treatise on freewill and destiny (26th Word). *Mektubat*, '12. Mektup,' RNK 1:364; *Letters*, 'Twelfth Letter,' 61.

symbolic world of the parable and the 'real' world that it represents. Moreover, the strange new place of the parable is set in three magnitudes at once: a palace, a city and a country. (For instance, the treatise sometimes refers to the 'lamp' in the 'palace' and sometimes the 'huge lamp' of the 'country,' both of which represent the sun in the real world.) The reason for his three-tiered metaphor may be that Nursi wants to highlight the immensity and the many dimensions of the real world that the parable represents. Nursi uses the parable to simplify the discussion and facilitate the understanding of dense matters, but he does not want the reader to forget that the universe it represents is utterly vast, infinitely complex and marvelous.

In the parable, the two men encounter creatures that seem to be speaking about serious things but in a foreign language. This detail seems to represent the Quranic notion that the universe praises the Creator in ways that human beings often fail to recognize: *the seven heavens extol His limitless glory, and the earth, and all that they contain; and there is not a single thing but extols His limitless glory and praise: but you [O human beings]* fail to grasp *the manner of their glorifying Him!* (Q. 17:44, emphasis added). (Incidentally, this verse is among the most often quoted ones in the *Risale-i Nur*.) Elsewhere, the Quran seems to relate such failure to grasp the speech of creation to willful rejection: *how many signs there are in the heavens and on the earth, yet they pass them by [unthinkingly], and* turn away *from them!* (Q. 12:105, emphasis added). One of the men in the parable rejects the speech of the creatures in the new land as gibberish and denies that there is a sovereign. The other man sets out to explain that the creatures in fact are 'speaking' about the sovereign, declaring his immense power, wisdom and beauty. The rest of the section consists of this 'reasonable friend' advising his 'stubborn friend' by means of thirteen 'proofs'. In the remaining part of our introduction to this parable, we shall highlight only several points from the discussion.

Starting from the 'Fourth Proof,' the parable emphasizes the greatness of the maker of the universe. In the 'Ninth Proof,' Nursi indirectly responds to a philosophical criticism of continuous creation: how can one single being be the maker and continuous sustainer of such a vast universe?[2] In response, Nursi suggests that our feeling of being overwhelmed is not a good reason to reject the factual reality of continuous coming into existence and the corresponding truth of continuous creation. In other words, the fact that such an amazing and vast universe is constantly renewed with everything within it, indicates and testifies to an amazing and incredible sustainer. A finite and limited being whose power we could humanly comprehend could in no way be the maker of an atom, let alone this amazing and vast universe. Therefore, it is utterly unreasonable to reject that amazing and incredible Maker of this universe simply because it is overwhelming to limited human beings. Furthermore, Nursi suggests, the alternative to confirming this appropriately—and overwhelmingly—great God is completely untenable. He demonstrates how the alternative to belief in One Infinitely Powerful Being is to believe in endless number of entities, each of which has god-like qualities. For instance, if we reject the One who is causing the atoms, the genes, the human body, the solar system and so on, to work in utmost harmony and interconnectivity with each other, we would have to accept that each part of that harmonious order is itself all-knowing and all-powerful, and aware of the whole, in order to be able to produce the observed vast order and creativity. Moreover, each part would have to have control over all other parts and yet at the same time, it would have to be subjugated to them as well. Thus, if we don't accept 'immense and tremendous lordship (*rubūbiyya*),' which is *completely appropriate and in place*,' we will have to accept a 'totally unreasonable and precluded' view.[3]

From the 'Seventh Proof' onwards, the treatise seems to focus on broader patterns in the world. Nursi highlights the *interconnectedness* of all things and how they are 'hastening to each other's aid and cooperating in answering each other's needs.' At the end of the

---

[2] Hume, for instance, surmises that one God maintaining the entire universe is too extraordinary. Hume, *Treatise*, pt. 8, para. 7/12, p. 184.

[3] Nursi, Lem'alar, '13. Lem'a, 13. Isaret,' RNK 1:627; *Flashes*, '13th Flash, 13th Indication,' 123.

'Tenth Proof,' Nursi prepares the reader to see not only the amazing aspects of the world but also its transience as a sign indicating the Creator. The Quran often mentions the flourishing and the withering away of things together such as life and death, gain and loss, abundance and scarcity, knowing and forgetting, and so on. The emergence *and* withering away, the excellence *and* the failure of the creatures *together* constitute a sign pointing to the qualities of the eternal creator beyond them. For instance, the Quranic verse *and some of you are reduced in old age to the weakest of ages, so that, they know nothing after having had knowledge. Truly, God is all-knowing, all-powerful!* (Q. 16:70, emphasis added) suggests that the fact that human beings can display knowledge *and* then lose it show that the knowledge they display is not from them, but is from an enduring source.[4] Using such Quranic cues, Nursi shows how the constant 'flow' of creatures bear witness to the enduring beautiful qualities of God, *al-asmā al-ḥusna*.

Finally, in the last two proofs, the Eleventh and Twelfth Proofs, Nursi considers the Prophet Muhammad—whom he presents as being confirmed by previous prophets—and the Quran as signs of God. The existence of God's messengers and the Quran are part of the indications to *tawhid* present in the universe because there are clear indications in the life of the Prophet and in the content of the Quran showing that they are sent by the one God. By crowning these two signs as containing the final and clearest evidences for God, Nursi effectively discloses that his reasoning in the previous 'proofs' was inspired by the prophetic message. In other words, this treatise is *not* an unaided reflection on nature that reaches the same conclusions of the Quran. Rather, it is a reflection based on scripture that increases belief (*tafakkur imanī*) that takes enlightening cues from the Quran, reflects on the world through them and discovers that the world confirms the truths of belief. Indeed, for Nursi one should not

---

[4] Similarly, the Quran calls attention to how life is brought out of the dead and death out of the living. (Q. 30:19). Also see, Q. 3:26; 6:1; 18:7–8; 22:5; 30:24; 87:1–5 etc.

reflect merely on the Quranic verses, but rather one should reflect *by means* of the Quranic verses (*tafakkur bi al-ayāt*).[5]

***

The World is Speaking of Tawhid: A Parable[6]

In the name of God, the Merciful, the Compassionate.

...And [thus it is that] God sets forth parables for people, so that they may remember.

—Quran 14:25

...And such parables We set forth for people, so that they may reflect.

—Quran 59:21

Once upon a time two men entered a pool, and in some unknown way they lost consciousness. When they opened their eyes, they found themselves in a strange land. A very ordered land, which seemed like a well-developed country, a perfect city, or an exquisite palace. They looked around in amazement; this was an incredible world: from one perspective, it looked like a well-ordered country, and from another perspective it looked like, a wonderful well-planned city. It looked like a palace comprising an incredible universe.[7]

---

[5] Nursi, *al-Mathnawi al-'Arabī*, 257.

[6] Nursi, *Sözler*, '22. Söz, Birinci Makam' (22nd Word, First Station), RNK I:115–120, title added by editors.

[7] As noted in our introduction, Nursi expects the reader to think about the 'new place' in the parable in three perspectives: as a palace, city, kingdom. Each of them serves the purposes of the parable adequately, for instance, to show the connection between order and its maker. Using three of them has the additional benefit of emphasizing the complexity and magnitude of the real world. For the sake of making the parable easier to follow, we usually kept only the 'palace' metaphor.

The two men walked around in this world and saw various odd creatures that spoke in a language they could not understand. However, from their gestures, it was clear that these creatures were performing important tasks and carrying out crucial duties.

One of the men told his friend: 'Surely this artful palace must have a maker. Let's find out who he is and get to know him. For it looks like he is the one who brought us here. If we don't get to know him, who can help us? What can we expect from these weak creatures around us who speak a language we don't understand and who ignore us? Surely, whoever fashioned this palace, and filled it with wonderful artifacts and decorated it with incredible art and exquisite wonders must want something from us and from all those who come here. Let's get to know him and see what he wants from us.'

The other man said, 'I don't believe that there is such a being and that he is taking care of this entire palace on his own.'

His friend said: 'Listen, if we ignore him and don't get to know him, we will gain nothing and we may lose much. On the other hand, it shouldn't be difficult to get to know him, and it will probably be very beneficial. It would be ridiculous to remain indifferent to him.'[8]

The foolish man replied, 'Well, I see my enjoyment and comfort in not thinking about him! I will not bother with these things that my mind does not comprehend. I don't want to think too deep! I believe that all these things around us are just random and chaotic. And, why should I care anyway?'

---

[8] Nursi does not explain why it is urgent for the men to find about the maker of the palace and understand its purpose. He simply states here (and several more times in the rest of the parable) that there is something personally at stake for them. This may be his way of hinting that the search for the Creator is not just an intellectual need for explanation but also a profound existential need. For his explanation of why *tawhid* is so important for human soul, see the previous chapters in this volume, for instance Chapters 3 and 8.

His sensible friend replied: 'Your stubbornness will put me and many others in trouble... It has happened that an entire country is ruined because of one bad-mannered person.'⁹

The foolish man turned and said: 'Either prove to me decisively that this huge palace has only one maker and that he is the one who rules everything or leave me alone.'

His friend responded: 'Well, given that you are so stubborn, let me show you twelve proofs that there is only one maker of this palace-like world and city-like country. I shall prove to you that this maker takes care of everything by himself and has no imperfections. While he is not visible to us, he sees everything, including us, and hears our conversation. All his works are astounding and wondrous. And all these creatures we see and whose language we don't understand are his employees.'

First Proof

Come, look around, and pay attention to everything. There must be a hidden hand behind all these activities. For instance, look: a tiny thing as small as a seed, which does not have an iota of strength, is lifting thousands of pounds! (This points to the seeds that are so tiny and yet carry huge trees on their 'heads,' that is, tiny seeds that yield huge trees.)¹⁰ And look, things that do not have the least consciousness are accomplishing wise tasks. (This points to the delicate plants,

---

⁹ The idea of entire society being in trouble because of one person's wrong-doing may sound a bit extreme. It may be helpful to recall that according to Nursi's Quranic reflection, rejecting *tawhid* is a major insult and injustice to the universe (see earlier Chapter 9). In response to such 'injustice,' if the 'sensible' person remains indifferent and does not attempt to remind his 'foolish' friend, he becomes culpable as well. Nursi seems to have in mind Quranic passages that remind of the duty to stand up for justice and right and try to prevent wrong (see for instance, Q. 9:71, 9:112, 22:4, 31:17) as well as Quranic verses that talk about the serious consequences of remaining silent to injustice, as in, for instance, Q. 8.25.

¹⁰ In the original, this sentence is in a footnote by Nursi. To make the parable easier to follow, we incorporated all his footnotes into the main text within brackets.

such as grapevine, that cannot go up on their own and cannot carry the weight of their fruits. These plants extend their delicate arms onto trees and put their weight on them.)[11] This means that these things do not accomplish such results on their own. Rather, a hidden hand of power is at work. If these things were happening by themselves, then everything in this palace would be a miracle in itself and a miraculous wonder of its own. And that is absurd.

Second Proof

Come, pay attention to the things that adorn these plains and fields. Each contains indications of that unseen being as if each is like a stamp or a signature acclaiming this being. For instance, look, right before your eyes at what he is making out of a tiny bit of cotton (This indicates a seed. For instance, look at a tiny seed like a poppy seed, a wild apricot seeds, and a melon seed. See how they offer to us from the treasure of mercy (*rahma*) leaves weaved better than baize, lovely white and yellow flowers brighter than batiste, and sweet and nourishing fruits tastier than candy and desserts!)

Look, from that tiny seed how many yards of baize, batiste and flowery fabric emerge!

Look also how many candies and tasty meatballs are made from it! So many people can be fed and clothed from these!

And look how he takes iron, soil, water, coal, copper, silver, and gold into his unseen hand and turns them into flesh. (This refers to the creation of living beings from elements, and the creation of life from a zygote.) Look and see!

Now, foolish friend, these activities can only be accomplished by a being who has the entire palace with all its amazing parts under his control, and to whose wishes all elements yield.

---

[11] In other words, for Nursi, the growth of the branches in purposeful directions is a wise action. And, yet these plants have no consciousness to plan such action. Thus, there must be a wise creator behind the scenes that is making this happen.

Third Proof

Come, look at these 'machine-like' dynamic and exquisite works of art. (This points to animals and human beings. For, an animal is like a small index of the entire universe. And human nature is like a small model of the entire creation; it is as if whatever exists in the universe has a corresponding sample in human beings). Each of them is crafted in such a way that it is a model of the entire palace. Whatever exists in this huge palace exists in these dynamic works of art as a minute sample.

Is it at all possible that anyone other than the maker of this wondrous palace can model this machine-like small work of art to contain the entire palace?[12] Is it at all possible that a small living work of art that contains the whole world may be the result of random and aimless activities?

It is clear then that all these visible works of living art are like signatures of that unseen maker. Each is like a herald and a declaration. Through their very being, their 'tongue of disposition,' (*lisān al-ḥāl*), they declare: 'We are the art of such a being who can make the entire universe with the same ease with which he makes us.'

Fourth proof

Come my stubborn friend! I shall show you something even more wondrous. Look at all the things and events in this palace: they all have changed and they are constantly changing. Nothing remains the same. Look carefully at how these lifeless and unconscious elements control their environment; it is as though each rules over all the oth-

---

[12] An example from the real world might be the fact that a single cell of an organism contains the code or the DNA of the entire organism. Moreover, Nursi frequently refers to a living being, especially a human being, as a 'microcosm' (*al-ʿālam al-saghīr*) 'containing' the entire universe in it. For an explanation see Chapter 6, 'First Indication.' Such a view of human being as microcosm is common in a number of classical Islamic Sufi texts, such as in the works of Ghazali, Rumi and Ibn al-Arabi, as well as in other religious and philosophical traditions.

ers. It seems as if all these lifeless containers have become like supreme rulers; it is as if they are subjugating everything to serve them.

For instance, look at this machine right next to us. (Here, 'machines' refer to fruit bearing trees. For, it is as if they have numerous workshops and factories within their thin branches: they weave, embellish and 'cook' wonderful leaves, flowers, and fruits and offer them to us! While trees like pine trees and turpentine trees have set up their workshops in dry stone, working incessantly.) It is as if it commands all the ingredients and materials needed for its adornment and operation to come to it, running from afar. Look, it is as if with one signal, that unconscious entity subjugates the greatest things, like the sun, and puts them at its service. Many similar things are happening all around us. It is as if each thing subjugates the rest of the world to itself.

Now, if you don't accept that there is a hidden wondrous being orchestrating all these events, then you will have to attribute all his skills, artistry and perfections to this palace's stones, soil, animals, and 'human-like creatures.'[13] You will have to assume that every single one of them is an absolute ruler in itself. Consequently, if you dispute the existence of one unseen incredible maker, you will have to say that all these beings are each such an incredible maker. That is, when you reject the existence of one single unseen glorious maker, you will have to accept that there are billions of amazing makers like him! Moreover, you will also have to maintain that these billions of miraculous makers oppose each other yet are also are subjugated to each other, so that the order in front of our eyes can be sustained without breaking down! What an absurd conclusion![14]

If there were just two authorities ruling over this palace, things would be chaotic. As is well-known, two cooks spoil the broth! In-

---

[13] This phrase may be Nursi's way of keeping to the parable's setting that the two men are in a strange land.

[14] Nursi thus highlights a major contradiction: each seems to be subjugating all others beings and things to itself and at the same time it is subjugated to each other being and things. In other words, each seems to have total control over all the rest of beings and to be at the same time under the control of all and each one of them.

deed, if there are two heads in a village, two mayors in a town, or two kings in a country, order will be spoiled. So, can you imagine how unreasonable it is to claim that innumerable absolute rulers can rule this palace at the same time and that the outcome is so orderly and harmonious![15]

Fifth Proof

Oh my perplexed friend!

Come look at this incredible palace's decorations! Look at the beautiful ornaments of this city. See the organization of this entire country.[16] And reflect on the artistry of this world.

Now look: if you deny that the pen of a hidden incredible artist, who has miraculous abilities, is at work here, you will run into absurdities. If you attribute all this beautiful artwork to causes such as unconscious things, blind chance and deaf nature, it would mean that every single stone and every single bit of grass is itself a wondrous tailor. It would mean that each is an incredible scribe who can inscribe an entire book within a single letter and incorporate millions of artistic ornaments within one pattern. Now be fair and think, can such an assumption be reasonable at all?

Look at the artistic engraving in these stones (The stones in palace refers in real life to the human being, who is the fruit of the tree of creation. It also refers to fruits, which carry the plan and index of their trees. For, the 'pen' of Divine power summarizes everything

---

[15] Here Nursi is clearly making use of the Quranic verse: *If there had been in them [i.e. heavens and earth] any gods other than God, surely both would have been corrupted! So glory be to God, Lord of the Throne [of almightiness] beyond what they describe!* (Q. 21:22) Nursi understands this verse to suggest that only when we accept one almighty being who has control over all things and thus is able to coordinate each thing that we avoid the absurd conclusion noted earlier.

[16] As noted earlier, Nursi uses within this parable three metaphors, a palace, city and country and we have retained only the 'palace' metaphor, and skipping Nursi's occasional references to the 'city' or 'country.' Here and in several other places below, we kept all three metaphors so as to highlight the complexity of the reality the parable represents.

that it wrote in the universe, the macrocosm, within human nature. And the 'pen' of destiny incorporates all that it inscribed in a huge tree within its tiny fruit.) Each one of them contains the artistry of the entire palace, its organizational laws, and its governance templates. Accordingly, making these engravings is as wondrous as making the entire palace. Each artistic engraving and each piece of art reveals the same unseen being and each bears his style and signature.

Now, as you well know, a letter reveals its scribe. Likewise, an artistic engraving inevitably reveals its artist. Then how do you suppose that an author who writes an entire book within a letter and incorporates thousands of inscriptions within one artistic engraving cannot be known through his book and art?

Sixth Proof

Come, we will go up to this open field! (This is a reference to the earth during spring and summer. During these seasons, thousands of diverse species are created within each other and 'written out' on the page of the earth. Each season, they are renewed with perfect order, without mistake or fault. Numerous feast tables of the Merciful are freshly brought in, set up and then cleaned up. Each tree becomes like a waiter serving food, and each orchard and field becomes like a huge pot in which nourishment is cooked.) See, there is a high mountain over there. Let's climb it to get a better view of the area. Let's also take with us some fine binoculars to see even better. For, in this place, extraordinary things are happening incessantly.

Look—all these fields, mountains, and cities are suddenly changing. And the changes are stunning: millions of incredible transformations are taking place one within the other in a very orderly manner.

Look: all the familiar flowery artifacts have disappeared. Now, other similar ones appeared in an orderly fashion and replaced them. It is as if these plains and mountains are each a page and thousands of different books are written on each page. What is more, all this incredible writing takes place without any error or oversight.

Now it is utterly impossible that these things are happening on their own. Indeed, it is completely impossible for these extremely artistic and fine-tuned events to happen by themselves. Clearly, these works are revealing their artist. This artist is such a glorious being that nothing is burdensome for him. To him, writing thousands of books is as easy as writing a single letter.

Moreover, look all around you: this unseen artist assigns everything in its right place with wisdom. He generously grants everyone the gifts that they deserve. He takes care of everyone's wishes by generously 'opening doors' for everyone. He sets such a multitude of lavish banquets that all people and all species of animals are served according to their needs and tastes. In fact, each individual receives customized servings specially marked with his/her name.[17]

Now, is it at all possible that all these events are taking place by chance or that they are meaningless and vain,[18] or that multiple agents are responsible in creating them?

Is it at all possible that the maker of all these events is not all-powerful or that everything is not subjugated to his power? My friend, what excuse can you make up to deny this maker? How else can you explain these amazing activities you witness before your eyes in a reasonable way?

Seventh Proof

Come, my friend. Putting aside these particular events, we shall now take a broader view of this place. We shall look at how parts of this palace-like world are positioned in relation to each other.

Look here. Such orderly comprehensive tasks and universal changes are carried out in this place in such a way that it is as if each stone, each piece of soil, each tree, and everything else, are acting in harmony with the overall order here. It is as if each is a conscious

---

[17] Here Nursi seems to have in mind Quranic passages such as *And how many a living creature is there that takes no thought of its own sustenance; God provides for it as [He provides] for you—since He alone is all-hearing, all-knowing.* (Q. 29:60) Also, he does not talk about the economic injustices and ecological crisis in this context, as they are related to human wrongdoing.

[18] Lit. 'without benefit.' By this rhetorical question, ('can they be without benefit'?) Nursi is suggesting that since these events are clearly beneficial, they cannot be by chance.

actor. And things that are very far from each other hasten to the aid of one another.

Look! A surprising caravan appeared suddenly (This represents the plants and trees that carry the provisions of all the animals). The 'camels' of this approaching caravan are trees, plants and mountains. Each is carrying a load of food. Look, they are bringing provisions that the animals here are waiting for.

Look, there is also a huge lamp under this dome (That huge lamp represents the sun). It both gives light and cooks their food so well! Each piece of food that needs cooking is attached so as to be exposed to this stove by an unseen hand (That stove and the food on it represent the thin branches of a tree and its tasty fruits.)

And over there, look at these delicate and weak animals. See how in front of them there are bottles with pure nourishment (which represents the breastmilk). The bottles are placed at their mouths so that they can enjoy their meal without any effort.

In sum: All things here assist one another as if they see each other's needs. They cooperate with each other and complete each other's tasks and work shoulder to shoulder all together. There are so many other examples of such cooperation.

Now, all these situations certainly show that there is a wondrous maker of this place, to whom everything is subjugated. Everything works on his behalf, in his name. All things are under his command. Everything is accomplished through his power. Everything acts with his command. All is arranged with his wisdom. Everything is made to assist one another on account of his generosity. Through his mercy everything hastens to the need of others; that is, he makes them help each other and collaborate with each other. O my friend, is there anything you can say against this proof?

Eighth Proof

O my friend, you consider yourself intelligent, but you make illogical statements, just like my ego! You do not wish to recognize the maker of this incredible palace. Yet, everything indicates him, points to him and bears witness to him. How can you reject all of these testimonies? If you do so, you might as well reject the existence of this palace, too. Can you say, 'There is no palace and no world'? Can you deny your own existence? No. Then, come to your senses and listen.

Look, there are basic elements that are constantly found throughout the palace. (These elements are air, water, light, and earth, which have very regular duties, and which hasten to the aid of all the needy with the permission of their Sustainer (*rabb*). They enter everywhere at the command of God, support life and nurse all living beings. They become the loom for the weaving of the 'fabrics' and 'embroideries' of Divine artistry.) It is as if everything that exists in this place is made up from these substances. This means that whoever owns those elements is the owner of all the things made up from them. Just like whoever owns the field owns its harvest and whoever owns the sea owns all that is within it.

For example, look at these embroidered beautiful fabrics; see how they are woven from the same few elements. Obviously the one who creates these substances, while making them into thread must be one and the same being because such a dynamic task can only be the work of one maker, who creates, sustains, and constantly changes the fabrics as well as their constituents. Such a dynamic, animate task does not admit partnership. Surely, all similarly woven, artistic fabrics must be his.

Also, look: the things that are woven and manufactured here are found throughout the country. They are all made at the same time, one within each other, following the same style. Thus, they must be the work of the one and same being; everything must be happening through his command. Otherwise, it is impossible for them to happen all at the same time, and display the same style and form, and share the same look.

Therefore, each of these works of art is bearing witness to that unseen maker; they all point to him. It is as if each flowery fabric, each well-designed machine, and each tasty bite is a *trademark, a stamp* and a *sign* indicating him. Each declares through its mode of being (*lisān al-hal*): 'Whoever made me is also the owner of the boxes and shops in which I am found.' Each embroidered pattern says: 'Whoever weaved me on this fabric is the same one who made the entire bolt.' Each tasty bite declares, 'Whoever is cooking me is the owner of the entire pot in which I am cooked.' Each machine says,

'Whoever manufactured me is the maker of all my kind that is found throughout the palace. Hence, he is the same one who owns the entire palace.[19] Moreover, only the one who rules the whole palace, and everything in it can be our maker.' Think of this metaphor: a state uniform, or even a button, that bears the state logo is clearly from the state factory. If an irregular soldier appropriated it, he would be told: 'Stop, that is state property!' and he would face consequences.

In sum: Given that the elements of this place are found throughout this amazing palace, [and that they exhibit qualities beyond their capacities] it can be deduced that whoever owns these elements owns the whole country. Similarly, the artwork, which is spread throughout the country and forms a unified embroidery indicates the same artist who rules over everything.

Hence, my friend, consider the sign of unity in this country and trademark of oneness on this incredible palace. Here there are simple elements that pervade the entire palace (this refers to things like air in reality). Other things are complex but they resemble each other and are found throughout the country. Thus, they also indicate a sort of unity. As a result, this oneness apparent in the palace reveals the One. That is, the maker, artist, and owner of such a unified whole must be One.

Furthermore, look at this: a thick thread is emerging as if out of nowhere or from behind the curtain of the unseen. (The thick rope refers to a fruit tree and its thousands of threads represent the tree's branches. As for the diamond, sign, and gifts attached to the tip of each thread, they represent the various flowers and different fruits.) Thousands of threads are issuing from this thick one. Look at the end of each thread: a diamond, a symbol, and a gift are attached to it. It offers an appropriate gift to everyone. Wouldn't you want to acknowledge and thank this artist sovereign, who brings out in such an incredible manner such wonderful gifts to all beings? One would have to be insane to reject him. For, if you don't recognize him, you would have to claim that 'All these threads are producing the dia-

---

[19] In this sentence and the next, the reference is to 'country' which we rendered as 'palace' to keep the parable easier to follow.

monds and gifts attached to them and offering them to us.' This would mean that each thread is an artist sovereign on its own. And yet, you see before your own eyes that these threads themselves are being made. An unseen hand is making these threads as well as the gifts attached to them. Therefore, in this palace everything points—more than to its own self—to that wondrous artist. If you reject him, you would have to deny all this reality before you...

Ninth Proof

Come my unreasoning friend! You not only do not recognize the maker of this palace, but you also do not wish to do so. For it seems too overwhelming to you. Since you cannot comprehend his miraculous art and ever-changing creations, you go astray and deny him. In reality, incomprehensibility and incongruity lie in rejecting him. For if we recognize him, then the existence of this entire palace, this entire world, will be as easy as that of one single thing. The abundance and ease we see before us become understandable.

If we were to reject him and if he did not exist, then the existence of every single thing would be as complicated and difficult as the existence of the entire palace, for every part is as sophisticated as the whole. [It requires for its existence the same all-encompassing power and knowledge as the entire palace; since everything is intricately interconnected and therefore one single thing can only exist within the whole world.] If he did not exist, there would not be the ease and abundance that we see throughout; we would not be able to obtain a single thing, let alone all these things around us.

As an example, just look at the sweet wholesome juice pack attached to the thread there. (Juice pack represent blessings of mercy, such as melons, watermelon, pomegranate, and coconut). If it did not come out of his unseen miraculous kitchen, we would not be able to afford it. Instead of being able to get these fruits for just a couple dollars at the market, we would not be able to get them even for thousands of dollars.[20]

---

[20] Nursi refers to 'cheapness' of fruits in the market to emphasize their abundance and ease with which these fruits are brought into being.

Indeed, rejecting him is overwhelming, very difficult, problematic, catastrophic[21] and unreasonable. Indeed, consider a tree: since a tree receives life from *one* root system, *one* center and through *one* principle, the formation of thousands of fruits is as easy as one fruit. If each of these fruits were connected to different centers, roots systems and principles, then each fruit would be as complicated as a tree. To give another metaphor, if all the uniforms for a company was made in one center, through one principle and in one factory, it would be as easy as taking care of one employee's outfit in the company. If each employee's uniform was made in a different place, you would need an entire factory for each employee's uniform.

Just like in the two examples above, in this well-ordered palace, if you attribute all these things to one being, everything will be so easy and effortless that it will result in the ease, abundance and generosity that we see. Otherwise, everything would be so complicated and difficult that we could not afford to obtain anything, even if we paid the whole world as a price.

Tenth Proof

Come, my friend, you've become a bit more reasonable. Look, we have been here for fifteen days now. (Fifteen days correspond to the fifteen years of age, which is the age of responsibility) If we don't learn about the procedures of this place and do not recognize the sovereign of this palace, we will face consequences.[22] We have no excuse any more. They have given us fifteen days to figure things out. Now it is clear that we are not just left to our own devices here. In the midst of all these beautiful, balanced, delicate, and meaningful works of art, we cannot act like animals messing around and messing

---

[21] Again, while Nursi does not explain here why rejecting *tawhid* is catastrophic, it is noteworthy that he makes occasional references to it. Nursi seems to highlight that *tawhid* does not have mere intellectual import, rather it is extremely important for human life and can lead to peace or suffering. He explains such existential importance of *tawhid* in earlier chapters excerpted in this volume.

[22] The consequences represent suffering in this world and the next as a result of turning away from the Creator.

up.[23] They will not let us spoil this place. The owner of this amazing palace must also have incredible chastisement.

See how the maker arranges this huge world ('ālam) like a palace, and takes care of it as if it were a house, without leaving anything lacking. You can understand how powerful and awesome the maker of this place is. Look: every now and then he fills up this palace, with utmost order and then empties it with utmost wisdom. He achieves all this as easily as filling a cup and emptying it. And, with the ease of setting up a table and cleaning it, he sets up manifold feasts throughout the palace. (The feast tables represent the face of the earth in the summer. Hundreds of fresh meals, which come out of the Divine kitchens of mercy, are laid out. Each vegetable garden is like a cooking pot, each tree like a server.) He brings in various dishes one after the other and feeds everyone. Also, if you would just reason, you would see and understand that within this incredible majesty there is abundant generosity.

And, just as all these things bear witness to the oneness of that unseen maker, the constant changes, shifts, and transformations point to his endurance. Caravans of beings pass one after the other, curtains are opened and closed, and new beings emerge and then disappear. Moreover, things as well as their seeming causes all decline

---

[23] As noted earlier, Nursi considers rejection of *tawhid* is an insult and transgression against the universe (as explained in Chapter 9). A contemporary Muslim scholar, S. Hossein Nasr, also highlights a connection between rejection of *tawhid* and the mistreatment of nature. According to this view, when human beings turn away from *tawhid* and reject that nature is a sacred sign of God, they not only harm themselves but also mistreat the environment, which leads to the environmental catastrophes. See Nasr, *Man and Nature: The Spiritual Crisis in Modern Man*. Nasr understands the following Quranic passage as indicating, among other things, environmental crisis *Corruption has appeared on land and sea as a result of people's actions and [God] will make them taste the consequences of some of their own actions so that they may turn back.* (Q. 30:41) Also see Ozdemir, *The Ethical Dimension of Human Attitude Towards Nature: A Muslim Perspective.* For a discussion of Nursi's approach, see Ozdemir, Ibrahim. 'Bediuzzaman Said Nursi's Approach to the Environment.'

and disappear.[24] And, after the demise of seeming causes, the results we attributed to them occur again. This shows that seeming causes were not actually the makers. Rather, this parade of beings, this constant flow, must be the work of someone enduring, a maker who is not passing or transient.

Consider this metaphor: there is a river flowing in front of us. As the river gushes forth, we see that bubbles rise up, they shine, and then fade away. New bubbles come after them and shine as well. That is, while the bubbles are passing, the light source that reflects on them is enduring. Likewise, given that things before us change quickly and are replaced with others with similar qualities, they must be the manifestations, mirrors, artworks and embroideries of one enduring and everlasting being.

Eleventh Proof

Come my friend! Now, I shall show you a proof that is as strong as the last ten proofs. Come, we will board a ship and sail to a faraway island which contains the answers to this mysterious palace and country.[25] (The ship represents history and the island represents the 'Era of Happiness,' the time of Prophet Muhammad, peace be upon him. Standing at the dark 'shore' of our present era, let us take off the 'clothes' of 'uncivil civilization,' plunge into the 'sea' of time, and board on the 'ship' of the prophet's biography. Let's go and visit the Pride of the World, peace be upon him, at work. We will realize that he is a shining proof of *tawhid* that has changed the face of the earth and enlightened the two 'faces' of time—the past and the future—and has extinguished the darkness of unbelief and misguidance.) Everyone looks to that island with high expectation and receives orders from there. Let's go there.

---

[24] For instance, not only does a child grows up and then pass away, but the parents who seemingly caused the child's life also die.

[25] To make it easier to follow the metaphor of traveling used here, in addition to 'palace,' we decided to include Nursi's reference to 'country' in this section of 'Eleventh Proof.'

Here, we have arrived at the island. Look, there is a very big gathering here. It is as if all the leading people of this place are gathered here for an important celebration. Look closely. See there is the head of this important committee. Let's approach further and get to know that leader.

Look, he is wearing so many shining medals. (These medals represent the miracles of the Prophet, peace be upon him, that number up to a thousand, according to several truth-seeking and discerning Muslim scholars[*muḥaqqiqīn*]).

Listen: his discourse is profound and powerful and his conversations with people are so enjoyable. During my stay here for two weeks, I have learned a little from what they say; and you may learn from me. Look, he is talking about the wondrous maker of this palace. He is saying that the glorious king of this place has sent him to us. Look, he is performing miracles that assure us that he is indeed a special envoy of that king.[26]

Pay attention: not only do the beings on the island listen to what he is saying, but surprisingly, his voice also reaches the entire

---

[26] Nursi is implicitly making use of the traditional view of miracles in Islamic theology. According to this view, God enables the prophets to perform extraordinary events as an evidence of their being a prophet. For a discussion of traditional Islamic views on the evidentiary value of prophetic miracles see Yazicioglu, *Understanding*, 18–19. While Nursi acknowledges this traditional view and considers miracles as part of evidences for Muhammad being a messenger of God, he emphasizes other evidences, such as the Quran. Indeed, as he puts in the introduction of his treatise on the Prophet's miracles ('*muʿjizāt aḥmadiya*'), 'All the states and acts of the Noble Messenger, upon whom be blessings and peace, testified to his veracity and prophethood, but not all of them had to be miraculous. For God Almighty sent him in the form of a human being so that he might be a guide and leader to human beings in their social affairs, and in the acts and deeds by means of which they attain happiness in both worlds. [Moreover, God sent him as a messenger] 'so that he might disclose to human beings the wonders of Divine art and His dispositive power that underlie all occurrences and are in appearance customary, but in reality are miracles of Divine power.' (*Letters*, '19th Letter, Fourth Sign, First Principle,' tr. by Vahide, *Letters*, 122).

world. Everyone, even from afar, is harkening to his speech. Not only people but also animals and even mountains listen to the commands he conveys (these represent the miracles of the Prophet). See how mountains are moving in response to him. Look how these trees move around and go to the places he points. He brings forth water from wherever he wishes. Look, when he signals to a lamp in the high dome of this royal palace, it splits and becomes two lamps (This 'royal lamp' represents the moon, which was divided into two at a gesture from the Prophet.)[27] This means that this entire palace acknowledges that he is appointed by the king. They obey him in a way as if they know that he is the most special and trustworthy envoy of the unseen wondrous owner. This person is a herald of the king, he deciphers for them the mysteries of the kingdom and reliably relays the orders of the king.

Indeed, all reasonable people around him confirm the truth of what he is saying. 'Yes, yes, certainly,' they say in response to him. Indeed, in this country, even the mountains, trees, and the major lamp (refers to the sun) that enlightens the whole country confirm this person's trustworthiness by obeying his commands.[28]

Now my deluded friend! Can you have any doubts about the message of such a person who carries thousands of medals from the royal treasury and who is acknowledged by wonderful and clear-headed people, as well as by all the leading people of this palace? Can you still doubt the wondrous maker that this envoy is speaking of and whose commands he is conveying? If this message were false, then we would have to assume that all the existence and the truth of

---

[27] Nursi continues his explanation in the footnote: 'As Mawlana Jami' said, 'That illiterate *ummi* prophet, wrote an *alif* on the sky with the pen of his finger and thus turned forty into two fifty.' That is, before being split, the moon looks like *mim* in the Arabic alphabet whose numerical value is forty. After the miracle of being split, it became two crescents, looking like a pair of *nuns* in the Arabic alphabet, each of which has a numerical value of fifty.'
[28] Nursi's footnote here reads: 'The sun's movement from east to west was momentarily reversed so that Imam Ali (may God be pleased with him), who was with the Prophet (peace and blessings be upon him) and was about to miss his late afternoon prayer, would be able to pray on time.'

this palace, lamps, and this community is false! However, that is clearly not the case. How about you use your reason and reflect?

Twelfth Proof

Come brother, you seem to have awakened a little. Now I shall show you a proof that is as powerful as the last eleven proofs. See, there is a shining decree descending from high above. (The shining decree represents the Quran and the seal on it is its miraculous nature [*i'jāz*]) Everyone is looking at it closely, with wonder or with awe. That person with a thousand medals is standing next to it and explaining its meaning to the public.

Look, the decree is so full of light that it attracts everyone's attention. And it talks about such serious and important topics that everyone feels compelled to consider it attentively. For it clearly explains/discloses the 'essential qualities,' (*shu'unāt*) actions, commands and attributes of the one who makes and sustains this incredible palace.

See, there is a major royal seal on this decree. You can also see authentic royal seal on every line and sentence in the decree. The truthful meanings and the wisdom expressed throughout the decree also indicate that only the king of the palace could have issued it. In sum, anyone who is not blind can see that this great decree reveals the great king, as clear as the sun on the sky.

Now, my friend! If you came to your senses, these proofs should suffice. What do you say? The stubborn man replied: 'In response to all these proofs, all I can say is 'Thank God, I now believe!' Indeed, I have believed with the clarity of the bright sunshine on a clear day that there is indeed one perfect owner of this palace. I recognize that there is one majestic maker of this world, and this palace has a beautiful artistic maker. Thank you so much! You have saved me from madness and obstinacy. I must admit that actually each one of the proofs you mentioned was sufficient by itself. Yet, as you expounded each proof, more profound, more lovely, more beautiful and brighter horizons of knowledge opened up. With each new proof, more and more curtains were unveiled and windows unto love were opened. That is why I preferred to keep silent and listen.'

This is the end of the parable, which points to the great truth of the oneness of God (*tawhid*) and the belief in God (*amantu billah*).

Now, we shall explain twelve 'flashes' from the sun of truth of *tawhid* that correspond to the twelve proofs in the story. Let us proceed, with the grace of the Merciful, blessings from the Quran and assistance from the light of belief (*īmān*). *And from God proceeds all success and guidance.*

13

SUPERFICIAL VS. TRUE *TAWHID*: UNPACKING THE PARABLE

If there had been in them [the heavens and the earth] any gods other than God, surely both would have been corrupted!

So, glory be to God, Lord (rabb) of the Throne, beyond what they describe!

—Quran, 21:22

There is no moving creature, which He does not hold by its fore-lock. Truly, my Sustainer (rabb) is on a straight path!

—Quran, 11:56

This selection is the 'Second Station' of the 22nd Word. It unpacks the extended parable contained in its first station (translated in Chapter 12). It contains 'twelve flashes' that correspond to 'twelve proofs' of the parable. Each 'flash' clarifies the parable's implications and adds substantial depth. The text resonates with the classical approaches in Islamic theology that infers God's existence, oneness and main attributes from nature, as seen in the works of theologians such as al-Baqillani (d.1013), al-Juwayni (d. 1085), al-Ghazali (d. 1111), and

Fakhr al-din al-Razi (d. 1210).[1] However, this text goes further than establishing the existence of God and emphasizes getting to know the Beautiful Names of God through contemplating nature. In that regard, Nursi's approach here has more affinity with mystical thinkers such as Jalaluddin al-Rumi (d. 1273) and Ibn al-Arabi (d. 1240) offering much more in that they considered proving the existence of God merely as a starting point, and emphasized focused on journeying into knowing and loving God.

The 'First Flash' acts as an introduction to the unpacking of the parable. It offers a crucial distinction between two types of tawhid: superficial (*al-tawhid al-zahiri*) and genuine (*al-tawhid al-ḥaqiqi*). The former is a popular but deficient inference of oneness of God from nature, while the latter is a detailed and well-grounded one. Nursi notes that the treatise is meant to offer 'flashes' that show the 'genuine tawhid.' Moreover, the first flash discusses the role of 'seeming causes' in creation. The seeming causes have no efficacy or power, and yet they are placed in the world for two main purposes. First, they serve as a 'screen' onto which divine power and qualities manifest. To give an example: we repeatedly observe that life appears along with water. Yet, upon reflection with Quranic cues, we realize that water is only a *seeming* cause of life. It has no power to give life, itself being lifeless and unconscious. Water is thus simply a *screen* onto which the glimpses of Divine power and qualities such as Life Giver reflect. In Nursi's words, water, like other seeming causes, is simply an 'announcer' of the Beautiful Names of God. Interestingly, the seeming causes have another purpose: to veil the Divine agency

---

[1] Their arguments that make use of 'signs' in the empirical world do not neatly fit in with the classification of arguments for God in Western thought. For instance, in the case of Baqillani, his argument 'presents a distinctive type of argument that cannot be classified under the classical types of ontological, cosmological, and design arguments.' It is an argument made up of sub-arguments such as 'argument from accidents, the argument from particularization, the argument from design, the argument for eternity, and the argument for uniqueness' for which Nazif Muhtaroglu coins the term 'cosmological argument from agency.' See: 'al-Baqillani's Cosmological Argument From Agency,' 271–289.

from the heedless people and their potential unjust accusations. The inner reality of all things, including death, is beautiful, however in the sight of the heedless, who cannot see beyond appearances, many things seem ugly. In those situations, seeming causes constitute a sort of veil that 'hinder' the heedless from seeing the divine agency so that they are deterred from accusing divine mercy. In this text, Nursi spends more time on this second wisdom behind the creation of seeming causes.

This treatise can be considered as another elaboration of Nursi's earlier treatise on *bismillah*, the 'First Word,' It shows in more detail how the universe is constantly speaking about God, declaring His beautiful names, glorifying and praising Him through their way of being or 'tongue of disposition' (*lisān al-ḥāl*), in the way they come into existence, change and pass away. As noted earlier, in classical Islamic sources, references to nature as praising God and as speaking of God are common. Nursi's distinctive contribution lies in explaining *how* the process of glorification happens by engaging with natural phenomena and causality in detail. Moreover, Nursi makes a cogent case for the dynamism of the creation. The universe is a *dynamic* 'book' that is being written continuously by a 'pen' of power. Or as Nursi also puts it elsewhere, 'the constant creativity in the universe is silent speech glorifying God.'[2] Things praise God constantly, in every moment, in their various states of being. Nursi intends to disabuse the reader from a static perception of creation—a world that is

---

[2] 'It was made known to me with complete certainty that the activity of divine power in the universe and the constant flood of beings are so meaningful that through them the All-Wise Maker causes all the realms of beings in the universe to speak. It is as if the beings of the earth and the skies and their motion and actions are the words of their speech; their motion is their speech. That is, the movement and transience arising from activity is speech glorifying God. The activity in the universe is the silent speech of the universe and that of the varieties of its beings; their being made to speak.' Nursi, *Letters*, 340, modified translation. For original text, see Nursi, *Mektubat*, '24. Mektub, Ikinci Remiz,' RNK 1: 481. For discussion of this passage and Nursi's understanding of the universe as speech glorifying God, see the introduction chapter of this book.

created once and continues to function on its own—to a world that is constantly undergoing change and transformation and therefore requires continuous creation, bringing into existence, and sustaining.

Another misunderstanding regarding the absolute Unseen Maker stems from misconception of natural laws. Some claim that the laws of nature are responsible for the unfolding of this amazingly complex and immense universe. They attribute power, knowledge and creativity to the so-called 'laws of nature.' Yet, the 'laws of nature' are simply descriptions of regularities in nature, they do not make such regularities happen. In other words, a law of nature is not an operant agent acting in the world. It is merely a description that expresses an observed regularity, as Nursi discusses elsewhere.[3] To appreciate that the 'laws of nature' cannot be responsible for the events in the universe, let us think about the case of a mother who has a very regular habit of making pancakes every Sunday morning. After having observed this regularity in the house, her child may infer a 'Sunday pancake rule or law,' on the basis of which he successfully predicts the breakfast menu for Sundays. However, 'Sunday pancake law' is only a useful description of what happens in the house, it is not an explanation and even less an active agent. Sunday pancake law does not make the pancakes! Similarly, as American philosopher Charles Peirce explains, 'no law of nature makes a stone fall, or a Leyden jar to discharge, or a steam engine to work.' Indeed, he notes that 'a law of nature left to itself would be quite analogous to a court without a sheriff.' Continuing the analogy, he rightly notes 'A court in that predicament might probably be able to induce some citizen to act as sheriff; but until it had so provided itself with an officer who, unlike itself, could not discourse authoritatively but who could put forth the strong arm, its law might be the perfection of human reason but would remain mere fireworks, *brutum fulmen*.

---

[3] Nursi, *Words*, 709; Nursi, *Flashes*, 246. Nursi also says, 'The imagination got deluded into reifying them (the natural laws) [collectively] as 'Nature,' and considered the latter as an external efficacious being and an operative reality, though it is no more than a mental estimation and a theoretical law.' Nursi, 'Preface to the Al-Mathnawī,' 341 (italics added).

Just so, let a law of nature—say the law of gravitation—remain a mere uniformity—*a mere formula* establishing a relation between terms—and *what in the world would induce a stone*, which is not a term nor a concept but just a plain thing, to act in conformity to that uniformity?'[4] In sum, it does not make sense to claim that natural laws are responsible for the universe.[5] To explain this amazingly complex and dynamic universe there is need for the agency of an amazing absolute maker.[6]

Moreover, as noted in the introduction to the previous chapter, being overwhelmed by the greatness of the Maker implied by the universe is not to be mistaken for a logical problem. Elsewhere, Nursi explains that the wise and fruitful way to channel such feelings of being overwhelmed is to remind oneself that we infer the existence and beautiful names of the Sustainer of the universe from our observations of the world. Certainly, the Maker Who sustains the whole universe and all beings within it at all times *must be* greater than anything human beings can comprehend. Therefore, the appropriate response to being at awe is to praise the Maker. Nursi notes that this is why the declaration of *allāhu akbar* ('God is the greatest') is repeatedly declared in all Islamic rituals, such as in daily worship and

---

[4] Peirce, *Collected Papers*, 5.48:1903.

[5] Similarly, Muhammad Basil Altaie, a contemporary Muslim physicist, notes that 'the laws of nature cannot stand alone. Some agency has to drive these laws in accordance with the algorithm they describe. [Moreover,] the laws of nature need to be coordinated for a fruitful result to be achieved.' ('Paving the Way for the Reformation,' in *Islam and Science*, 80). For his detailed analysis see: Altaie, *God, Nature and the Cause: Essays on Islam and Science*, 27–50.

[6] In another treatise, entitled 'Treatise of Nature,' Nursi analyzes in detail three major claims presented as alternatives to *tawhid:* 1) Natural causes are creating things and events, 2) Things are coming into being and happening by themselves, 3) Nature or natural laws are making things happen. Each of these claims fails to explain the fact that things in the universe are happening very wisely and with immense, and utterly harmonious interconnection with the rest of the world while *tawhid* is the only viable explanation. See 'Treatise of Nature,' in 26th Flash, *Flashes*, 232–254.

during the pilgrimage (*hajj*). Through the 'light' of *allāhu akbar*, 'the hearts of utterly limited and weak human beings' become capable of recognizing the immense truths of Divine power.'[7] Like he did in the case of *bismillah*, Nursi once again shows how key motifs in Islamic rituals, such as *allāhu akbar*, are linked to the purpose of the creation. He demonstrates how sacred Quranic phrases used in Islamic worship and rituals serve as guides and pointers of the reality of the world, as well as landmarks and the best responses to it, as expressions of awe and gratitude.

***

SIGNS OF *TAWHID* IN THE UNIVERSE[8]

God is the Creator of all things, and He alone has the power to determine the fate of all things. Unto Him belong the keys of the heavens and the earth. (Q. 39: 62–63)

Limitless, then, in His glory is He in whose hand rests the mighty dominion over all things; and unto Him you all shall be brought back! (Q. 36:83)

And there is not a thing but its (inexhaustible) treasures are with Us.
And We do not send it down except according to a well-defined measure. (Q. 15:21)

Behold, I have put my trust in God, [who is] my Sustainer as well as your Sustainer: for there is no moving creature, but that He holds by its forelock. Truly, my Sustainer is on a straight path! (Q. 11:56)

Note: We have explained the evidences for belief in God, which is the heart of the pillars of belief elsewhere in more detail. For in-

---

[7] Nursi, *Lem'alar*, '13. Lem'a, 13. Isaret,' RNK 1:627; Nursi, *Flashes*, '13th Flash, 13th Indication,' 123.

[8] Nursi, *Sözler*, '22. Söz, Ikinci Makam' (22nd Word, Second Station), RNK 1:121–131, title added by editors.

stance, in the Treatise 'Droplet' (in *Mathnawi al-Nūrī*) we have noted how all beings indicate and bear witness to the necessity of His existence and His Oneness in fifty-five ways. Similarly, in the Treatise 'Point' (in *Mathnawi al-Nūrī*), we have noted four major proofs for the existence and oneness of God, each of which is as strong as thousands of proofs. Moreover, in my twelve treatises composed in Arabic, we have noted hundreds of pieces of evidence for belief in One. Referring to the reader to such detailed treatments of the topic, here we shall only briefly expound on Twelve Flashes from the light of belief in God.

First Flash

Belief in the oneness of God (*tawḥid*) is of two types. Let's explain these two types through the following analogy. Say a great variety of goods manufactured by the same great producer arrived to all the markets in town. There are two ways you could understand that these goods belong to this great producer.

The first is an unspecific and common people's way. You say, 'Wow! All these great goods can only be from so-and-so company, no local production or merchant could produce or possess these many goods and with this great variety.' Such a statement is not based on careful analysis of evidence but on mere quantity. If you were entrusted with the protection of these goods, you would not be able to recognize all kinds of possible 'petty' stealing from the merchandise. Indeed, many people could claim parts of the merchandise as theirs and get away with it as long as it remained limited in amount.

There is also a second way of recognizing that all these goods belong to the same great manufacturer. It is to see the logo of the producer in every single thing. This way, you note the manufacturer's signature in every shirt, every towel, every furniture item, every ad, and so on. That is how you can conclude, 'All these goods belong to that great manufacturer.' That is, you see how each item points to the same great maker.

Just like the two approaches in this parable, there are two types of *tawhid,* i.e. of recognizing the oneness of God. First, there is the superficial and popular *tawhid,* which amounts at declaring: 'There is only one God, He has no partner or like. This entire universe belongs to God.' The second is the authentic and genuine *tawhid*. You see in every single thing the stamp of the One's power and the logo of His sustainership (*rubūbiyya*). Through genuine *tawhid*, you find a window on to God's light in each being. You affirm that every single thing comes from God's hand of power and that He has no partner in His divinity, sustainership and property (*mulk*). Genuine tawhid is an affirmation that is almost as certain as directly witnessing and thus brings a sense of being in His presence at all times (*al-ḥuḍūr al-daimī*). In this treatise, we shall note 'gleams' that reveal such sincere and elevated genuine *tawhid*.

An important reminder

O heedless person who is stuck in seeming causes! Realize that seeming causes are a mere veil to the One; they are not the real cause of events. This veil is wisely placed by the One who has dignity and grandeur. At the same time, His oneness and majesty mean that all events are executed only by the power of the Eternally Self-Sufficient One on whom everything depends (*al-qudra al-ṣamadāniyya*). Indeed, note this well: the employees of this Eternal King are not in any way assisting in the ruling of His kingdom. Rather, these employees—the seeming causes—are merely declaring His power and bearing witness to His sustainership. The wisdom behind God's employment of such means in His creation is to reveal the dignity/honor (Tk. *izzet*, Ar. *'izza*) of His power and to disclose the majesty/grandeur of His sustainership. In 'lowly' events, these seeming causes hide the connection to Divine power from the sight of the heedless. Thus, these seeming causes and veils do not help God in the execution of any task; the Eternal King is not like human kings who, out of weakness, need ministers and helpers to rule. God creates all things and sustains them into existence, including the seeming causes.

In other words, seeming causes are placed in the creation in order to protect the glory of Divine power from the misperceptions and false assumptions of superficial, heedless reasoning.

For, all created things have two aspects like the two sides of a mirror. One apparent aspect, which looks to the world (*mulk*), and another inner aspect.

The apparent aspect of things is like the dark side of a mirror as it reflects various 'colors,' conditions and situations. The other inner aspect of things (*malakūt*) looks to their Maker. It is like the shiny side of the mirror, always bright and clear. In the apparent aspect there are states that are at variance with the dignity and perfection of the power of the Eternally Self-Sufficient One on whom everything depends. So, seeming causes have been placed as the point of re-course and root of those states. However, as far as the inner aspect that looks to reality is concerned, everything is transparent and beau-tiful; it is befitting of being directly associated with divine power, as it is compatible with divine dignity and glory. Accordingly, seeming causes are superficial only. In actual fact, they possess no real effect.

Another wisdom behind the creation of seeming causes is that they divert unjust complaints and baseless objections from the Abso-lutely Just One. Instead, such unfair complaints and objections are directed to seeming causes. [Indeed, from the viewpoint of heedless-ness, the only discernible aspect of things is the one looking to seem-ing causes.] Therefore, the imperfections associated with this aspect pertain to the shortcomings and inability of seeming causes. Here is a symbolic narration that elucidates this mystery:

It is said that 'Azra'īl, the angel of death (upon whom be peace), said to God: 'Your servants will resent me when it is time to take their souls.' Through the tongue of wisdom God replied to him, 'I shall place between you and them the veil of calamities and sickness, so that they will not resent you for death; rather, they will blame the calamity or sickness.'[9]

See, sickness is a veil that deflects the unfair complaints lodged because of the imagined ugliness in the appointed hour. In reality, there is beauty and wisdom in 'Azra'īl's (peace upon him) task of seizing souls. At the same time, the angel of death is also a veil: he has

---

[9] In other words, the true believers in God, those who know Him with His most beautiful names and trust His wisdom and mercy, are aware of the inner beautiful aspect of things that looks to their Maker. Hence, they real-ize that death is not annihilation but the passage to eternal paradise, and therefore it a cause of joy and gratitude, not of distress. As a result, they do not resent the angel of death, who only obeys God's commands.

been appointed as an 'observer' of and a veil to divine power so that seemingly merciless affairs that are incompatible with the perfection of divine mercy may be ascribed to him.

In sum, exaltedness and grandeur require that seeming causes be a veil to Divine power for those with superficial vision. While, divine oneness (*tawhid*) and majesty require that seeming causes 'give up' any claim to agency and the creation of effects.

Second Flash

Look at this garden of the universe! And, pay attention to the garden of earth and to the lovely face of the heavens embellished with stars! You shall see that there is on each work of art a *trademark* (*sikka*) that is unique to the Creator of All. Similarly, on each created thing there is a *stamp* (*khātam*) exclusive to the Maker of All. And, you shall see that there is an *exclusive signature* (*turra*) of the Divine 'pen' of power 'inscribed' on the 'pages' of night and day, summer and spring.

Now, we shall give some examples of such trademarks, signatures and stamps of the One. For instance, among the innumerable 'trademarks' of God, see the one placed on *life*: *He makes many things from one thing and one thing from many things.* Indeed, He creates innumerable organs from a drop[10] and from water.

Now, making so many things from one thing must certainly be the work of the Absolutely Powerful One. Similarly, to turn innumerable and various types of food, including animal-based and plant-based nutrition, into a well-organized specific organ or skin or tissue can only be the feat of an All-Knowing One who has power over all things. Indeed, through His wisdom and a law proceeding from His command, the Creator of Death and Life sustains life so miraculously that it is clear that only one who has total control over the entire universe can enforce such a law.

Now, if your mind is still sane and your heart has not turned blind, then you will understand that to transform one thing and make it into so many things with perfect ease and order, and to turn

---

[10] This drop is interpreted as a fluid mixture of the seminal fluid and egg.

many things into one thing with remarkable precision and balance is a trademark unique to the Maker and Creator of All.

For instance, if you see a miracle worker take an ounce of cotton and from it produce hundreds of yards of various fabrics, including linen and silk. He also makes many foods such as cakes and sweets from it. And then you see him take some iron and stone, honey and butter, water and soil into his hand, and turn it into fine gold. If you see all this, you will certainly conclude that he possesses a unique and exceptional skill since all the elements of the earth are under his command and submit to his will. Now, the manifestations of power and wisdom in life are tremendously more impressive than this example. Thus, is one of the many *trademarks* of the Divine on the phenomenon of life!

Third Flash

Look at the living beings in this flowing universe! You will notice that on each living being there are numerous *stamps* of the Living and Enduring One (*al-ḥayy al-qayyum*). One example of such stamps is thus:

A living being, such as a human being, is like a small 'sample/summary' of the entire universe. That is, the human being contains samples from most of the various realms in the universe;[11] he is like the fruit of the tree of creation and the seed of this entire world. It is as if this living being is a drop drawn out/distilled from the entire universe in a very delicate and balanced measure. Hence, to create and sustain this living being requires complete command over the entire universe.

- To make a word of power, such as a honey bee, into a minute index of nearly everything in the universe

- To write in one page, such as a human being, most matters of this book of the universe

---

[11] For a brief explanation of how a human being is connected to many different realms in existence, see Chapter 6, 'First Indication.'

- To include in a tiny 'dot', such as a fig seed, the program of a huge fig tree.

- To show in one 'letter', such as the human heart, all the traces of the Most Beautiful Names (*al-asmā al-ḥusnā*) manifested throughout the 'pages' of this macrocosm, which they encompass.

- To insert a huge library, containing innumerable collections and pieces of information in the human memory.

- To include in the human brain a detailed summary of all events-pertaining to creation.[12]

All these examples constitute a special stamp of the Creator of all things and the Majestic Sustainer of the universe.

If one stamp of the Sustainer yields such light and draws attention to the reading of the Sustainer's signs (*āyāt*), imagine if you could perceive and behold the stamps of the Sustainer all together, wouldn't you exclaim, '*Glory be to the One who is hidden because of the intensity of His manifestation!*'?[13]

---

[12] Nursi's reference here to the human mind having 'a detailed summary of all events in the creation' may remind of the American thinker and scientist Charles Peirce's reflection on the connection between human mind and the universe. To start with, Peirce highlights the role of intuition in formulating a hypothesis. Theoretically, the number of possible hypotheses is endless, and if we were not gifted the capacity to guess correctly more quickly, testing them out would take forever and we would not be able to discover any laws or arrive at any scientific theories. And yet, Peirce rightly points out, we have been able to decipher many patterns in nature and advance in scientific knowledge. This must be because 'man's mind must have been attuned to the truth of things in order to discover what he has discovered.' (Peirce, *Collected Papers*, 6.476: 1908)

[13] This statement is in Arabic in the original (*subḥāna man ikhtafā bi shiddati zuhurihi*).

Fourth Flash

Now, look and pay attention to the colorful creatures and various works of art swimming in the ocean of existence, in the heavens and on the earth! You will see that in each of them there are inimitable signatures of the Eternal Sun. Just as we saw some of His *trademarks* on life, His *stamps* on living beings, He also has *signatures* on the *giving of life (ihya)*. Since metaphors facilitate the understanding of profound meanings, we shall use the following metaphor to illustrate this truth.

Think of the sun. The sun has a 'signature' on so many various things, from the planets to water drops, to shining snowflakes and small pieces of glass. In each, you see a reflection of the sun, a trace of light from the sun. Now, if you do not accept that all these reflections and 'tiny suns' manifest and mirror the sun's light, you will have to make a preposterous assumption, such as claiming that each water droplet, each piece of glass and any other transparent object that reflects light contains a genuine, real sun.

Similarly, *giving of life (ihya')* is among the luminous manifestations of the Eternal Sun. Even if all the seeming causes were to unite and each were a conscious agent possessing will (*fa'il mukhtār*), they would not be able to imitate this signature. For, living beings, which are all 'miracles of Divine power', are each like a focal point of the beautiful names stemming from the Eternal Sun.

Suppose you do not attribute the incredible artistic pattern, the wisely planned order and the mystery of unicity (*ahadiyya*) to the One on whom everything depends (*al-ṣamad*). Then, you will have to claim that within every single living being, even within a fly or a flower, there resides limitless creative power. Moreover, you will have to assume that each living being has knowledge that encompasses everything and a will that manages the entire universe. In fact, you will have to accept that eternal qualities unique to the Necessarily Existent (*wājib al-wujūd*) are contained within each particle. This would entail the preposterous conclusion that each particle of a fly or a flower is a god in itself!

For, these particles, especially the particles in seeds, behave in a way that takes into account the entire life of that living being such as a flower or a fly. They conform to the overall order of that living being. In fact, they even cohere with the entire species of that living being. For instance, look, how a seed functions in the process of reproduction: a seed is produced and spread around in such a way that it aims to continue the species of the living being it belongs to. It is as if a seed vies to 'waive the flag' of its species on earth, takes on wings and finds efficient ways to spread around and populate the earth with that species. In fact, a living being acts in a way that takes into account its needs from all other beings and its relationship and interdependence on others. Now, if these particles were not employed by an Absolutely Powerful One (*al-qadir al-mutlaq*), if they were disconnected from the Absolutely Powerful One, then each particle would have to possess a vision and a consciousness that comprehends everything [including the entire process and all the interrelationships that it involves].

In sum, let's remember our sun metaphor: if we do not attribute all the traces of light and the colors on water droplets and pieces of glass to the reflections of the sun, then we would have to accept the existence of innumerable suns in all of them as opposed to accepting one sun outside of them. A ridiculous belief indeed! Just like this, if we do not attribute all things to the Absolutely Powerful One, then we would have to believe in as many gods as the number of all the particles of the universe, instead of assenting to the existence of One God! That is the alternative to belief in One God is totally nonsensical and utterly unreasonable.

Thus, from each particle there opens up three windows onto the light of oneness and the necessary existence of the Eternal Sun:

First Window: Each particle is like a soldier. A soldier has a relation to its own unit, division, regiment, and so on, and he has a duty pertaining to his position within each of them. Similarly, a lifeless particle in your eyeball, for instance, has a relation to your eye, motor and sensory nerves, arteries and veins—that carry blood, your defense mechanisms, your powers of reproduction, attraction and repulsion—and to your species and so on. And it has a role and duty within each of these contexts. Thus, the particle reveals, to all who are willing to see, that it is the work of art of the Absolutely Powerful One and that it is employed and directed by the One who holds all under His power.

Second Window: Each molecule of air can visit any plant, flower or fruit. It can enter and work within any of them. Now if this particle of air were not employed by the Absolutely Powerful One who sees and knows all, then that roaming molecule of air would have to know all the various structures of each flower and fruit; it would have to be an incredible 'tailor' that knows how to 'weave' different 'outfits' and forms suitable for each plant.

Look, how this molecule of air reflects the light of divine oneness (*tawhid*) so clearly! You can compare particles of light, water and soil to the air. All these four elements are the basis of all beings after all. (To be sure, in contemporary science, the four basic building blocks are instead identified as hydrogen, oxygen, carbon and nitrogen, which are all parts of the former four elements.)[14]

Third Window: Let's take some soil, which is made up of particles and put it in a flower pot. And let's take any seed and place it in the soil. Plant seeds, like the 'seeds' of animals, do not differ from one another substantially, all are made from the same organic elements: carbon, nitrogen, hydrogen and oxygen. The seeds only differ from one another in regards to the abstract 'program' that the pen of divine decree and destiny has written in each of them. Now if we place different seeds in this pot of soil, one at a time, each will grow in its unique way, with its particular wonderful 'equipment' and form.

Now, if you do not ascribe these particles of soil to the One who knows all conditions and states of every single thing and is able to grant each of them an appropriate existence as well as everything necessary to sustain that existence; the One to whose power everything is easily subjugated, what could you say? If these particles are not employed by the One for whom all things are easy, if they are not His obedient servants, then there must be in each particle of soil factories to the number of various flowers and fruits, so that these particles could produce all the various species of plants, each of whom display vastly different structures and shapes. Each particle of soil would have to possess comprehensive knowledge and power so as to produce all these various plants. Thus, if you disconnect them from

---

[14] This bracketed sentence is in the original text.

the Creator, you would have to accept gods to the number of the particles of the soil! And that would be a most far-fetched fantasy!

In contrast, if each particle is a servant, then you can easily explain these things. A regular soldier of a great king can easily perform great things relying on the power of the king—he can make an entire population migrate; he can combine two seas and subdue a governor. Similarly, with the command of the Eternal King, a fly can subdue a Nimrod, an ant can bring down the palace of Pharaoh, and a tiny seed of a fig can turn into a huge fig tree.

Moreover, in each particle there are two trustworthy witnesses to the existence and oneness of the Maker (al-ṣāniʿ). First, each particle, despite its utter weakness, carries out enormous tasks. Moreover, despite being lifeless, it displays a comprehensive consciousness by acting in accordance with the universal order. Thus, each particle through the language of its weakness (ʿajz) bears witness to the necessary existence of the Absolutely Powerful (al-qādir al-muṭlaq). And, through the language of its obeying the order of the cosmos, it declares the *unity (waḥda)* of the Powerful. *And, just as in each particle there are two witnesses to the necessary existence and oneness (waḥda) of the One, in each living being, there are two signs pointing to the Unique One (aḥad) on whom everything depends (al-ṣamad).*[15]

Yes, indeed, on each living being there is a trademark of the Unique One and a signature of the Self-Sufficient One on whom everything depends (al-ṣamad). For, each reflects in its own mirror all the names (al-asmāʾ) that manifest throughout the universe. Each living being is like a focal point where the Greatest Name (al-ism al-aʿẓam) of the Ever-living and Self-Subsisting (al-ḥayy al-qayyūm) shines! Hence, each living being shows a shadow of the unicity of the Divine Essence (aḥadiyya dhātiyya) under the veil of the Giver of Life (muḥyī) thus bearing the trademark of unicity.

Moreover, given that each living being is a small summary of the entire universe and a fruit of the entire tree of creation, it shows the signature of the One on whom everything depends. For, its endless needs are met from unexpected corners of the universe with ease.

---

[15] This italicized sentence is in Arabic in the original text.

Hence, each living being has a Sustainer (*rabb*) whose regard is worth the entire universe. Even if all things were to unite, they could not replace the attention and regard of the One. *Yes, the Sustainer is sufficient for each thing from everything so that it needs no other thing than Him. And without Him, all things cannot be sufficient for even one single thing.*[16]

Besides, this situation shows that its Sustainer does not need anything and nothing decreases from the Sustainer's treasure and nothing is difficult for His power. This is a kind of signature that shows a reflection of the One on Whom Everything Depends.

Thus, each living being carries a trademark of the Unique One (*aḥad*) and a signature of the Self-Sufficient One on whom everything depends (*al-ṣamad*). Indeed, each living being recites *Say: 'He is the One God (aḥad), God the one on whom everything depends (al-ṣamad)'* (Q. 112 :1–2)

In addition to these two signs, there are several other important 'windows' opening to the One. We will skip it here, since we have explained it elsewhere. Thus, each particle presents three windows and two openings, and each living being opens two doors unto the unity (*wāḥidiyya*) of the Necessarily Existent One. You can deduce from this how all the levels of beings from particles to the sun spread the light of the Majestic One. See how there are endless degrees of spiritual progress in knowledge of God and in awareness of His presence.

Fifth Flash

Think of a handwritten book; only a pen is needed to write it. However, if you say that it was printed, then there is need for a whole printing press for it. There would need to be iron letters to the number of letters in the book. Besides, if the book contains big special letters that contain within it the summary of the entire book written in small letters and thin calligraphy, then you would need special tiny iron letters for printing just one such big letter. Instead of one pen,

---

[16] The italicized is in Arabic in the original.

you would thus need many different iron 'pens' to print that single book.

Similarly, if you attribute this book of the universe to the 'pen' of power of the Self-Sufficient One on whom everything depends and a message from the Unique One (*aḥad*), then things are easily explained. This explanation is so reasonable and so easy as to be necessary. In contrast, if you were to ascribe this book of the universe to nature and natural causes, your position would be so fraught with difficulties and so problematic as to be impossible; such delusion is intolerable. For, you'd have to assume that in each bit of soil and air, in each drop of water, there are millions of printing presses and intangible factories that produce the countless various flowers and fruits. Or you would have to claim that each bit of soil, air, and water possesses comprehensive knowledge and infinite power capable of producing all those beings.

For each bit of soil, water and air can be a source for most plants. Yet, each plant, especially the ones bearing fruits and flowers, is so well-ordered, so balanced, and each is so different from others, that for each plant, an intangible factory or a printing press would be necessary. In other words, if nature is not a work of art but an artist itself, you'd have to assume that in every single thing there are factories producing plants and everything else.

As you can see, this thought amounts to deifying nature and worshipping it. When analyzed closely, it is clear that it is totally preposterous. See how the people, who deem themselves so rational, end up with such irrational dogmas when they reject God. You make your decision accordingly.

In sum: Each letter of a book points to itself to the extent of its size. At the same time, the same letter also points to its author, in various other ways that exceed the extent of the letter itself. While it is only one letter, it speaks many words about its author. For instance, it says, 'My author has beautiful handwriting. His pen is red, and so on...' Similarly, a letter in this great book of the universe points to itself to the extent of its size. However, it describes the Names of its Eternal Calligrapher (*al-naqqāsh al-azalī*) to the length of a poem, and through its various states and shapes it points to His Names (*asmā*) and bears witness to its Owner. Thus, even if you were to subscribe to skepticism and deny everything, you should not go so far as denying the Majestic Maker![17]

Sixth Flash

The Majestic Creator has placed a trademark of uniqueness and unicity (*aḥadiyya*) on each being and every single part of His creatures. We have already seen some examples of such logos. Similarly, He has placed in a shining and bright way a trademark of unicity (*aḥadiyya*) on each species and a stamp of unity (*wāḥidiyya*) on each universal, and various signatures of oneness (*waḥda*) over the entire world. Now, from among all these various trademarks, stamps and signatures, let us witness just one logo and one stamp placed on the 'page of the earth' during the spring season.

During the spring and summer seasons, the Eternal Artist (*al-naqqāsh al-azalī*) resurrects hundreds of thousands of animal and plant species on the face of the earth. He does so with incredible distinction and order, without any confusion between the species, even though all the 'ingredients' of the species are totally intermingled. This state of affairs constitutes a clear and shining trademark of the oneness of God (*tawḥīd*) as clear and bright as the spring season!

Indeed, only the one who possesses endless power, comprehensive knowledge and a will that encompasses the entire universe can perform such a feat. Resurrecting hundreds of thousands of species out of a lifeless earth and creating innumerable beings without any fault, deficiency, or disorder, with complete order and perfection is a shining 'trademark' of the One. Only such a Glorious Maker, such a Powerful One full of Perfection and such a Wise One full of Beauty could accomplish all this. Thus, the Wise Quran, declares: *Observe then the vestiges of God's mercy—how He revives the earth after its death! Truly, He is the One Who brings the dead to life for He is Powerful over all things!* (Q. 30:50)

---

[17] In other words, even if we were to accept the skeptical view that this world is just a dream, the creator of such an elaborate and magnificent dream would still be necessary.

Yes, indeed, it is certainly easy for the Creative Power, which resurrects hundreds of thousands of species within several spring days, to resurrect a human being after death. Think of someone incredible who removes huge mountains with a swift wave of his hand. Would it be reasonable to doubt that he can remove a big stone on our path? Similarly, regarding the One who has created heavens, mountains and earth in six days, and constantly fills and empties them with endless creatures—will you suspect his ability to resurrect you? Would it be reasonable to wonder whether this Powerful Wise One, this Generous Merciful One, can remove the layer of grave soil from us so that we can attend his feast in the hereafter? Would it be fair to be skeptical about whether he can reform the earth to carry us to life after death?

Thus, we have seen a trademark of oneness (*tawhid*) on the face of the earth during spring and summer. Now, look at this: there is a clear stamp of unity (*wāḥidiyya*) on these astonishing transformations of the spring, which are carried out with utmost wisdom and discernment. This stamp emerges from the following fact: all these spring transformations take place with extreme comprehensiveness, (spring comes to the entire hemisphere) *and* extreme speed (in a couple of days the face of the earth changes) *and* with extreme generosity. At the same time, such a comprehensive project with such richness and speed is executed with utmost order and utter artistic beauty. This fact constitutes a shining stamp of the One: only one who has limitless knowledge and power can accomplish such a feat.

Indeed, we observe this also on the face of the entire earth. There is constant activity and creativity at work all over the world. And, that comprehensive action and creation proceed with utter speed. Moreover, we see that things are created with utter ease, in addition to being carried out on an extensive scale and so swiftly. Furthermore, we notice utter profusion in the number of individuals of all species. Within this astonishing comprehensiveness, speed, ease and abundance, we notice that each species and each individual display profound order, excellent art and perfect creation. In other words, we notice the profusion of individuals and completeness of their creation at the same time. Similarly, exquisite art comes into being with the utmost speed. [Often increase in quantity is achieved at the expense of decrease in quality. Therefore, the fact that profusion and speed do not affect the perfect art and excellence of the creation is an indication to immense and comprehensive power and knowledge.] Additionally, we witness intermingled substances separated with perfect precision. Finally, we notice very precious works coming into being in great numbers, things across far distances being in sync with each other and utterly artistic things coming into being with so much ease. All these facts are a stamp, revealing the One who is present everywhere and at all times, without being at any particular location. Nothing can be hidden from this Maker. And nothing is difficult for Him. Particles and stars are equal before His power.

To give a small example from the gardens of the Merciful One of Beauty: the other day, I reflected on one tiny 'cluster' of His miracles on a grapevine. I counted the clusters that were hanging from the grapevine that was merely two inches thick. It turned out to have 150 clusters. Next, I counted the grapes on a single cluster: 120. I thought: If this vine were a faucet through which juice flowed continuously, then it might have been sufficient for it to feed all these grapes with the syrup of mercy in this hot weather. However, in this climate it gets only a little humidity. Thus, the one who achieves this must be powerful over all things. *Glory be to the One whose art dazzles the minds!*

Seventh Flash

Look attentively, you can see the stamps of the Unique and Eternally Self-Sufficient One on whom everything depends (*al-aḥad al-ṣamad*) on the face of the earth. Raise your head, open your eyes and gaze at this great book of the universe, you shall see a bright stamp of unity. For, all the beings in the universe are helping each other and working shoulder to shoulder—like the various parts of an organism...They answer the needs of one another and cooperate with each other. They join efforts so as to serve and assist living beings. They obey the Wise One who administers all things (*al-mudabbir al-ḥakīm*) towards a purpose.

Indeed, we see that the sun and moon, day and night, winter and summer as well as the plants hasten to help the needy animals. And the animals hasten to the aid of the weak and noble human beings. We even see this universal principle of cooperation in the hastening of nourishment to the needs of delicate babies as well as fruits. Similarly, food particles hasten to the aid of cells. Anyone who is not prejudiced will understand that this universal cooperation is happening by the power of an extremely Generous Nurturer and the command of an extremely Wise Director (*al-mudabbir al-ḥakīm*).

Thus, this solidarity, cooperation, collaboration, assistance and order in the universe demonstrate that the universe is being managed and directed by a single Disposer and Nurturer. Moreover, the universe also carries another bright stamp of oneness of God. This stamp is revealed through the comprehensive wisdom manifest in the artistry of all beings, and the comprehensive mercy, providence and beneficence shining all over the universe.

It is clearly apparent in the nourishment spread over that mercy and dispersed so as to meet the needs of all living beings, i.e. in the comprehensive nurturing of all living things.

Indeed,

- A 'curtain' of wisdom is spread all over the universe. This comprehensive wisdom reveals intentionality, consciousness and will.

- Over this curtain of wisdom, a curtain of graciousness has been spread out. This comprehensive beneficence (*'ināya*) reveals that acts of favoring, adoring, and beautifying are at work.

- Over this adorned cover of beneficence, a cloak of mercy that reveals flashes of generous hospitality and bestowal has been spread and has encompassed the entire universe. This enveloping mercy indicates that the Creator wishes to be known and loved.

- And, over this shining curtain of universal mercy, a feast of universal sustenance has been spread out. This feast reveals the beautiful caring, kind attention and benevolent favor.

In other words, this whole existence—from particles to suns, including individuals and species, everything big and small—has been dressed with

- An incredible shirt sown from the fabric of *wisdom*, adorned with patterns of *purpose* and *beneficial consequences*.

- A beautiful shawl of beneficence adorned with flowers of generosity and hospitality has been spread over this shirt of wisdom, appropriate for each being.

- A badge of mercy flashing with love, care and compassion has been placed over the shawl of beneficence.

- And a fulfilling feast has been spread over all these layers of existence. Meal tables sufficient for all the living beings have been placed on earth.

All these accomplishments reveal the infinitely Wise (*hakim*), Generous (*karim*), Merciful (*rahim*), All-Providing (*razzāq*) One full of Beauty.

Now, we may ask, how is this so? Does everything really need sustenance (*rizq*)?

Yes, it does. Just as a person needs sustenance, all the beings in the universe, especially the living beings, big and small, universal and particular, have so many material and spiritual needs for their existence and for the continuation of their lives. Moreover, they need things that are utterly beyond their power and reach. And yet, we see before our eyes that all these needs are being met *from places they do not expect* [Q. 65:3][18] with complete order and wisdom at the appropriate time. Thus, while these beings are utterly poor and needy, their needs are taken care of from the unseen (*ghayb*), and assistance is sent to them. This indicates clearly a Wise Majestic Nurturer and a Beautiful Merciful One who administers all things.

Eighth Flash

A seed planted in a field indicates that the field must be under the control of the owner of the seed, and vice versa, the seed must be at the disposal of the one who possesses control over the field.

Similarly, the basic elements, which are the building blocks of all beings in the world, are like a field. From such a simple and unified 'field,' we see the 'harvest' of various creatures: inanimate beings,

---

[18] Nursi cites this Quranic phrase in Arabic, without explicitly noting that it is a Quranic phrase, presumably because it is a well-known one.

plants and animals. All these creatures are 'crops' of mercy, miracles of power, and words of wisdom. The 'field,' i.e. the basic elements, are universal and comprehensive, and the 'harvest,' i.e. various inorganic and organic creatures, are disseminated throughout the world in similar forms. This shows that they are under the control of one single Miraculous Maker, and that each flower, fruit, and animal, is like a trademark, stamp and signature of the Maker. Wherever it is found, it proclaims: 'I am the trademark of the Maker of this place. Whosoever stamp I am, this place is His letter. Whosoever signature I am, this homeland of mine is his weaving.'

Thus, the sustainer of the smallest being can only be the one who has authority over all the elements. It is obvious—to anyone who has eyes to see—that to manage and regulate one simple animal can only be the work of the Sustainer who nurtures and administers all animals, plants and other beings.

Indeed, each being speaks of the One through the 'tongue' of its similarity to other beings. It says, 'Only the one who owns my species can be my owner. Anyone less than that cannot be my owner.' Similarly, each species say: 'Only the one who owns the entire earth can be my owner. Anyone less than that cannot be my owner.' And, the earth speaks through the 'tongue' of its relations with other planets and its collaboration with the heavens: 'Only the one who owns the entire universe can be my owner. Anyone less than that cannot be my owner.'

Hence, for instance, if someone was to tell an apple: 'You are my product,' the apple would respond, through the tongue of its disposition (*lisān al-ḥāl*), 'No way! If you are able to form all the apples in the world, manage all the other similar fruit species, and administer all other gifts of mercy, only then you can claim to be my sustainer.' Thus, the apple would silence such a foolish claim.

Ninth Flash

So far, we have indicated some of the trademarks, stamps and signatures on parts and particulars, wholes, universals and on the entire universe. We have seen them on life, living beings and in the giving of life. Now, we shall point to one of the many trademarks, present on *species*.

Consider a fruit tree. Its many fruits are produced through 'one law,' from one center, through one management and therefore, they are much easier to make than one single fruit managed from multiple centers. In the latter case, for each fruit a separate effort as complicated as that of the entire tree would be needed. To use another metaphor: the factories required for the equipment of the whole army are needed to equip one single soldier. Indeed, it is easier for many things to proceed from one center, than for one thing to proceed from many centers. In other words, when a task passes from unity to multiplicity, complications increase in proportion to the quantity of individuals involved. Thus, the remarkable ease clearly visible in each species must be the result of unity and oneness.

In sum: All the species of a kind and the individuals of a species declare through their similarity and resemblance that they are the works of a single Maker. Moreover, the oneness of their script and the unity of their trademark entail this. Similarly, this absolute ease and effortlessness, which are clearly visible, indicate that they are all artifacts of One Maker. Otherwise, there would be such incredible difficulties that it would be impossible for any species or kind to exist.

In conclusion, when attributed to the Almighty, all things are as simple as one single thing. If things are attributed to seeming causes, every single thing becomes as difficult as the entire universe. Thus, this astonishing and benevolent abundance before our eyes reveals a bright 'trademark' of oneness. If, the exquisite fruits we receive in abundance were not the work of the Only and Unique One (*al-wāḥid al-aḥad*), we would not be able to afford a single pomegranate even if we paid the entire world as the price.

Tenth Flash

As a manifestation of divine beauty, life is a bright evidence of unicity (*aḥadiyya*)—in fact life is a manifestation of unity (*waḥda*). Similarly, as a manifestation of divine majesty, death is also a clear evidence of unity (*wāḥidiyya*).

Let us consider a metaphor, keeping in mind that *to God belongs the highest parable* (Q. 16:60).[19] Imagine a big river flowing under the glowing sun. As the water bubbles in the river shine, they point to the sun. The water bubbles testify to the sun not only through their shining but also through vanishing and losing light. For, as shining water bubbles move on and vanish, new bubbles follow them and reflect the sunshine. While the bubbles and all transparent things keep changing and renewing, the sunshine remains constantly reflected without any loss or blemish. This shows that all these reflections of light are from one constant, enduring sun. That is, by appearing on the scene, the sparkling bubbles point to the existence of the sun, to the through their vanishing and passing, they point to the sun's permanence, continuation, and oneness.

Similarly, through their existence and coming to life, the flow of creation points to the Necessarily Existent One and to His oneness. And through their departure and death, they point to His eternity, permanence, and unicity (*aḥadiyya*).

Indeed, the beautiful and delicate creatures that are renewed through the alternation of the day and night, of winter and summer, and the passing of ages point to the existence, permanence and unity of an exalted, eternal possessor of constantly manifested beauty. Likewise, the fact that these creatures die along with their seeming and lowly causes shows that the seeming causes were no more than a mere veil, and possessed no power whatsoever. This situation shows clearly that all these works of art, embroideries, and reflections are the renewed work of art, the constantly transforming embroideries, the moving mirrors, the flowing signatures, the wisely changing stamps of a Beautiful One full of Majesty, whose names are all sacred and beautiful.

---

[19] Nursi invokes this verse so as to indicate that no parable can ever fully represent Divine Reality. In other words, even though a parable is used to explain infinite Divine power, it is to be kept in mind that parables have limits due to being brought from finite world and God is above any parable or similitude.

In sum, this great book of the universe teaches us the creational signs (*al-ayāt al-takwīniyya*) of the existence and oneness of the Author. Moreover, it testifies to the attributes of perfection, beauty and majesty of the Majestic One. Finally, it proves the flawless and impeccable perfection of His essence. For, it is obvious that:

- Perfection in an artifact reveals the perfectness of the *act* behind that artifact,

- As for the perfectness of the act, it points to the perfection of the *name*, which in turn points to the perfection of the *attribute*,

- As for the perfection of the attribute, it points to the perfection of the essential capacity (*sha'n dhati*)

- And the perfection of the capacity (*sha'n*) points intuitively, necessarily, and clearly to the perfection of the possessor of that capacity (*sha'n*).[20]

For instance, consider an impeccable palace with perfect architecture and decorations. These show the perfection of a builder's *acts* behind them. And the perfection of the acts shows the perfection of the *titles* and the *names* of the builder that show his rank. And the perfection of the titles and the names of the builder shows the perfection of the builder's *attributes* pertaining to his *art*. And the perfection of the art and the attributes show *the essential capacity* and abilities of the builder, which is also called *sha'n dhati*. And the perfectness of the essential qualities and abilities show the perfection of the builder's essence.[21]

---

[20] For an explanation of *sha'n* see introductory note to 23rd Window in Chapter 2.

[21] Nursi explains how the metaphor of builder applies to inferences about the perfection and beauty of the Divine essence. However, this reasoning doesn't apply to limited human beings. In the case of a human being who is a builder for instance, the perfection of the essential quality pertains only to the area of art of building. The application of perfection is limited because human qualities are not inherent to human beings; they can deteriorate or be lost. Moreover, a human being can be an amazing surgeon but a bad

Similarly, this impeccable and faultless cosmos with all its aspects, and this well-ordered universe with all its artistry, clearly bears witness to the perfect acts of a Powerful Sovereign. Thus, the cosmos manifests the mystery of the verse *do you see any fault?* (Quran, 67:3). The perfection of the acts clearly shows the perfection of the *names* of the Majestic Doer. Such perfection of the names necessarily points and testifies to the perfect *attribute* of the beauteous One to whom these names belong. And the perfection of that attribute certainly indicates and testifies to the perfection of the essential qualities (*shu'ūnāt*).

And the perfection of the essential qualities indicates with certainty the perfection of the essence of the possessor of those qualities. Through this certain indication, it is understood that all the variety of perfections observed in the entire universe are just a weak shadow of His perfection; all the perfections in the world are signs of His perfection, hints of His majesty and tokens of His beauty.

Eleventh Flash Shining Strong Like Many Suns

The greatest sign of the great book of the universe (*al-kitāb al-kabīr*) and the greatest name (*al-'ism al-a'ẓam*) in that macro-Quran (*al-qur'ān al-kabīr*) is Muhammad, peace and blessings be upon him. He is the 'seed' as well as the most shining 'fruit' of the 'tree' of creation, the sun of the palace of the universe and the radiant full moon of the world of Islam. He is the harbinger of the sovereignty of Divine sustainership and the wise revealer of the mystery of creation. Through his 'wing' of messengership, he includes all the prophets and through his 'wing' of Islam he takes all the world of Islam under his protection; with these wings he glides through the layers of truth. He takes behind him all the messengers, all the saints (*al-awliya'*) and the veracious ones (*al-ṣiddiqīn*), all the purified ones (*al-aṣfiya'*) and the discerning scholars (*al-muḥaqqiqīn*). With all his strength, he

---

cook. Whereas the true creator of beautiful things is the source of all beauty, including our sense of beauty and justice, and therefore He must be beauteous in His essence.

shows the oneness of God (*waḥdāniyya*) and opens up the path to the throne of unicity (*aḥadiyya*). Can there be any suspicion or doubt about such a fortified and proven belief in God and divine unity (*waḥdāniyya*)? How can any delusion conceal this radiant proof?

We have already talked about this definite proof elsewhere, in the Nineteenth Word and Nineteenth Letter; where we briefly reviewed the various miracles of the Messenger (peace and blessings be upon him) through 'Fourteen Droplets' and 'Nineteen Indications' from the life-giving knowledge of that Clear Evidence (i.e., the Messenger of God). We shall thus skip a detailed discussion here. Instead, let us conclude with a prayer on the Messenger (*salawāt sharīfa*), which outlines the core points, which witness to that proof of Divine unity and confirm his veracity:

O dear God! Bestow your mercy and grace on the one who points to Your necessary existence, and oneness, and bears witness to Your majesty, beauty and perfection; the one who is the truthful witness confirmed by the entire universe and all the prophets and saints; the one who is the speaking proof supported by the research of discerning scholars; the one who is the head of all the prophets and messengers and who is the recipient of the mystery of all their consensus, confirmation and miracles...[22]

Twelfth Flash Shining with the Strength of Many Suns

This Flash of the Twenty Second Word shows how the Quran is a witness for *tawhid*.

The Quran is an ocean of truth; all the 22 Words are just twenty-two drops from that ocean. The Quran is a dazzling source of light; and these 22 Words are just twenty-two flashes from that sun...Each verse of the Quran is like a bright star in the sky of the

---

[22] Here, Nursi continues on to complete a long prayer of blessing for the Messenger Muhammad in Arabic, the rest of which we skipped due to difficulty of translating in an easily readable form. The prayer notes the variety of ways in which the prophet showed the unity of God and ends by asking God to bless and give peace to him abundantly.

Quran. And these Words or chapters are just flashes from one of those stars. Each verse is like a river flowing from this ocean of the Criterion of truth and falsehood (*furqān*) and these Words are like droplets from that river. The Book of God is an exalted treasure and each of its verses is a trove, whereas these Words are just a single pearl from the treasure of one of the verses.

As we briefly described in the '14th Droplet' of the 19th Word, the Quran is the speech of God descending from the Greatest Name, the Highest Throne, the greatest manifestation of sustainership. The Quran speaks with such a comprehensiveness and majesty that it connects the earth to the Divine Throne (*'arsh*) and with all its strength and the certainty of its verses/signs (*ayāt*), it repeatedly declares *there is no god except Him*, taking the entire universe as its witness. Indeed, the entire universe recites/celebrates in unison *there is no god except Him*...[23]

In sum, the Noble Messenger, peace and blessings be on him, and the Wise Criterion is each like a sun.

- The first one bears witness to the truth of *tawhid* from the World of the Seen (*'ālam al-shahāda*). Islam and messengership, which is supported by a thousand miracles and confirmed by all the prophets and the purified ones, are powerful evidences of this truth of *tawhid*.

- The second one, the Quran, is a witness of *tawhid* from the World of the Unseen (*'ālam al-ghayb*). It clearly shows *tawhid*, through its truthfulness and guidance, which is supported by its manifold miraculousness as well as all the creational signs of the universe.

O stubborn deluded human being! How can you oppose these powerful witnesses with your limited and dim reason? Do you imagine that you can extinguish these two bright suns by blowing on them? These 'tongues' of the seen and the unseen 'speak' in the name of the

---

[23] Here we skipped a paragraph that briefly mentions the strength and impeccability of the Quran, which may be too dense to be clear for a first time reader. An expanded and explained version is to be found in the beginning of '25th Word' of *Words*.

Sustainer of all the worlds, the Owner of the Universe, and they prove the truth and reality of *tawhid*. Given that you are needier and more vulnerable than a tiny fly, how can you belie the Glorious Owner of the universe?

Conclusion

O friend whose mind is alert and heart is awake! If you have understood this 22nd Word so far, then behold the Twelve Flashes and see how they constitute a powerful shining lamp of truth. Hold onto the verses/signs (*ayāt*) of the Quran that descend from the Highest Throne ('*arsh al-'azam*), ride on the divine mount (*burāq*) of success raise to the heavens of truth, and ascend to the throne ('*arsh*) of Knowledge of God (*ma'rifatullah*). And, proclaim: 'I bear witness that there is no god except You, You are the only one, You have no partner' (*ashadu an lā ilāha illa anta wahdaka la sharīka laka*).

And, together with all the beings of the universe in the great mosque of the world declare the oneness of God by saying: 'There is no god except God. He is one; He has no partner. To Him belongs all sovereignty. To Him all praise and thanks are due. He gives life, and He deals death. He is Ever-living, and dies not. All good is in His hand. He has power over everything. And with Him is all journeys' end.'

> *Glory to You! We have no knowledge except what You have taught us. Surely, You are the All-Knower, the All-Wise.* (Q. 2:32)[24]

> *O our Sustainer! Take us not to task if we forget or make mistakes! O our Sustainer! Don't lay on us a burden like that which You laid on those who were before us! O our Sustainer! Do not*

---

[24] Nursi often ends his chapters with this verse (Q. 2:32). This is also the verse that Nursi stopped at in his *Isharat al-I'jaz*, which is a line-by-line commentary he wrote in Old Said period. He later notes that his entire *Epistles of Light* is from the 'sea' of this verse and each chapter implicitly starts with it and is a continued commentary on it. (See his final footnote in *Isharat al I-jaz*). At the end of long chapters, as is here, Nursi adds other passages from the Quran as a concluding prayer.

place on us that which we have not the strength to bear! And pardon us, forgive us, and have mercy upon us! You are our Protector, help us, then, against the disbelieving people! (Q. 2:286)

O our Sustainer! Let not our hearts swerve after You have guided us and grant us mercy from Your Presence. Truly You are the Bestower. O our Sustainer! Verily, You are the Gatherer of humankind unto a Day about which there is no doubt: truly, God never breaks His promise. (Q. 3: 8–9)

O God grant peace and blessings onto the one whom you sent as a mercy to all the worlds and onto all of his family and companions. And have mercy upon us and have mercy upon his community (*umma*) from your endless mercy O Most Merciful!

And the conclusion of their supplication is 'All praise is due to God, the Sustainer of all the worlds!' (Q. 10:10)

BIBLIOGRAPHY

Abdel Haleem, M. A. S. *The Qur'an: A New Translation*, Oxford University Press, 2004.

Akkach, Samer. *Cosmology And Architecture in Premodern Islam: An Architectural Reading of Mystical Ideas*. New York: SUNY Press, 2006.

Altaie, Muhammad Basil. 2014. "Paving the Way for the Reformation of Islam: Conversation with Mohammed Basil Altaie." In *Islam and the Quest for Modern Science* by Stefano Bigliardi, 71–102. Istanbul: Swedish Research Institute.

——. *God, Nature, and the Cause: Essays on Islam and Science*. UAE: Kalam Research & Media, 2016.

Asad, Muhammad. *The Message of the Qur'an*. Gibraltar, Spain: Dar al-Andalus, 1984.

Chittick, William. *Self-Disclosure of God: Principles of Ibn al-'Arabi's Cosmology*. Albany, NY: SUNY Press, 1998.

al-Daghamin, Ziyad Khalil Muhammad. 'The Aims of the Qur'an in Bediuzzaman Said Nursi's Thought.' In *A Contemporary Approach to Understanding the Qur'an: The Example of the Risale-i Nur, 20th–22nd September, 1998*, 353–79. Istanbul: Sözler Yayinevi, 2000.

Ghazālī, Abū Ḥāmid. *The Faith and Practice of al-Ghazālī [translation of Al-Munqidh min al-ḍalāl]*. Translated by W. Montgomery Watt. London: G. Allen and Unwin, 1967.

——. *Faith in Divine Unity and Trust in Divine Providence* [translation of Kitāb al-Tawḥīd wa'l-tawakkul, book 35 of *Iḥyā' 'ulūm al-dīn*]. Translated by David Burrell. Louisville, Ky.: Fons Vitae, 2001.

——. *The Foundations of the Articles of Faith* [translation of *Al-Kitāb Qawā'id al-'aqāid*, from *Iḥyā' 'ulūm al-dīn*]. Translated and annotated by Nabih Amin Faris. Lahore: Sh. Muhammad Ashraf, 1963.

Grice, Herbert P. *Studies in the Way of Words.* Cambridge, MA: Harvard University Press, 1989.

Madigan, Daniel. *The Qur'an's Self-Image: Writing and Authority in Islam's Scripture,* NY: Princeton University Press, 2001.

Marinis, Marco de. *The Semiotics of Performance.* Bloomington & Indianapolis, IN: Indiana University Press, 1996.

Mattson, Ingrid. *The Story of the Qur'an.* NY: Wiley-Blackwell, 2008.

Mermer, Yamina Bougeuenaya. 'Bediuzzaman Said Nursi's Scriptural Approach to the Problem of Evil' *Journal of Scriptural Reasoning,* (4:1, July 2004),

——. 'Islam: A Dissenting Prophetic Voice,' in *Scripture, Reason, and the Contemporary Islam-West Encounter,* ed. by Basit B. Koshul and Steven Kepnes. New York: Palgrave Macmillan, 2007: 67–104.

——. 'Principles of Qur'anic Hermeneutics,' *The Journal of Scriptural Reasoning,* 5:1 (2005), published online at <http://jsr.lib.virginia.edu/vol-5-no-1-april-2005-islam-and-scriptural-reasoning/principles-of-Qur'anic-hermeneutics/>.

——. *Living with Genuine Tawhid: Witnessing the Signs of God through Quranic Guidance,* Maryland: Receiving Nur, 2016.

——. and Redha Ameur. 'Beyond the Modern: Sa'id al-Nursi's View of Science.' *Islam and Science* 2 (Winter 2004): 119–60.

——. and Isra Yazicioglu. 'Said Nursi's Qur'anic Hermeneutics,' in *The Companion to Said Nursi Studies*. Edited by Ian Markham & Z. Sayilgan, Pickwick Publications, 2017, 51–66.

Muhtaroglu, Nazif. 'al-Baqillanī's Cosmological Argument from Agency,' *Arabic Sciences and Philosophy* 26:2, 271–289.

Nasr, S. Hossein. *Man and Nature: The Spiritual Crisis in Modern Man*. Chicago, IL: ABC International Group, 1996.

Nursi, Bediuzzaman Said. *The Flashes: From the Risale-i Nur Collection*. Translated by Şükran Vahide. Istanbul: Sözler Yayinevi, 1995.

——. *Ishārat al-iʿjāz* [Signs of Eloquence] Ed. by Ihsan Qasim al-Salihi. Istanbul: Sözler Yayinevi, 1994.

——. *Işarat al-iʿcāz*. *Risale-i Nur Kulliyati*. Vol.1, Istanbul: Yeni Nesil Yayinlari, 1996.

——. *al-Mathnawi al-ʿArabi al-Nuri*. Istanbul: Sözler Yayinevi, 1999.

——. *The Letters*. Translated by Sukran Vahide. Istanbul: Sözler Yayinevi, 1994.

——. *The Rays: From the Risale-i Nur Collection*. Translated by Şükran Vahide. Istanbul: Sözler Yayinevi, 2002.

——. *Emirdag Lahikasi-I* in *Risale-i Nur Kulliyati*. Vol.2, Istanbul: Yeni Nesil Yayinlari, 1996.

——. *Lem'alar* in *Risale-i Nur Kulliyati*. Vol.1, Istanbul: Yeni Nesil Yayinlari, 1996.

——. *Mektubat* in *Risale-i Nur Kulliyati*. Vol.1, Istanbul: Yeni Nesil Yayinlari, 1996.

——. *Mesnevi-i Nuriye*, in *Risale-i Nur Kulliyati*. Vol.2, Istanbul: Yeni Nesil Yayinlari, 1996.

——. *Muhakemat*, in *Risale-i Nur Kulliyati*. Vol. 2, Istanbul: Yeni Nesil Yayinlari, 1996.

——. *Sözler* in *Risale-i Nur Kulliyati*. Vol.1, Istanbul: Yeni Nesil Yayinlari, 1996.

———. *Şualar* in *Risale-i Nur Kulliyati*. Vol.1, Istanbul: Yeni Nesil Yayinlari, 1996.

———. *The Words: From the Risale-i Nur Collection*. Revised ed. Translated by Sukran Vahide. Istanbul: Sozler Publications, 2004.

Ozdemir, Ibrahim. *The Ethical Dimension of Human Attitude Towards Nature: A Muslim Perspective*. Istanbul: Insan Yayinlari, 2008.

Ozdemir, Ibrahim. 'Bediuzzaman Said Nursi's Approach to the Environment.' Paper delivered at the Fourth International Symposium on Bediuzzaman Said Nursi: A Contemporary Approach towards Understanding the Qur'an: The Example of *Risale-i Nur*, Istanbul, Turkey, 20–22 September 1998.

Peirce, Charles S. *The Collected Papers of Charles Sanders Peirce*. Ed. by Charles Hartshorne and Paul Weiss. Cambridge, MA: Harvard University Press, 1931–1935.

Rumi, Mawlana Jalal al-din. *Mathnawi*. Book III and IV. Translated By R. A. Nicholson. Gibb Memorial Trust, 2016.

Sells, Michael. *Approaching the Qur'an: The Early Revelations*. 2nd ed. Ashland, Or.: White Cloud Press, 2007.

Smith, William C. *The Questions of Religious Truth*. NY: 1967.

Tuna, Mustafa. 'At the Vanguard of Contemporary Muslim Thought: Reading Said Nursi Into The Islamic Tradition. *Journal of Islamic Studies* 28:3 (2017) pp. 311–340.

Turner, Colin *Islam: the Basics*. Second Ed. New York: Routledge, 2011.

———. *The Qur'an Revealed: A Critical Analysis of Said Nursi's Epistles of Light*. Berlin: Germany, Gerlach Press, 2013.

Yazicioglu, Isra. 'Perhaps their Harmony is not that Simple: Said Nursi on the Qur'an and Modern Science,' *Theology and Science*, 11:4 (2013), 339–355.

——. 'Redefining the Miraculous: Al-Ghazālī, Ibn Rushd, and Said Nursi on Qur'anic Miracle Stories.' *Journal of Qur'anic Studies* 13, no. 2 (2011): 86–108.

——. 'Saʿid Nursi,' in *The Princeton Encyclopedia of Islamic Political Thought*. Edited by G. Bowering, P. Crone, W. Kadi, D. J. Stewart, M. Q. Zaman and M. Mirza. Princeton and Oxford: Princeton University Press, 2011, 110–112.

——. *Understanding the Qur'anic Miracle Stories in the Modern Age*. University Park, Penn.: Penn State University Press, 2013.

——. 'Affliction, Patience and Prayer: Reading Job (p) in the Qur'an.' *Journal of Scriptural Reasoning*. 4:1, July 2004.

——. 'A Graceful Reconciliation: Said Nursi on Free Will and Destiny.' In *The Companion to Said Nursi Studies*. Edited by Ian Markham & Z. Sayilgan, Pickwick Publications, 2017, 129–145.

INDEX

NAMES AND DESCRIPTIONS OF GOD

SUBJECTS/THEMES